New Digital Troubleshooting Techniques

Other books by the Author:

New Ways to Test Meters: A Modern Guide to Electronic Servicing

Troubleshooting Electronic Equipment Without Service Data

NEW DIGITAL TROUBLESHOOTING TECHNIQUES

A Complete, Illustrated Guide

Robert G. Middleton

Prentice-Hall, Inc.
Business and Professional Division

Englewood Cliffs, New Jersey

Prentice-Hall International, Inc., *London*
Prentice-Hall of Australia, Pty., Ltd., *Sydney*
Prentice-Hall of Canada, Inc., *Toronto*
Prentice-Hall of India Private Ltd., *New Delhi*
Prentice-Hall of Japan, Inc., *Tokyo*
Prentice-Hall of Southeast Asia, Pte., Ltd., *Singapore*
Whitehall Books, Ltd., *Wellington, New Zealand*
Editora Prentice-Hall do Brazil Ltda., *Rio de Janeiro*

© 1984, *by*

PRENTICE-HALL, INC.

Englewood Cliffs, N.J.

Editor: George E. Parker

Library of Congress Cataloging in Publication Data

Middleton, Robert Gordon
  New digital troubleshooting techniques.

  Includes index.
  1. Digital electronics.   2. Electronic apparatus and
appliances—Maintenance and repair.   I. Title.
TK7868.D5M524   1984   621.381'028'8   83-16157
ISBN 0-13-612275-2

Printed in the United States of America

A Word from the Author on the Unique, Practical Value This Book Offers...

Electronic technicians who are unfamiliar with digital troubleshooting procedures tend to suppose that this is one of the "black arts." The *fact of the matter* is that digital troubleshooting is *easier than analog troubleshooting—ALTHOUGH THE DIGITAL TROUBLESHOOTER MUST "LEARN THE ROPES."*

The "secret" of learning the ropes is to start at the beginning; get the knack of digital test procedures and trouble analysis while becoming at home with digital circuitry and terminology. It is also a "must" to get your hands on some digital devices and digital test equipment. This need not be an expensive activity—as explained in the following chapters, you can build your own digital test equipment. *You can also put some of your familiar analog test equipment to good use in digital troubleshooting procedures.*

Many never-before-published troubleshooting techniques are explained in this book, with case histories to show how the new techniques are applied and evaluated in actual practice, step-by-step. Included among these unique troubleshooting techniques are:

* Example of Latch Troubleshooting with Charge-Storage Probe
* Simple Two-Tone Logic-Level Indicator
* Ohmmeter Tests of NOR Gate

* Temperature Quick Checks
* Ohmmeter Wipe Test
* Short-Circuit Localization
* Logic Probe with Pulse Memory
* Logic Probe with Supplementary Sound Indicator
* Single-Shot Pulse Generators
* Digital Activity Quick Test
* Pulse Trains vs. Static High Level
* How to Monitor Intermittents with Logic-High and Logic-Low Probes
* Double-Ended Single-Shot Pulser
* Piezo-Buzzer IC Quick Checker
* Simple Counter Readout Probe
* Negative Fan-Out Test
* Normal and Abnormal Current Flow (UL:E/I/R)
* Short-Circuit Localization with Service-Type DVM
* Localizing Short-Circuits to V_{cc}.
* Troubleshooting Short-Circuited PC Conductors
* Phone-Tone Count Indicator
* Changing Negative-Going Square Waves into Positive-Going Square Waves
* Checking the Direction of Data Flow
* Generalized Resistance Tests
* Continuity Quick Check
* Digital Word Recognizer

You will find that this digital troubleshooting guide is your best workbench "tool." It starts at the beginning and explains why particular trouble symptoms are investigated to best advantage by making specific tests and measurements. It continues by pointing out where new kinds of tests and measurements can provide valuable troubleshooting data.

Numerous new ideas in digital troubleshooting are introduced in this guidebook. As an illustration, it shows how to quickly determine which way digital data is flowing in a PC conductor. Logic-high and logic-low levels can be checked (or monitored over extended periods of time) by audio tones, thus "liberating" the troubleshooter from the necessity of continually rechecking visual displays.

Important general principles are discussed with respect to speedup of troubleshooting operations. For example, it is shown how much digital circuitry normally "looks like an open circuit" to an ohmmeter (applied in suitable polarity). In turn, the troubleshooter can quick-check many nodes for faults on the basis of simple ohmmeter indication (or continuity-check tone indication).

Many troubleshooters who are well experienced in analog tests and measurements are handicapped by a "mental block" when confronted by a digital troubleshooting situation. Fortunately, there is an easy way to overcome this "mental block." It consists of hands-on construction projects with follow-up tests and measurements, as described in the following chapters. Unexpectedly, perhaps, *learning digital troubleshooting expertise can be easy and interesting— even exciting, as you realize the speed with which you are progressing.*

In the words of the editorial reviewer, troubleshooting digital circuits has always seemed rather arcane to those whose original training was in linear (analog) circuits. The parallel proliferation of integrated circuits, where you cannot even see the internal circuitry, has not helped at all; it has only made the inscrutable also invisible!

Obviously, since the troubleshooter can't see inside of an IC, he is in the position of a veterinarian. The troubleshooter must diagnose the "disease" from its symptoms, and the "patient" can't tell the troubleshooter where it hurts. This means that he must have a thorough understanding of the "animal's" anatomy and normal behavior.

This, then, is the approach that is used in this book. It starts with the simpler digital devices, and describes their circuits, operation, and problems. It then proceeds to show how to troubleshoot these devices with familiar bench test equipment . . . but, the reader is also introduced to the idea of level indication with a home-made LED probe.

In this way, the book leads the reader step-by-step from familiar analog troubleshooting methods into digital troubleshooting methods that are more concerned with discrete voltage levels. The book also shows the reader how to make current tests without breaking circuit connections—a very valuable technique in the real world, considering the difficulties and hazards involved in removing components from printed-circuit boards.

From this point, the reader moves up, step-by-step, to more complex digital circuits and to more sophisticated testing techniques, until he (or she) ultimately reaches the altitude of professional digital troubleshooting, using expensive test equipment. (This is where a retro-reader—one who reads books from back to front—would be in deep trouble!)

Accordingly, this book will serve as an excellent training manual for those who are learning digital troubleshooting. Additionally, it provides valuable practical tips, data, and tricks of the trade for the hobbyist/experimenter. He or she (the hobbyist/experimenter) does not, as a general rule, construct equipment using very complex circuits. Consequently, the hobbyist/experimenter is more concerned with the down-to-earth troubleshooting techniques and "how it works" information presented in the earlier chapters. *Many never-before-published techniques are explained for the benefit of BOTH hobbyist/experimenter and professional troubleshooter.*

Experienced digital troubleshooters know that time is money, and that knowledge is power. *Your* success in the practice of digital troubleshooting is limited only by the horizons of your technical know-how. The unique, practical application techniques, new methods, trouble-symptom analyses, case histories, troubleshooting guidelines, and technical reference data in this workbench "tool" provide key stepping-stones from your present position to your goal.

Robert G. Middleton

TABLE OF CONTENTS

Note: /...../ indicates a new troubleshooting technique.

guage Code * Hardware and Software for Start, Stop, and Clock * Detecting Start, Stop, and Data with the Clock * Fault Isolation of Bused Devices * Read and Write as Clock Assists Fault Location * RS-232C Port

New Digital Troubleshooting Techniques

1
Digital Troubleshooting Basics

RS Latch Troubleshooting with a Charge-Storage Probe and DC Voltmeter • CMOS NOR Gate • Bad Region • Latch Troubleshooting • Inverter Latch Circuit Action • From the RS Latch to the D Latch • Trick of the Trade • "Floating" Input • Temperature Quick Checks • Practical Note

RS LATCH TROUBLESHOOTING WITH A CHARGE-STORAGE PROBE AND DC VOLTMETER

A reset-set (RS) latch is the basic type of bistable multivibrator. Latches are typically used as a simple form of digital *memory*, for temporary storage of binary data. (The basic RS latch must be elaborated, however, before it can store a logic-high or a logic-low state.) A simple charge-storage probe shows at a glance whether a latch input or output terminal is in a logic-high state or in a logic-low state. Latches are often configured from NOR gates (see Fig. 1-1).

The charge-storage probe depicted in Fig. 1-1 is suitable for troubleshooting transistor-transistor logic (TTL). Most of the digital logic circuitry that you will encounter employs TTL logic levels. Note the following electrical relations in Fig. 1-1:

1. A type 7402 NOR gate is typical. The power supply has an output of approximately +5 volts. Its maximum permissible value is +5.25 volts, in this example. If the supply voltage accidentally rises above +5.25 volts, the NOR gate is likely to be damaged.

2. When the gate input terminals are at a potential from zero (ground) to +0.8 volt, the gate normally responds to a logic-low input. This response is a logic-high output level, inasmuch as NOR action occurs.

3. When the gate input terminals are at a potential from +2 volts to +5 volts, the gate normally responds to a logic-high input. This response is a logic-low output level, inasmuch as NOR action occurs.

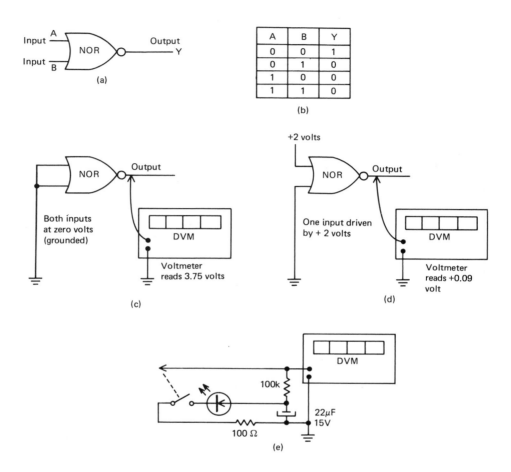

Visual Indication with DVM (or VOM). A 22μF capacitor charges through a 100k resistor when the test prod is touched to a logic-high point. As the troubleshooter increases the pressure on the prod, a microswitch closes and the charged capacitor discharges through the LED, giving a bright flash.

Fig. 1-1. NOR gate checkout with charge-storage probe and voltmeter. (a) Symbol; (b) truth table; (c) output check with inputs logic-low; (d) output check with one input logic-high; (e) charge-storage logic probe used with voltmeter.

4. A TTL logic-high output level is a voltage in the range from +2.4 to +5 volts.

5. A TTL logic-low output level is a voltage in the range from zero (ground) to +0.4 volt.

CMOS NOR Gate

Although most of the digital logic circuitry that you will encounter employs TTL logic levels, CMOS gates are sometimes utilized. From the troubleshooter's viewpoint, the difference between TTL gates and CMOS gates is the comparatively higher or lower supply voltages that are used. Different values of supply voltage correspond to different logic-high and logic-low threshold voltages.

Troubleshooters will find CMOS gates normally operating from supply voltages in the +3 to +15-volt range. From a practical viewpoint, CMOS logic-high and logic-low levels are defined as follows:

1. If the supply voltage is in the range from 3 to 10 volts, the normal logic-high level is a voltage greater than 0.7 of the supply voltage ±0.5 volt. The normal logic-low level is a voltage less than 0.3 of the supply voltage ±0.5 volt.

2. If the supply voltage is in the range from 10-18 volts, the normal logic-high level is a voltage greater than 0.7 of the supply voltage ±1 volt. The normal logic-low level is a voltage less than 0.3 of the supply voltage ±1 volt.

The bottom line is that when you are troubleshooting CMOS circuitry, a charge-storage logic probe may be suitable for checking logic-high and logic-low levels. On the other hand, a charge-storage probe may be completely unsuitable —a dc voltmeter should be used in this situation to check logic-high and logic-low CMOS states.

Note on Commercial Logic Probes

In following chapters, we will consider the use of commercial logic probes in troubleshooting both TTL and CMOS circuitry. At this time, it may be noted that most commercial logic probes are provided with a TTL/CMOS switch, and that CMOS logic states are correctly indicated regardless of the supply voltage value.

Bad Region

Digital troubleshooters are often concerned with circuits that check out in the bad region. For example, TTL input levels are separated by a *bad region* from $+0.8$ to $+2$ volts—a range of 1.2 volts. Therefore, if we are tracking down a trouble symptom, and we happen to measure $+1.6$ volts at an input terminal (*as we might very well measure in a trouble situation*), we will conclude that this input terminal is "in the bad region," and that there is a defect inside of the IC, or outside in the branch circuit (node).

Next, we observe that the output state levels are separated by a *bad region* from $+0.4$ to $+2.4$ volts—a range of 2 volts. Therefore, if we are tracking down a trouble symptom, and we happen to measure $+1$ volt at an output terminal (*as might very well occur in a trouble situation*), we will conclude that this output terminal is "in the bad region," and that there is a defect inside of the IC, or outside in the associated node.

LATCH TROUBLESHOOTING

A basic RS latch may be configured from cross-connected NOR gates, as shown in Fig. 1-2. You will sometimes hear this arrangement called a flip-flop —however, it is a latch from a technical viewpoint. In other words, a latch is an asynchronous device; it is unclocked and it can be triggered at any time. On the other hand, a flip-flop is a synchronous device; it is clocked and it operates in step with the clock pulses, as explained subsequently.

Troubleshooters often state that the latch in Fig. 1-2 is *loaded* by inputting a logic-high (1) level to the S input and inputting a simultaneous logic-low (0) level to the R input. As seen in the truth table, when the latch is loaded, its Q output goes logic-high and its $\bar{Q}$ output goes logic-low. Conversely, the latch is *unloaded* by inputting a logic-low level to the S input and inputting a simultaneous logic-high level to the R input.

If the RS latch fails to respond in this manner, the digital circuit is malfunctioning. If the V_{CC} supply voltage is normal, the failure will be tracked down to a defective gate or an external circuit fault.

Note on Digital Logic Test Equipment

It is sometimes supposed that ordinary analog test equipment such as voltmeters and ohmmeters have little or no application in digital troubleshooting procedures. However, this is not so—a VOM, TVM, or DVM may not be as

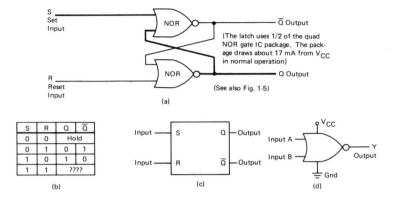

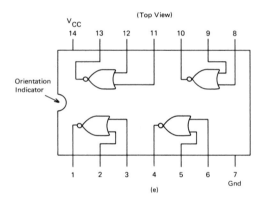

Note: The RS latch shown in (a) is a form of bistable multivibrator with the following characteristics:

1. When both inputs are logic-low (grounded), the outputs simply remain in their previous states.
2. If S is logic-high (at V_{CC} potential) and R is logic-low, Q normally goes logic-high and $\bar{Q}$ goes logic-low.
3. If S is logic-low and R is logic-high, Q normally goes logic-low and $\bar{Q}$ goes logic-high.
4. If S and R are both driven logic-high, the Q and $\bar{Q}$ states will be unpredictable. (It is "forbidden" to drive S and R logic-high simultaneously.)

Fig. 1-2. Basic RS latch. (a) Cross-connected NOR gates; (b) truth table; (c) logic symbol; (d) NOR gate as viewed by the troubleshooter; (e) type 7402 quad two-input positive NOR gate IC package.

convenient as a logic probe, but it does provide more comprehensive test data. We have seen, for example, that V_{CC} can be measured with a dc voltmeter; whereas, a logic probe can only indicate that the V_{CC} value is not below the logic-high threshold.

As explained in the next chapter, you can easily construct a new kind of logic-level indicator which provides sound output (instead of light output). In other words, this new logic tester produces a high-pitched tone output when the test lead is applied to a logic-high point. On the other hand, it produces a low-pitched tone output when the test lead is applied to a logic-low point.

Note that an elaborate DVM may provide a supplementary logic-level tone indication. For example, a typical DVM in this category produces a tone output when the test lead is applied at a point which is at the logic-low threshold or lower. (The DVM provides no logic-high tone indication.) We will return to this topic subsequently.

INVERTER LATCH CIRCUIT ACTION

Digital troubleshooting is greatly facilitated by a good understanding of circuit action. Observe that a NOR gate provides voltage amplification. In turn, multivibrator action is obtained in the configuration of Fig. 1-2. It is helpful to consider the experimental inverter latch arrangement depicted in Fig. 1-3.

This latch can be easily constructed from a Radio Shack hex-inverter IC package, type 7404; it is powered from a 5V supply. As indicated in the diagram, *one output will be latched logic-low, and the other output will be latched logic-high.* (In this simple configuration, the output from one inverter is the same as the input to the other inverter.)

Observe the IC package pinout depicted in Fig. 1-4. The inverter latch arrangement can be constructed on a perf board, or, an experimenter socket such as the Radio Shack No. 276-174 may be used. This experimenter socket has the advantage of flexibility and provides push-in connection facilities.

When the inverter output voltages are measured, as shown in Fig. 1-3(b), it will be observed that one output is logic-low and that the other output is logic-high. It is impossible to predict which output will go high and which output will go low when V_{CC} is applied to the inverter latch. In other words, the initial output states depend on device tolerances. *However, in normal operation, one inverter output will rest in a logic-high state, and the other inverter output will rest in a logic-low state.**

---

*Since device tolerances are "permanent," the start-up states will always be the same.

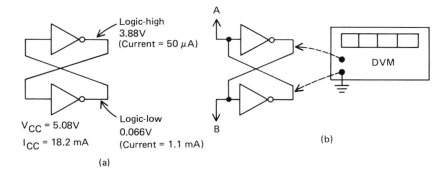

Fig. 1-3. Inverter latch arrangement. (a) Cross-connected inverters; (b) latch changes output state when input A or input B is suitably driven.

Note: Each inverter in the IC package has a V_{CC} connection and a Gnd connection. These connections are customarily implied (not explicitly shown in the inverter's logic symbol).
Troubleshooters who are not entirely familiar with NOR gate circuit action will find it helpful to construct this experimental inverter latch and to check out its operation.

Note: Keep in mind that the I_{CC} value indicated in (a) is the current demand of the complete hex-inverter IC package.

> If inputs A and B are tied together, they assume a bad-level potential of 1.3 volts, approximately.

Since the output from one inverter is the same as the input to the other inverter in this configuration, one inverter input will normally rest in a logic-low state, and the other inverter input will rest in a logic-high state. Now, observe the following circuit actions:

1. If the DVM if Fig. 1-3(b) shows that the upper inverter has a logic-high output, touch input lead B to Gnd (Ground). In normal operation, the upper inverter will "flop" to a logic-low output.

2. If the DVM in Fig. 1-3(b) shows that the upper inverter has a logic-low output, touch input lead B to V_{CC}. In normal operation, the upper inverter will "flip" to a logic-high output.

3. If the DVM in Fig 1-3(b) shows that the upper inverter has a logic-high output, touch input lead A to V_{CC}. In normal operation, the upper inverter will "flop" to a logic-low output.

4. If the DVM in Fig. 1-3(b) shows that the upper inverter has a logic-low output, touch input lead A to Gnd. In normal operation, the upper inverter will "flip" to a logic-high output.

If these responses are not obtained, the troubleshooter should check his connections for possible error. In case all connections are correct, check the V_{CC} voltage to determine whether it may be subnormal. Finally, if all connections are correct, and V_{CC} is normal, an inverter may be found defective—select another pair of inverters in the IC package, and repeat the experiment.

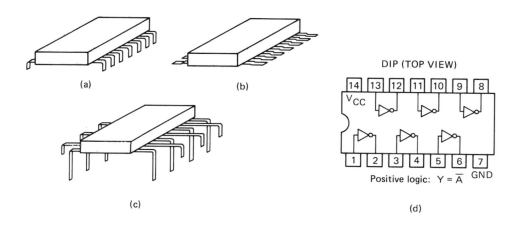

DIP (TOP VIEW)

Positive logic: $Y = \overline{A}$

(a)

(b)

(c)

(d)

Note: Positive logic means that the logic-low state is at ground potential, or near ground potential. In turn the logic-high state is considerably above ground potential, such as 3.88 volts (as in the example of Fig. 1-3).
The logic equation $Y = \overline{A}$ is read "Y equals *not* A." It means that when A (an inverter input) is driven logic-high, the result will be that the Y (the inverter output) will go logic-low. Conversely, when A is driven logic-low, the result will be that Y will go logic-high.

If you are not familiar with the various types of ICs and their functions, refer to pages 111 through 344 in *Encyclopedia of Integrated Circuits* by Walter H. Buchsbaum, Sc.D.

Fig. 1-4. IC package types and pinout. (a) In-line, through-board mounting type; (b) in-line, surface-mounting type; (c) quad-formed, lead-mounting type; (d) dual in-line package (DIP) pinout of type 7404 hex inverter.

Now, refer back to Fig. 1-2. With the understanding of inverter-latch circuit action gained from the preceding experiment, it is easy to follow RS latch operation. *Observe that the RS latch becomes an inverter latch if both inputs of each NOR gate are tied together.* This is just another way of saying that a NOR gate functions as an inverter when its inputs are tied together.

To understand RS latch operation completely, note that when one input of a NOR gate is driven logic-high, and its other input is driven logic-low, the result is that the logic-high input takes precedence—the gate output will go logic-low. *A NOR gate waits for one of its inputs to be driven logic-high.* This is just another way of saying that an RS latch has no response when both of its inputs are driven logic-low (the latch outputs will merely remain unchanged, regardless of the Q and Q̄ states).

Also, it is now apparent why both inputs of an RS latch should not be driven logic-high simultaneously. For example, if S is driven logic-high, and R is driven logic-high (Fig. 1-2), the outputs of both NOR gates go logic-low. *These output logic-low states are applied to the NOR-gate inputs, whereby the outputs of both NOR gates attempt to go logic-high. Since this is an "impossible" circuit action, the resulting states will depend upon device tolerances—and the resulting states will be unpredictable.*

The technician should note that when we say "the resulting states will be unpredictable," we mean that a normal RS latch selected at random will have unpredictable output states if both of its inputs are driven logic-high. On the other hand, we do not mean that the *same* RS latch will have unpredictable output states after we determine how this *particular* latch responds to having both of its inputs driven logic-high. This is just another way of saying that a particular latch will always respond in the same way to having both of its inputs driven logic-high.

From the RS Latch to the D Latch

Troubleshooters are often concerned with D latches, such as depicted in Fig. 1-5. The designation "D" denotes that a single data input line is employed; by way of contrast, an RS latch has a pair of data input lines. The D input of a D latch is comparable to the S input of an RS latch.

Practical Note: To drive the input of a latch logic-high, a test lead may be connected between the latch input terminal and the V_{CC} source. This is usually a permissible test procedure. On the other hand, you may encounter latch circuitry in which V_{CC} is at its upper limit and in which this voltage exceeds the maximum-rated input voltage for the latch. Therefore, it is good foresight to use a 100-ohm resistor in series with the test lead.

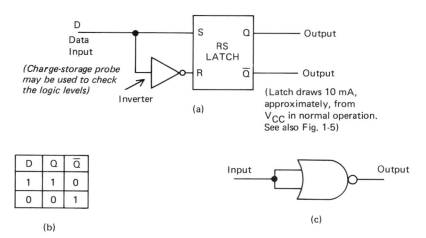

(a)

(b)

(c)

Note: A D latch consists of an RS latch and inverter, as shown in (a), and has the following characteristics:
1. The D latch has only one input, called the data (D) input.
2. This latch has a Q output which "follows" the D input.
3. A D latch is an asynchronous device (it is not clocked).
4. Advantages of the D latch are that the "forbidden" condition of the RS latch is eliminated and only one input line is required.
5. The Q and $\bar{Q}$ outputs are complementary; if Q goes logic-high, $\bar{Q}$ normally goes logic-low (and vice versa).
6. If the D input is driven +2 volts logic-high, the Q output typically goes +3.75 volts logic-high. Or, if the D input is driven logic-low (grounded), the Q output typically goes +0.09 volt logic-low.

Observe that the foregoing logic levels are typical of transistor-transistor logic (TTL). Circuit action of TTL configurations is explained in Chapter 2.

Fig. 1-5. D latch. (a) Logic diagram; (b) truth table; (c) NOR gate connected to operate as an inverter.

Trick of the Trade: With reference to Fig. 1-5, if you switch off the V_{CC} voltage, you can quick-check the D, Q, and $\bar{Q}$ terminals of the latch with the ohmmeter function of the DVM. Since the latch employs TTL circuitry with NPN devices, the D, Q, and $\bar{Q}$ terminals will normally check out at practically infinite resistance when the ohmmeter test lead is applied with positive polarity.

If the ohmmeter indicates other than an extremely high resistance, the troubleshooter concludes that the RS latch is defective, or that there is a fault in the associated circuitry. Sometimes the IC package is plugged into a socket—in such a case the IC can be easily removed for an out-of-circuit cross-check.

Note that many DVM's provide a lo-pwr ohms function. If you check the resistance at the latch terminals with the DVM operating on its lo-pwr ohms function, the ohmmeter test-lead polarity may be disregarded. We will return to consideration of resistance tests in digital circuitry in succeeding chapters.

"FLOATING" INPUT

The "bad region" of a gate was noted previously. With reference to Fig. 1-6, note that when a charge-storage probe is used to check latch circuitry, a "floating input" causes the LED to flash dimly; whereas, the LED will flash brightly if the input level is logic-high.

Practical Reminder

Since the logic-low level in Fig. 1-6 is normally about 0.1 volt above ground, the troubleshooter does not expect to measure zero volts. In other words, if the DVM happens to indicate zero volts, look for a short circuit to ground—the short circuit may be inside of the IC package, or it may be in the external circuitry.

Again, since the logic-high in Fig. 1-6 is normally about 3.75 volts above ground, the troubleshooter does not expect to measure 5 volts. This is just another way of saying that if the DVM happens to indicate 5 volts, look for a short circuit to V_{CC}. The short circuit may occur inside of the IC package, or it may occur in the external circuitry.

TEMPERATURE QUICK CHECKS

A helpful quick check that can often "spot" a short-circuit condition is shown in Fig. 1-7. The operating temperature of the IC is measured with a temperature probe and DVM. Since a short circuit to ground, for example, draws an abnormal amount of current, the power dissipated as heat by the IC increases accordingly. For example, a 7402 IC package has an absolute maximum temperature rating of 70°. In turn, if you happen to measure 75° (or even 70°), look for a short circuit.

Precise temperature quick checks can be made on a comparative basis, if you happen to have a similar unit of digital equipment available which is operating

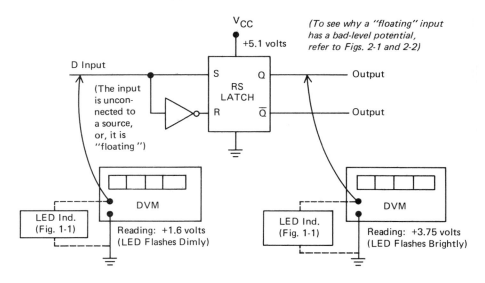

Fig. 1-6. Although the D input is in the "bad region," and is neither logic-high nor logic-low, the Q output is logic-high because a "floating" input "looks like a logic-high level" to the latch.

normally. Observe that a subnormal operating temperature indicates malfunction, just as an abnormal operating temperature indicates malfunction. As an illustration, if the ambient temperature is 21°C, and the IC package is operating at 22°C, it is indicated that malfunction is present.

LOGIC PROBE WITH SUPPLEMENTARY TONE INDICATOR

This one is not really "new," but it is of sufficient practical importance that it should be mentioned here. As shown in Fig. 1-8, a transistorized logic-probe arrangement may include supplementary tone indication. A logic-high level

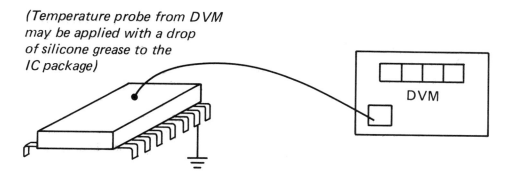

(Temperature probe from DVM may be applied with a drop of silicone grease to the IC package)

EXAMPLE: With an ambient temperature of 21°C, the typical "idling" temperature of the IC package will be 25°. One output shorted to ground, 28°; two outputs shorted to ground, 31°.

Fig. 1-7. Temperature check of integrated circuit.

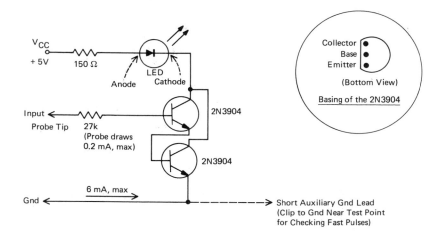

Note: LED glows brightest when probe tip is touched to a V_{cc} point ($+5.1$ volts).

LED glows bright when probe tip is touched to a logic-high point ($+3.75$ volts).

LED glows dimly when probe tip is touched to a "bad level" point ($+1.61$ volts).

Fig. 1-8. Simple LED logic-probe arrangement.

causes the LED to glow, and also causes the piezo buzzer to sound. A Radio Shack 273-060 solid-state buzzer is suitable.*

HIGH-Z LOGIC PROBE

Another one that is not really "new," but which is of basic importance to the troubleshooter is shown in Fig. 1-9. The distinctive feature of this logic probe is its very high input resistance. In turn, it is better suited to checking out CMOS logic circuits than is the probe depicted in Fig. 1-8. (The internal resistance of CMOS circuitry is often much higher than the internal resistance of TTL circuitry.)** Note also, that this high-Z probe is designed to operate in

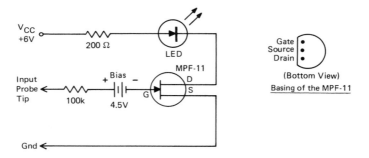

Note: LED glows when the probe tip is applied at a logic-high point. LED is dark when the probe tip is applied at a logic-low point. *If the probe tip is "floating," the LED will glow because the gate-source circuit is open-circuited (JFET is not reverse-biased).*

Note: When the probe tip is "floating" it will be observed that the brightness of the LED depends considerably on the position of the troubleshooter's hand, and where the probe tip is placed on the bench. The reason for this variation is the very high input impedance of the JFET, with the result that it responds to stray fields.

Fig. 1-9. High-impedance LED logic-probe arrangement uses a junction field-effect transistor.

---

*A variation of the basic probe circuit with "memory" is shown in Chapter 2.

** This configuration can be slightly elaborated to provide probe "memory," as shown in Chapter 2.

circuits with a V_{CC} supply of 5 or 6 volts. In other words, if a CMOS circuit operates with a V_{CC} supply of 3 volts, or 16 volts, don't use this probe—use your DVM instead.

PRACTICAL NOTE

Troubleshooters will find that a large percentage of digital circuitry involves NAND implementation. This means that you are likely to find various NAND-gate configurations in networks that would seem to require other kinds of gates.

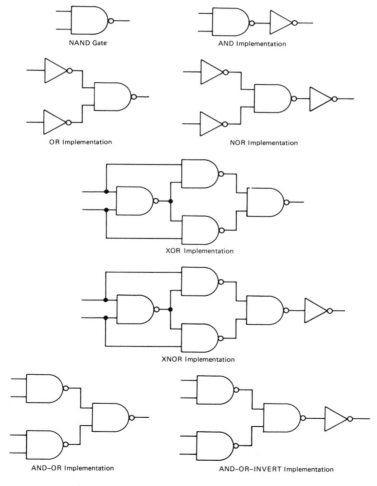

Fig. 1-10. Some typical NAND implementations.

The reason for this is that NAND gates were produced by manufacturers before other kinds of gates were made available. In turn, NAND implementation got a "head start" in commercial logic circuitry.

We have seen that a NAND gate may be operated with its inputs tied together to function as an inverter. With reference to Fig. 1-10, an AND gate may be devised by connecting a NAND gate in series with an inverter. A NOR gate may be devised by inverting the inputs of the NOR arrangement. Again, an OR gate may be devised by negating the inputs of a NAND gate.

Four NAND gates are often connected as shown in Fig. 1-10 to function as an XOR gate. If this arrangement is followed by an inverter, it functions as an XNOR gate. Three NAND gates may be connected as shown to function as an AND-OR gate. If this arrangement is followed by an inverter, it functions as an AND-OR-INVERT gate. We will return to this topic in subsequent chapters.

2

Latch Troubleshooting Procedures

Two-Tone Logic Probe • Ohmmeter Wipe Test • D Latch Source Resistance Requirement • Circuit Action with Subnormal V_{CC} • CMOS Inverter Latch • Alternate Latch Symbolism • Logic Probe with Pulse Memory • AND-NOT Gates • OR-NOT Logic Probe with Pulse Memory • Single-Shot Pulse Generators • Double-Ended Single-Shot Pulser • Lo-Pwr Ohmmeter Reminder • Piezo-Buzzer IC Quick Checker

TWO-TONE LOGIC PROBE

Digital troubleshooters sometimes prefer to use logic probes that provide audio tone output; it may be less distracting to listen to sound signals than to watch LED indicators. The simplest two-tone logic-level probe arrangement is shown in Fig. 2-1. It consists of two piezo buzzers, a 3-volt battery, and an SPDT switch.

In the exemplified arrangement, a spring-leaf loaded SPDT switch is used; however, any SPDT switch will serve the same purpose. When the probe tip is touched to a logic-high point, current flows into piezo buzzer PB1, and a high-pitched sound is outputted. On the other hand, when the probe tip is touched to a logic-low point, piezo buzzer PB1 remains silent.

Next, the probe tip is pressed firmly against the test point. If the point is logic-low, current flows from the 3-volt battery into piezo buzzer PB2 and a low-pitched sound is outputted. However, if the point is logic-high, PB2 remains silent because of cancellation by the 3-volt battery.

Note that if the test point is a "bad level," PB1 will output a weak sound; PB2 will remain silent. Again, if both PB1 and PB2 remain silent, the troubleshooter concludes that the test point is an open circuit. Note also that this two-tone probe should be used only in TTL circuitry—it is not suitable for CMOS circuit testing.

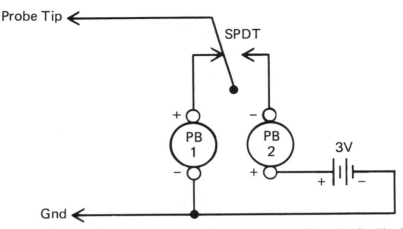

Note: Piezo buzzer PB1 is the logic-high indicator. It may be a Radio Shack 273-060. Piezo buzzer PB2 is the logic-low indicator; it has a lower pitch than PB1. Piezo buzzer PB2 may be a Mallory Sonalert 5C628.

Fig. 2-1. Simplest two-tone logic-probe arrangement.

OHMMETER WIPE TEST

One of the most useful quick checks in TTL circuitry is an ohmmeter wipe test. The troubleshooter connects the negative lead of his ohmmeter to ground, and "wipes" the positive test lead along the pins of the IC packages. Thereby, various defective nodes can be easily "spotted." (See Chart 2-1.)

As noted in the previous chapter, most gates have multi-emitter inputs and totem-pole output with NPN implementation. Accordingly, input and output terminals on the IC will normally "look like" open circuits in a wipe test. If the ohmmeter "kicks," the troubleshooter should check out the associated node for a possible defect.

Observe in Chart 2-1 that the V_{CC} terminal normally has finite resistance to ground, such as 28 kilohms. Therefore, the ohmmeter will normally "kick" at a V_{CC} terminal in a wipe test. A "false alarm" could occasionally be caused by certain expandable-AND circuits, or by a wired-AND circuit. We will return to this topic in later chapters.

> *Caution:* If a hi-pwr ohmmeter is used that operates with a 9-volt battery on its Rx10,000 range, a good NOR gate will *seem* to fail the reverse-resistance test. *This "false alarm" is due to zener action from the comparatively high test voltage.* To avoid this misleading situation, operate the ohmmeter on its Rx1000 range.

CHART 2-1

How a Normally Operating NOR-Gate IC Package "Looks" to an Ohmmeter

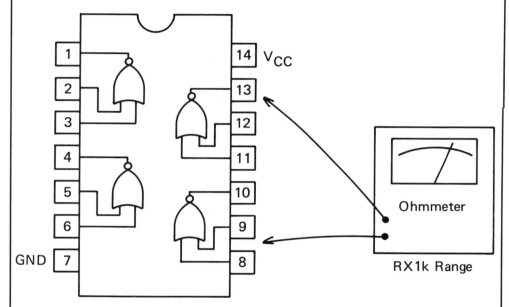

QUAD 2-INPUT NOR GATE

Pin 14 to any other pin (except pin 7) with pin 14 negative, infinite ohms.

Pin 14 to pin 7, with pin 14 negative, 28 kilohms.

Pin 14 to pin 13, 10, 4, or 1, with pin 14 positive, 40 kilohms.

Pin 14 to pin 12, 11, 9, 8, 6, 5, 3, or 2, with pin 14 positive, 16 kilohms.

Pin 14 to pin 7, with pin 14 positive, 28 kilohms.

Note: The finite resistance values listed above are typical; they may be somewhat lower or higher in practice, depending upon the VOM that is used.

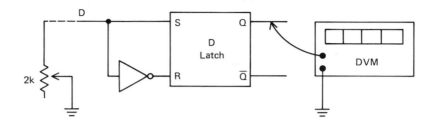

Note: This demonstration shows that TTL is basically a low-impedance family, and that high-resistance sources or open circuits can cause system malfunction. Although the actual impedance of TTL circuits encountered by the troubleshooter will vary considerably, a rough rule of thumb states that the internal resistance of a TTL circuit is 150 ohms.

Fig. 2-2. Demonstration of D-latch source-resistance requirement.

D-LATCH SOURCE RESISTANCE REQUIREMENT

This simple experiment demonstrates the source resistance range that is required for normal operation of a D latch. The procedure is as follows:

1. With reference to Fig. 2-2, connect a dc voltmeter at the Q output.
2. With the D input "floating," note that the Q output is logic-high.
3. Connect the D input through a 2-kilohm potentiometer to ground; this potentiometer functions as the internal resistance of the logic-low source.
4. As the potentiometer resistance is reduced, a point will be noted at which the Q input goes logic-high (voltmeter reading rapidly increases from +0.09V to +3.75V).
5. Disconnect the potentiometer and measure its resistance; this value will be approximately 600 ohms.

Accordingly, we recognize that TTL circuitry is low-impedance circuitry. A driving source must have an internal impedance of less than 600 ohms to ensure normal operation of the driven circuit. *In normal operation, a TTL circuit has a dynamic internal resistance in the range from 100 to 200 ohms.*

> *Practical Example:* The logic-high level at the output of the foregoing D latch measures +3.75V. When a 1000-ohm resistor is shunted from the output terminal to ground, the logic-high level is reduced to 3.31V. This is a decrement of 0.44V at a current flow of 3.31 mA. Accordingly, the dynamic internal resistance is equal to 133 ohms.

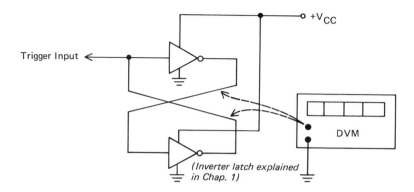

Trigger Input

+V_{CC}

DVM

(Inverter latch explained
in Chap. 1)

Note: As V_{CC} decreases from its normal value of +5.1V to lower values, the logic-high voltage becomes less than normal, and the logic-low voltage becomes greater than normal. For example, when V_{CC} is +5.1V, the logic-high voltage is 3.88V, approximately, and the logic-low voltage is about 0.07V. On the other hand, when V_{CC} is reduced to +2.1V, the logic-high voltage becomes 1.44V, and the logic-low voltage becomes 1.04V. The latch will still trigger at this value of V_{CC}. However, when V_{CC} is reduced to 2.0V, the logic-high voltage becomes the same as the logic-low voltage, or 1.26V. In turn, the latch will no longer "flip" or "flop."

Fig. 2-3. Demonstration of circuit-action change due to subnormal V_{CC} voltage.

Circuit Action with Subnormal V_{CC}

It was previously noted that obscure digital trouble symptoms can be caused by subnormal V_{CC} voltage. Observe that when the V_{CC} voltage for an inverter latch is subnormal, its circuit action becomes modified as shown in Fig. 2-3. This trouble symptom appears as "bad-level" logic-high and logic-low voltages, although the latch will continue to trigger until V_{CC} decreases below 2.1V, approximately.

CMOS Inverter Latch

Since digital troubleshooters may encounter CMOS latch circuitry, it is helpful to observe the normal logic-high and logic-low voltages when the inverters in Fig. 2-3 are implemented with CMOS NOR gates. (When the two inputs of a NOR gate are tied together, the gate operates as an inverter.) If you wish to make the experiment, you may use a 4001 COS/MOS quad two-input gate IC package.

The supply voltage for this inverter latch can range from 3 to 18 volts. It is instructive to power the latch from a 5.1V source, just as the previous TTL latch was powered. In this case, you will measure approximately 5 volts at a logic-high node, and virtually 0 volts at a logic-low node.

ALTERNATE LATCH SYMBOLISM

We must be alert for alternate latch symbolism, as exemplified in Fig. 2-4. The RS latch described in Chapter 1 was configured from NOR gates, and it operated with active-high input. In other words, when the S input was driven logic-high and the R input was simultaneously driven logic-low, the Q output went logic-high.

Next, observe the common NAND implementation of an RS latch, depicted in Fig. 2-4(a). This logic circuit looks similar to the NOR implementation— but its operation is quite different. Note than when the $\overline{S}$ input is driven logic-low and the $\overline{R}$ input is simultaneously driven logic-high, the Q output will go logic-high. This is called an active-low RS latch.

The inversion bars over $\overline{R}$ and $\overline{S}$ in Fig. 2-4(a) denote that to output a logic 1 at Q, $\overline{S}$ must be driven 0, and $\overline{R}$ must simultaneously be driven 1. Note that $\overline{1} = 0$. We will often encounter active-low circuitry as we proceed with explanations of digital troubleshooting techniques.

Another active-low NAND implementation of an RS latch is shown in Fig. 2-4(b). In this example, the NAND function is performed by a negated-OR

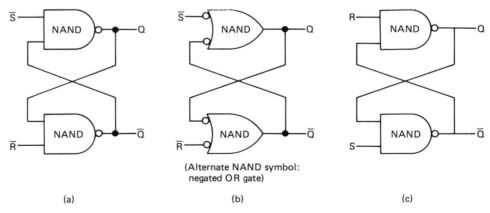

(Alternate NAND symbol: negated OR gate)

(a)   (b)   (c)

Fig. 2-4. Alternate latch symbolism. (a) Active-low RS latch with NAND implementation; (b) active-low RS latch with negated-OR implementation; (c) active-high RS latch with NAND implementation.

gate; stated otherwise, when inverters are connected in series with the inputs to an OR gate, the arrangement operates as a NAND gate. A useful general rule states that if all the level indicators for an AND gate are inverted, the AND symbol is replaced by the OR symbol to retain the original function.

We can restate this general rule in the form: If all of the level indicators for an OR gate are inverted, the OR symbol is replaced by the AND symbol to retain the original function.

Observe next the NAND RS latch implementation shown in Fig. 2-4(c). This is similar to the configuration depicted in (a)—with one important difference. Note that the latch inputs in (c) are indicated R and S; whereas, the corresponding inputs in (a) are indicated $\overline{S}$ and $\overline{R}$. In other words, this "switch" makes the NAND RS latch implementation in (c) active-high.

LOGIC PROBE WITH PULSE MEMORY

A logic probe with pulse memory can be constructed as shown in Fig. 2-5. This is an important type of probe for practical test procedures because it will

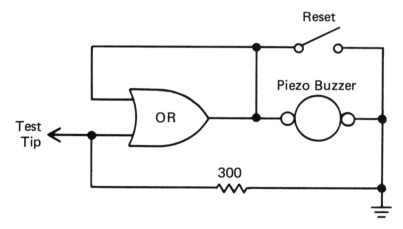

Note: The 300-ohm resistor serves only to prevent the test tip from "floating" while it is not connected to any test point.

In other words, if the 300-ohm resistor were omitted, the test tip would float to a bad level whenever the test tip was unconnected from a test point. This bad level would be interpreted as a logic-high level, and the piezo buzzer would output an audio tone. Thus, the 300-ohm resistor prevents "false alarms" in practical test procedures.

Fig. 2-5. Logic probe configuration with pulse memory.

"catch" and "hold" a momentary change in logic levels. In turn, this probe is particularly useful for monitoring intermittent digital circuits. It is a TTL device, and can be implemented with a 74LS32 OR gate.

Observe that one of the OR-gate inputs in Fig. 2-5 is fed back to the output terminal. This feedback connection provides the pulse-memory function of the logic probe. Operation is as follows:

1. When the reset switch is closed, both inputs are logic-low, and the output is logic-low. The piezo buzzer is silent.

2. When the reset switch is then opened, both inputs remain logic-low, and the output remains logic-low. The piezo buzzer is silent.

3. If a logic-high pulse is applied to the test tip, one input goes logic-high. The output goes logic-high, and the piezo buzzer outputs an audio tone.

4. After the pulse has passed, the test tip goes logic-low. However, the output remains logic-high because the output is feeding back a logic-high level to the input. (This is the pulse memory function.)

5. The piezo buzzer will then continue to output an audio tone until the reset switch is closed.

6. Then, when the reset switch is opened, the probe is "armed" once again. The piezo buzzer will remain silent until the test tip is driven logic-high.

AND-NOT GATES

An AND-NOT gate consists of an AND gate with one or more negated inputs, as exemplified in Fig. 2-6. A two-input AND gate with one negated input

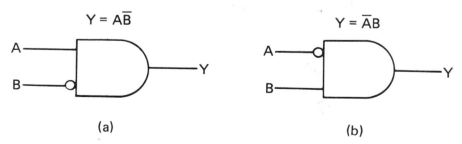

$$Y = A\overline{B} \qquad\qquad Y = \overline{A}B$$

(a)   (b)

Note: A "bubble" at the input of a gate denotes that the applied signal is inverted before it passes into the gate. This is called a negated input.

Fig. 2-6. Examples of AND-NOT gates. (a) A AND-NOT B gate; (b) B AND-NOT A gate.

is shown in Fig. 2-6(a). This is an A AND-NOT B gate. Next, a two-input AND gate with negated A input is shown in (b). This is a B AND-NOT A gate. If a three-input AND gate has its B input negated, it is termed an A AND C AND-NOT B gate. An AND gate with all of its inputs negated is called a NEGATED-AND gate. A NEGATED-AND gate differs from a NAND gate, as seen in Chart 2-2.

Observe in Chart 2-2 that if the output from an A AND-NOT B gate is inverted, it becomes equivalent to a B OR-NOT A gate. Similarly, if the output from a B AND-NOT A gate is inverted, it becomes equivalent to an A OR-NOT B gate. These relations follow from the logic law which states that if all of the level indicators on an AND gate are inverted, it becomes equivalent to an OR gate. Similarly, if all of the level indicators on an OR gate are inverted, it becomes equivalent to an AND gate.

CHART 2-2
AND-NOT and OR-NOT Gate Relations

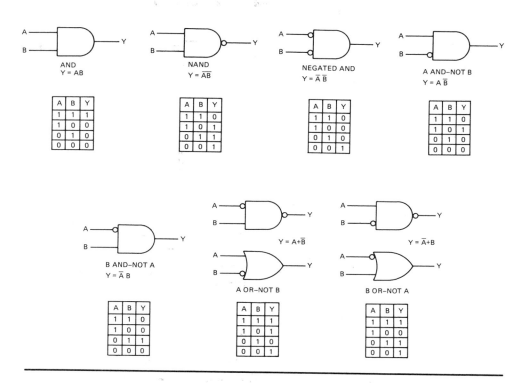

OR-NOT LOGIC PROBE WITH PULSE MEMORY

Next, an OR-NOT logic probe configuration with pulse memory is depicted in Fig. 2-7. We will note that this probe employs the same basic principle as the probe depicted in Fig. 2-5, except that an OR-NOT gate is used, instead of an OR gate. The OR-NOT gate makes the probe responsive to a momentary logic-low level. Operation is as follows:

1. When the reset switch is closed, both inputs are logic-low if the test tip is connected to a logic-high test point. The output goes logic-low, and piezo buzzer is silent.

2. When the reset switch is then opened, both inputs remain logic-low, and the output remains logic-low. The piezo buzzer is silent.

3. If the test tip momentarily goes logic-low, the probe output goes logic-high, and the piezo buzzer outputs an audio tone.

4. After the logic-low pulse has passed, the test tip again goes logic-high. The piezo buzzer continues to sound because the output is feeding back a logic-high level to the input. (This is the pulse memory function.)

5. The piezo buzzer will then continue to output an audio tone until the reset switch is closed.

6. Then, when the reset switch is opened, the probe is "armed" once again. The piezo buzzer will remain silent until the test tip is driven logic-low.

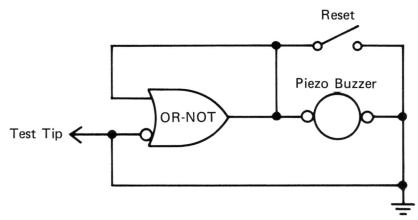

Note: The OR-NOT gate may be implemented from a 74LS32 two-input OR gate with an inverter consisting of a two-input 7402 NOR gate with both inputs tied together.

Fig. 2-7. Another logic-probe configuration with pulse memory.

SINGLE-SHOT PULSE GENERATORS

Most digital troubleshooters know that a single-shot test-pulse generator can be improvised from a 0.05-μF fixed capacitor. If the capacitor is connected between the V_{CC} and ground points in a TTL circuit, it becomes charged to about 5 volts. Then, if the charged capacitor is touched between a device input terminal and ground, a positive pulse is injected into the device.

Note that in the case of an active-low device, a negative-going pulse can be injected into the device. In other words, the troubleshooter reverses the terminals of the charged capacitor and applies a corresponding negative pulse to the device input terminal. This is a useful trick of the trade in practical troubleshooting procedures.

Busy digital technicians may prefer to use a convenient high/low single-shot pulser, such as shown in Fig. 2-8. This pulser operates on the basis of charging current flow. The 5-meg bleeder resistors function to discharge the capacitors after a pulse test has been completed. This pulser speeds up practical test work inasmuch as the SPDT switch permits ready pulsing of either active-high or active-low devices.

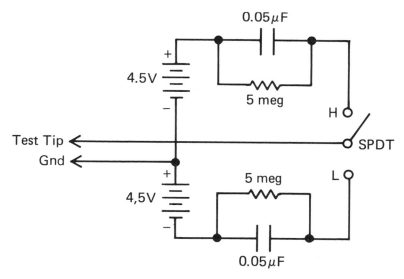

This simple quick checker provides fast and easy pulse tests in digital circuits.

Fig. 2-8. A handy high/low single-shot pulser.

DOUBLE-ENDED SINGLE-SHOT PULSER

Most pulse-injection tests involve single-ended positive pulses or single-ended negative pulses. Occasionally, double-ended (complementary) pulses need to be injected. An example is an RS latch; the latch has two inputs which must be driven by high/low or by low/high pulses. It is essential that the test pulses be applied simultaneously. This consideration rules out mechanical switching arrangements. Instead, logic switches are needed, as exemplified in Fig. 2-9.

Observe that this double-ended single-shot pulser is configured around a D latch with capacitively coupled output to the circuit under test. The pulser may

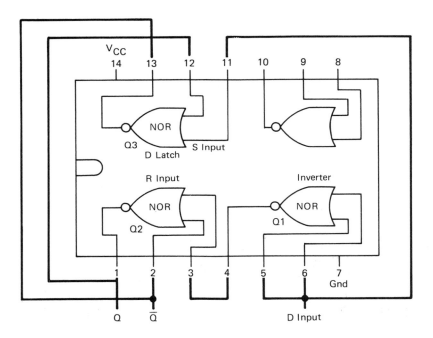

Operating Note: If the D input is connected to a logic-high point, there is no pulse output until the D input is disconnected from the logic-high point, and connected to a logic-low point (or ground). Then a single pair of pulses is outputted. Next, a complementary pair of pulses will be outputted when the D input is disconnected from the logic-low point and connected to a logic-high point. (Remember too, that a "floating" D input looks like a logic-high input to the D latch.)

Fig. 2-9. **Configuration for a double-ended single-shot pulser.**

be constructed from a 7402 quad two-input positive NOR gate IC package. Note that when the D input is connected to a logic-high point, test-tip one outputs a positive-going pulse and test-tip two outputs a negative-going pulse. Next, if the D input is connected to a logic-low point, test-tip one outputs a negative-going pulse and test-tip two outputs a positive-going pulse.

LO-PWR OHMMETER REMINDER

When using lo-pwr ohmmeters, troubleshooters should keep in mind that there are two varieties of such ohmmeters in common use. One type of lo-pwr ohmmeter applies less than 0.1V between the test points, and can be used to check circuitry that has either silicon or germanium devices, or both. On the other hand, the other type of low-pwr ohmmeter applies less than 0.5V between the test points; it is suitable only for checking circuitry that has silicon devices.

PIEZO-BUZZER IC QUICK CHECKER

Instead of using an ohmmeter, the digital troubleshooter often prefers to use an audio-tone resistance quick checker for preliminary tests of TTL IC packages and circuitry. With reference to Fig. 2-10, a piezo-buzzer and battery can be arranged to apply either a positive test voltage or a negative test voltage to IC pins or digital circuit nodes.

If a NOR-gate IC package is under test, for example, the troubleshooter may use the quick checker to apply a positive test voltage to the IC pins. In turn, he normally expects the piezo buzzer to remain silent except when the test tip is applied to pin 14 or pin 7 (V_{CC} and Ground pins). Otherwise, the IC is defective and should be discarded.

A follow-up test can be made with the quick checker to apply a negative test voltage to the IC pins. In this test, the troubleshooter expects the piezo buzzer to output an audio tone when the test tip is touched to any pin. Otherwise, the pin is "open," and the IC is defective.

Observe that when power is removed from a TTL circuit, such as the configuration shown in Fig. 2-9, the same test results are normally expected when the troubleshooter uses the quick checker to apply a positive test voltage or a negative test voltage at any node in the circuit. Otherwise, there is a defect present which should be investigated.

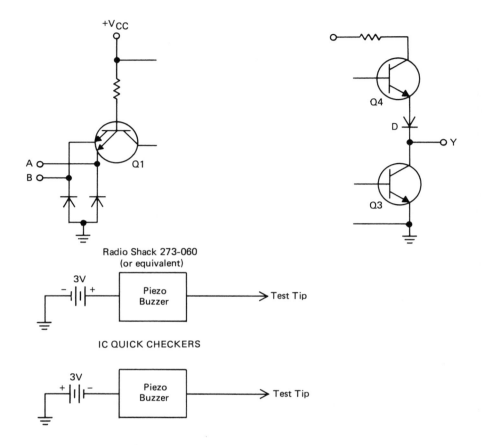

IC QUICK CHECKERS

Technical Note: Since most TTL circuitry employs multi-emitter inputs and to-tem-pole output, input and output terminals normally present an extremely high resistance to a positive test voltage, but present a low resistance to a negative test voltage.

Fig. 2-10. Piezo-buzzer IC quick checker for TTL devices.

3

Counter Troubleshooting Techniques

Counter Action • Counter Circuitry • Toggle-Latch Chain Operation • Active-High/Active-Low • Asynchronous Counter Experiment • Slow-Pulse Generator Operation • Unexpected Generator Action • Count-Down Ripple Counter • Subnormal V_{CC} Voltage • Count-Up/Count-Down Ripple Counter • Simple Counter Readout Probe • Asynchronous Decade Ripple Counter Action

COUNTER ACTION

A counter is a logic circuit which counts input pulses. For example, a widely used type of counter outputs a pulse each time that it inputs a predetermined number of input pulses. Counters are also called dividers. There are two basic forms of counters:

1. An asynchronous counter can input pulses at any time. It is unclocked and its operating speed depends only on the signal propagation through the circuitry, rather than on clock pulses as in synchronous counters.

2. A synchronous counter is clocked, and its operations take place in step with clock pulses.

Asynchronous counters are also called serial or ripple counters. An asynchronous counter comprises a chain of latches. The term "serial" means that trigger pulses are applied to Latch 1, after which Latch 2 is triggered from Latch 1, and so on. The term "ripple" means that the carry bit from Latch 1 is passed into Latch 2, from which it may be passed into Latch 3, and so on. The speed of ripple carry depends on the latch propagation time. A latch has a typical propagation delay of 15 ns. (See Chart 3-1.)

CHART 3-1

Toggle-Latch Chain Operation

A single toggle-latch unit is depicted below. If a pulse is applied at its input, it changes to its "on" state. When a second pulse is applied, it returns to its "off" state, and also produces an output pulse. Finally, if a third pulse is applied, it changes to its "on" state.

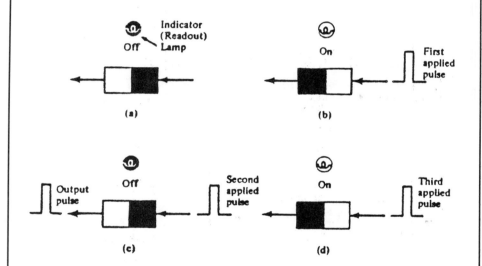

Changes of state in an electronic-switch device. (a) Electronic switch is off; (b) pulse is applied to switch and switch changes to on state; (c) a second pulse is applied to switch and switch changes to off state as it produces an output pulse; (d) a third pulse is applied to switch and switch changes to on state.

The toggle latches may use a configuration such as shown in Fig. 2-4.

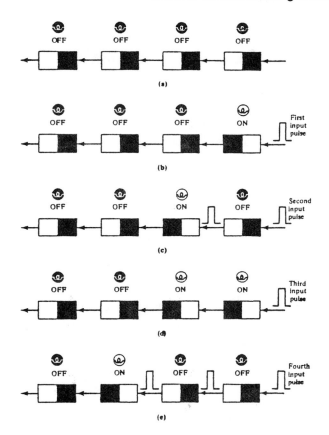

Electronic-switch chain operation: (a) Resting state of chain; (b) first input pulse applied and first switch device changes state; (c) second input pulse applied and first switch device changes state as an output pulse is produced and second switch device changes state; (d) third input pulse applied and first switch device changes state; (e) fourth input pulse applied and the first switch device changes state as two output pulses are produced and the second and third switch devices also change state.

(Reproduced by special permission of Reston Publishing Co. and Lloyd Rich from Understanding Microprocessors*)*

COUNTER-CIRCUITRY

A counter consists of a chain of latches. Note that simple latches, such as the RS and D latches that have been described, must be elaborated before they can operate in counter circuits. In other words, a suitable latch must output one pulse for every two input pulses. This is called a toggle latch. In the current state of the art, master-slave flip-flops are ordinarily configured as toggle latches.

The master section of a master-slave toggle latch loads an input pulse; it holds (stores) this input pulse until another pulse is inputted. Thereupon the stored pulse is unloaded into the slave section, and the second input pulse is stored. This "see-saw" action continues as long as input pulses are applied. This is just another way of saying that a toggle latch counts to 2_{10} (10_2), and then starts over again.

Digital troubleshooters should carefully note the following fact, because it is a bit tricky: The master-slave flip-flops used in asynchronous counters are the same master-slave flip-flops used in synchronous counters. A master-slave FF utilized in an asynchronous counter is not clocked. On the other hand, a master-slave FF utilized in a synchronous counter is clocked.

Note carefully that the clock input terminal of a master-slave FF employed in a toggle latch is connected as a trigger (signal) pulse input terminal. (See Fig. 3-1.) On the other hand, the clock terminal of a master-slave FF employed in a

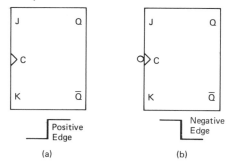

(a)   (b)

Note: A positive-edge triggered flip-flop can accept J and K data input only during the brief moment while the clock pulse is rising from logic-low to logic-high. On the other hand, a negative-edge triggered flip-flop can accept J and K data input only during the brief moment while the clock pulse is falling from logic-high to logic-low.

An edge-triggered flip-flop differs from a level-triggered flip-flop in that the latter can accept J and K data input at any time while the clock pulse is logic-high.

Fig. 3-1. Symbols for edge-triggered flipflops. (a) Positive-edge triggered; (b) negative-edge triggered.

toggle flip-flop is connected as a clock-pulse terminal. Beginners sometimes become confused when they observe a "clock" terminal on a master-slave FF connected as a data signal terminal.

Most counter circuitry is implemented with JK master-slave flip-flops. A JK FF is somewhat similar to an RS FF or RS latch, with one important difference: Both inputs of a JK FF can be driven logic-high, and the output is predictable—the output will be the complement of the preceding Q and $\bar{Q}$ states. Thus, a JK FF is more versatile than an RS FF. (The letters J and K have no particular meaning, other than their truth-table significance.)

A widely used JK master-slave FF logic circuit is shown in Fig. 3-2. The master section is in the lower portion of the diagram; the slave section is in the upper portion of the diagram. Note the clear and the preset inputs. The clear input is similar to a reset input; when driven logic-low, the Q output will be forced to 0 at any time. The preset input is similar to a set input; when driven logic-low, the Q output will be forced to 1 at any time.

Active-High/Active-Low

Digital troubleshooters must make careful distinction between active-high and active-low inputs for JK flip-flops. Otherwise, a trouble symptom is likely to be incorrectly evaluated. With reference to Fig. 3-3, an active-high input produces circuit action when the input signal goes logic-high. On the other hand, an active-low input produces circuit action when the input signal goes logic-low.

Note that active-high and active-low inputs relate to the same logic function, but denote a half clock-cyle difference in clock time for initiating circuit action. An active-low flip-flop can be operated as an active-high flip-flop by inserting an inverter in series with the clock line.

Asynchronous Counter Experiment

Unless you have had considerable experience in troubleshooting digital circuitry, you will find it both interesting and instructive to construct and check out the asynchronous counter depicted in Fig. 3-4. Note that negative-edge triggered JK flip-flops are used—but the circuit is unclocked and the clock-input terminals function as data signal-input terminals.

The counter may be driven from a pulse generator or from a square-wave generator—the generator should output a very low frequency signal, so that the counter action can be easily followed. You can monitor the output at each Q terminal with a logic probe. If you have four probes, and connect one at each Q output, the count readout is evident at any time.

Most counter trouble symptoms are caused by open circuits or by short cir-

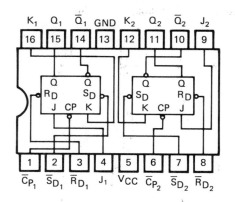

Package Pinout

t_n		t_{n+1}
J	K	Q
0	L	Q_n
L	1	L
H	L	H
H	H	$\bar{Q}_n$

NOTES:

t_n = Bit time before clock pulse.
t_{n+1} = Bit time after clock pulse.

Positive logic:
    LOW input to preset sets Q to HIGH level
    LOW input to clear sets Q to LOW level
    Clear and preset are independent of clock

Truth Table

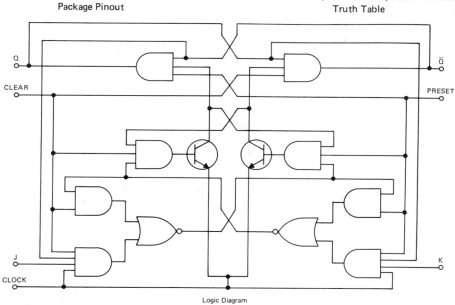

Logic Diagram

Technical Note: JK master/slave flip-flops are commonly manufactured with two units in the same IC package, as exemplified above. In this example, the preset, clear, and clock terminals for each flip-flop are individually pinned out. On the other hand, other dual IC packages have both clock terminals connected to the same pin; separate "clocks" are not provided. Similarly, another dual IC package may have both clear terminals connected to the same pin; separate "clears" are not provided. The counter experiments discussed in this chapter require JK flip-flops with separate clocks.

Fig. 3-2. JK master-slave flip-flop with separate presets, clears, and clocks.

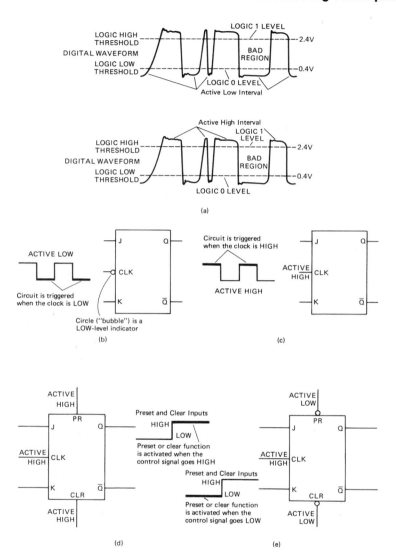

Fig. 3-3. Active-high and active-low examples. (a) Active-high and active-low intervals in digital waveforms; (b) qualified clock input (with circle) denotes that the clock input is active-low; (c) unqualified clock input denotes that the clock input is active-high; (d) preset and clear inputs are active-high; (e) clock input active-high, preset and clear inputs active-low.

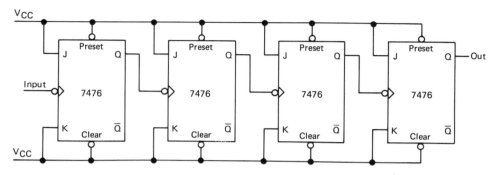

Construction Note: This asynchronous counter is configured from two 7476 dual JK flip-flops. The preset and clear inputs are tied to V_{CC} so that they have no effect on counter action. The J and K inputs are also tied to V_{CC} in order to make the flip-flops toggle in response to input pulses.

The start-up states of the flip-flops are unpredictable. When input pulses are applied (as from a square-wave generator), the counter will be cleared after 15 pulses have been loaded.

Observe that this is an "up" binary counter: the count progresses 0000, 0001, 0010, 0011, 0100, 0101, 0110, 0111, 1000, 1001, 1010, 1011, 1100, 1101, 1110, 1111, and then repeats.

Observe also, that since pulses are inputted to the lefthand toggle latch, that the count must be read out "backwards"—from right to left.

Fig. 3-4. Experimental asynchronous counter.

cuits, either inside IC packages or in the external circuitry. "Noisy" V_{CC} lines and subnormal V_{CC} voltage will also cause counter malfunction.

Experiment: With reference to Fig. 3-4, disconnect one of the preset terminals from the V_{CC} line. An open circuit is now present. Does a trouble symptom result? *Hint:* A "floating" TTL input appears logic-high to the circuit inside of the IC.

Experiment: Disconnect one of the preset terminals from the V_{CC} line, and connect it to ground. A short circuit is now present. Does a trouble symptom result? *Hint:* A logic-low preset forces the Q output to 1.

Experiment: Remove the short circuit to the preset terminal, and reconnect the preset terminal to V_{CC}. Normal counting action is then restored. Now, disconnect one of the J terminals from V_{CC}, and connect it to ground. A short circuit is now present. Does a trouble symptom result? *Hint:* Unless the J and K terminals of the flip-flop are both maintained logic-high, the flip-flop will not toggle.

Experiment: Disconnect the trigger source from the input of the counter. Trigger the counter manually with a test lead connected to the input of the counter. The input will be logic-high ("floating") while the test lead is open-ended. Next, when you touch the end of the test lead to ground, the input is pulsed logic-low. Observe that as you make and break contact to ground repeatedly, the counting action is erratic and unpredictable. Why does the counter malfunction? *Hint*: Mechanical switching is notorious for "bounce."

SLOW-PULSE GENERATOR OPERATION

Counter troubleshooting is often facilitated by driving the input line with a slow-pulse generator such as depicted in Fig. 3-5. This test unit outputs a very low frequency square wave which permits the troubleshooter to easily check the counter response with a logic probe. Note that the operating frequency of the generator can be changed, if desired, by changing the values of the coupling capacitors.

Unexpected Generator Action

In practice, confusion could result from unexpected generator action in the arrangement of Fig. 3-5. In other words, if you disconnect the V_{CC} supply from the slow-pulse generator, the counter continues to operate somewhat erratically. This unexpected situation results from the "sneak voltage" that backs up from

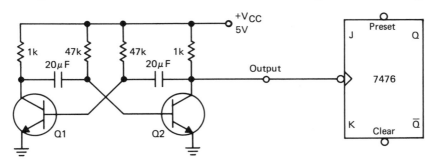

Technical Note: When the V_{CC} line is disconnected from the slow-pulse generator, the bad-level voltage from the input of the JK flip-flop "backs up" into the generator. In turn, the generator is energized and continues to operate.

Fig. 3-5. Slow-pulse generator continues to operate when V_{CC} line is disconnected.

the JK flip-flop input to the collector of Q2. This "bad level" voltage is sufficient to provide marginal operation of the slow-pulse generator.

To avoid this unexpected generator action, a $0.05\mu F$ coupling capacitor can be connected in series with the Q2 output from the slow-pulse generator. This capacitor passes the ac pulse voltage into the JK flip-flop, but prevents the "bad level" dc voltage from "backing up" from the input terminal into the generator.

Count-Down Ripple Counter

Troubleshooters will find count-down configurations such as shown in Fig. 3-6 in various digital networks. JK toggle latches are commonly employed; the clock input terminal is driven from the $\bar{Q}$ output of the preceding latch to obtain count-down action. Note that although 7476 JK flip-flops are exemplified in Fig. 3-6, any flip-flop in the same family may be utilized.

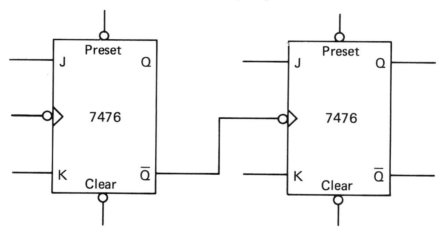

Note: The counter arrangement in Fig. 3-4 is rearranged as shown above to obtain binary "down" counter action. In other words, the count progresses 1111, 1110, 1101, and so on down to 0000. The cycle then repeats. Note that since pulses are inputted to the lefthand toggle latch, that the count must be read out "backwards"—from right to left.

Troubleshooting Hint: Counters sometimes develop erratic counting action which cannot be tracked down with usual digital test equipment. A "tough dog" problem of this type is likely to be caused by very narrow glitches from the power supply. For a quick check, disconnect the power supply and check counter operation with the digital system powered from an emergency source such as batteries.

Fig. 3-6. A count-down ripple counter arrangement.

Subnormal V_{CC} Voltage

Unnecessary waste of time is sometimes incurred in troubleshooting digital systems because the technician forgot to measure V_{CC} first. In the case of the ripple counters that have been described, counting action becomes unreliable at V_{CC} potentials less than 3V. When V_{CC} drops to less than 2.5V, counter action completely stops. Subnormal V_{CC} voltage is usually tracked down to a defective power supply. Excessive loading due to a short circuit somewhere in the digital system can also result in subnormal V_{CC} voltage.

COUNT-UP, COUNT-DOWN RIPPLE COUNTER

You will encounter quite a few count-up/count-down counter arrangements in digital systems. A simple asynchronous configuration that provides NAND-gate switching from count-up to count-down modes of operation is shown in Fig. 3-7. Unless the circuit action is properly recognized, trouble symptoms

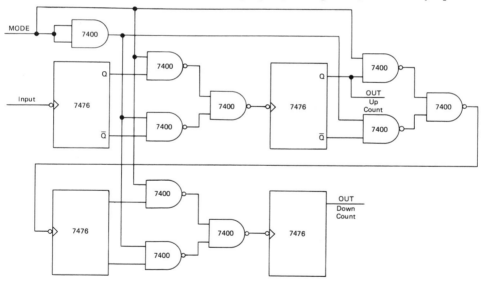

Circuit Action Note: When the mode line is logic-high, the upper toggle latches operate as in the basic up counter. However, operation of the lower toggle latches is inhibited. Conversely, when the mode line is logic-low, the lower toggle latches operate as in the basic down counter, and operation of the upper toggle latches is inhibited.

Fig. 3-7. Asynchronous count-up/count-down ripple counter configuration with NAND-gate mode switching.

could be incorrectly evaluated. The essential requirement is to understand and to observe the mode-switching action.

Each group of three NAND gates functions as an AND-OR gate, as previously explained for NAND implementation. You will observe that when the mode line is logic-high, the upper toggle latches operate as in the basic up counter, inasmuch as the toggle-latch outputs pass through the AND-OR gate and effectively apply a Q output to the following toggle latch.

On the other hand, when the mode line is logic-low, the lower toggle latches operate as in the basic down counter, since the toggle-latch outputs pass through the AND-OR gate and effectively apply a $\bar{Q}$ output to the following toggle latch. Observe also that while the mode line is logic-low, the up-counter section is inhibited, due to sustained blocking of signal flow by the AND-OR gate.

Digital troubleshooters must take particular care to identify an up-counter arrangement, a down-counter arrangement, and an up/down counter arrangement; in the latter situation, close attention must also be given to the mode-control circuitry. Sometimes the service manual will provide a counter truth table. On the other hand, if a truth table is not available, the troubleshooter must fall back on his knowledge of logic-circuit action.

SIMPLE COUNTER READOUT PROBE

A simple counter readout probe is shown in Fig. 3-8. It provides readouts up to eight bits, and can be connected into counter circuitry so that the display is in standard form from left to right. Micromini LED's such as Radio Shack 276-032 are suitable. The components and devices may be mounted on a small PC board in "flat pack" form. This tester is also useful in decoder troubleshooting, as explained subsequently.

ASYNCHRONOUS DECADE RIPPLE COUNTER ACTION

Another widely used type of counter in digital systems is the decade ripple counter configuration exemplified in Fig. 3-9. It is called a decade counter because it automatically recycles after ten pulses have been inputted. Note that the display is in binary form; in other words, the display progresses from 0000 to 1010. It is important for the troubleshooter to recognize this basic distinction between the decade ripple counter and the basic binary ripple counter.

Observe in Fig. 3-9 that the clear line will remain logic-high until the count has progressed to 10_{10} (1010_2). Thereupon, both of the NAND gate inputs go

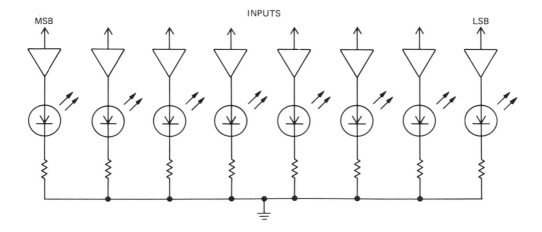

Note: Eight LED indicators are utilized with eight buffers and eight 330-ohm resistors. The buffers may consist of AND gates with the inputs of each gate tied together. This is a "piggy back" arrangement that is powered from V_{CC} in the circuit under test.

Fig. 3-8. Simple counter readout probe.

logic-high, and its output goes logic-low. Consequently, the clear line is driven logic-low, and the counter automatically clears. In practice, the clear line is extended into the digital system circuitry, so that the counter can be cleared at any time by application of a clear pulse from an external circuit.

Note that when the decade counter is first switched on, its readout is indeterminate (like any type of toggle-latch counter). In turn, the digital system is designed to apply a clear pulse to the counter before trigger pulses are inputted. Since a counting cycle might comprise two pulses, five pulses, or nine pulses, the digital system is further designed to apply a clear pulse to the counter at the end of each counting cycle.

Troubleshooters will encounter decade counters with modulus 100, or modulus 1000, for example. A mod 100 counter is configured from two mod 10 counters connected in series. The most significant bit from the first counter is used as the input to the second counter. Similarly, a mod 1000 counter is configured by connecting three mod 10 counters in series. The MSB from the second counter is used as the input to the third counter. Note that a mod 10 counter actually displays readouts from 0 to 9; a mod 100 counter displays readouts from 0 to 99; a mod 1000 counter displays readouts from 0 to 999.

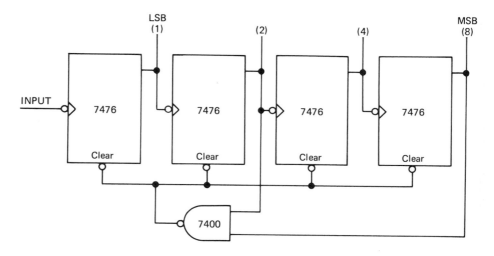

Note: Controlled feedback via the NAND gate is utilized in this decade counter to limit its total number of states to 10. In the absence of feedback, the total number of states would be 16. The decade counter is termed a modulus 10 (mod 10) counter. If no feedback were used, it would be termed a mod 16 counter.

Troubleshooting Hint: "Tough dog" problems involving erratic counting action are sometimes tracked down to "hot" ground circuits. Digital systems require very low resistance ground conductors throughout.

Fig. 3-9. Asynchronous decade ripple counter configuration.

Reminder: As was indicated in Fig. 3-3, the TTL logic-high threshold is 2.4V, and the logic-low threshold is 0.4V. In turn, erratic counter action can be caused by marginal trigger-pulse amplitude. If this possibility is overlooked, the troubleshooter could occasionally have a "tough dog" problem to contend with.

4

Troubleshooting Synchronous Counters

Counter Troubleshooting with the Oscilloscope • Synchronous Up-Counter Operation • Synchronous Down-Counter Operation • Novel Digital Activity Indicator • Synchronous Counter with Ripple Carry • Programmable Down-Counter • Basic Frequency Counter • Main Gate Demonstration • Short-Circuit Localization with Service-Type DVM

COUNTER TROUBLESHOOTING WITH THE OSCILLOSCOPE

When the cause of counter malfunction eludes tests with a logic probe, an oscilloscope can occasionally show the trouble area, even if it does not identify the specific defect. As an illustration, typical four-bit binary counter output waveforms are shown in Fig. 4-1, along with the train of input trigger pulses. As a practical note, this complete display requires a five-channel scope; most troubleshooters use two-channel scopes, and the counter waveforms must be displayed in pairs.

Observe in Fig. 4-1 that in normal operation, FF1 outputs a pulse for each two input pulses; FF2 outputs a pulse for every four input pulses; FF3 outputs a pulse for every eight input pulses; FF4 outputs a pulse for every 16 input pulses. All of the waveforms normally have about the same amplitude. Although these waveshapes are not ideal, they are within normal tolerance limits.

An oscilloscope will show whether the waveforms are stable, or whether "jitter" (sometimes with varying amplitude) may be present. Similarly, pulses with excessively slow rise and/or fall will be evident in the pattern. Noise glitches (unless they are quite narrow) will be displayed. In case of an intermittent counter, the troubleshooter should tap the PC board lightly, while watching the scope pattern. A blast of hot air may be directed on the flip-flops, followed by application of a coolant spray.

Flip-flops usually fail catastrophically, although intermittents can occur either inside of an IC package, or in the external circuitry. Remember too, that there

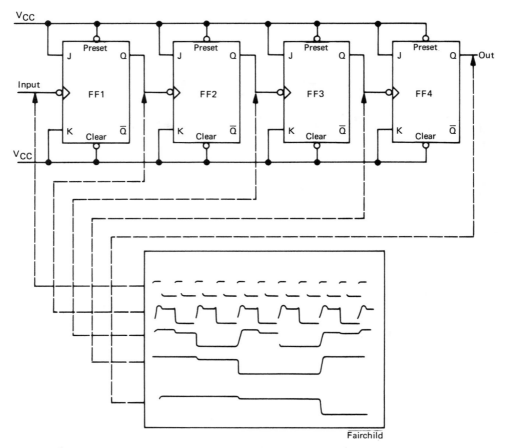

Fig. 4-1. Typical four-bit binary counter output waveforms.

is an off-chance that a flip-flop will develop marginal operation. In such a case, a normal scope pattern is displayed when the input trigger pulse rate is slowed down, but the pattern becomes "unglued" at rated clock frequency. In such a case, of course, the troubleshooter must replace the marginal IC package.

SYNCHRONOUS UP-COUNTER OPERATION

Digital troubleshooters encounter synchronous counters more frequently than asynchronous counters. A synchronous counter is clocked continuously. A synchronous counter such as depicted in Fig. 4-2 is configured to avoid ripple carry. In turn, it has an application advantage in elimination of unwanted gating

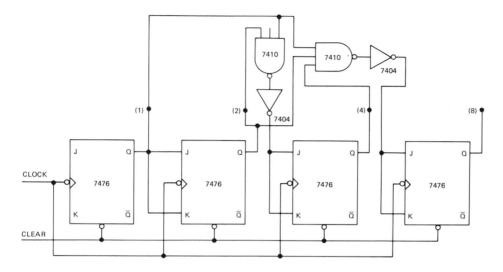

Note: The unconnected inputs "look" logic-high to their associated circuitry inside of the IC's. Clock pulses will be counted as long as the clear line is
held logic-high. Counting is synchronized with the sequence of clock
pulses. On the other hand, the clear function is asynchronous. The
counter may be cleared at any time by driving the clear line logic-low.
This clearing action is independent of the clock pulses.

Fig. 4-2. A widely used synchronous up-counter arrangement.

spikes and/or shortened pulses that can result from the cumulative delay time
in a ripple-carry counter. A less elaborate synchronous counter arrangement,
called a synchronous counter with ripple carry, will also be encountered occasionally, as explained subsequently.

With reference to Fig. 4-2, synchronous counters have the output from each
flip-flop connected to all more-significant-bit inputs via a series of gates. Each
gate selectively controls the time when each more-significant-bit flip-flop is to
change state (toggle) on the next clock transition. This control action permits a
common clock to synchronize data transfer—all flip-flops in the synchronized
counter will change state simultaneously.

Troubleshooters may recall that an asynchronous counter requires the output
from one flip-flop to change state in order to trigger the next flip-flop (ripple). In
turn, the maximum operating frequency is comparatively limited. On the other
hand, a synchronous counter is configured to change the state of all flip-flops simultaneously, thus providing a much higher maximum operating frequency.

Observe in the synchronous up-counter configuration (Fig. 4-2) that the AND gates (7410-7404's) are connected to all of the more-significant flip-flops in parallel. This type of gate circuit permits any number of flip-flops to be included in a chain with only one additional gate propagation delay added to the set-up time of each more-significant bit. Note that for each flip-flop that may be added to the chain, one more input will be required on each AND gate.

All flip-flops normally change state simultaneously in the synchronous arrangement of Fig. 4-2 because all flip-flops in the chain change state on a common clock edge. In turn, the flip-flop output data is available simultaneously, without waiting for ripple carry. Note also that each gate receives data from all of the less-significant flip-flops when more-significant bit inputs are to be enabled.

Troubleshooting of synchronous counters can usually be accomplished readily with logic pulsers and probes, since most IC failures are catastrophic. In more difficult situations, as when glitches are suspected, a high-performance oscilloscope can provide test data that cannot be "caught" by simple logic probes. Note, however, that the simple logic probe with pulse memory that was shown in Fig. 2-5 can "catch" glitches that are not unduly narrow.

SYNCHRONOUS DOWN-COUNTER OPERATION

Troubleshooters should make careful distinction between up- and down-counter arrangements; otherwise, trouble symptoms will be falsely evaluated, and a "good" counter could be unnecessarily replaced. The down-counter configuration exemplified in Fig. 4-3 is superficially similar to the up-counter arrangement previously noted. However, the down counter employs the preset line for resetting the flip-flops, and the $\bar{Q}$ terminal of each FF is used to drive the next FF.

NOVEL DIGITAL ACTIVITY INDICATOR

An unusual and effective digital activity indicator is depicted in Fig. 4-4. This is not a level indicator—it functions as a transition indicator. In other words, if the point under test is going from logic-high to logic-low (or vice versa), the miniature amplifier outputs a loud click. It indicates whether or not a change in level is occurring.

The Archer (Radio Shack) 277-1008 mini-amplifier with speaker is suitable for this application. It has high gain and it can be easily held in the hand while probing digital circuitry. A convenient test prod can be fashioned from a 4-inch length of No. 14 copper wire, with its end sharpened to a point. The other end

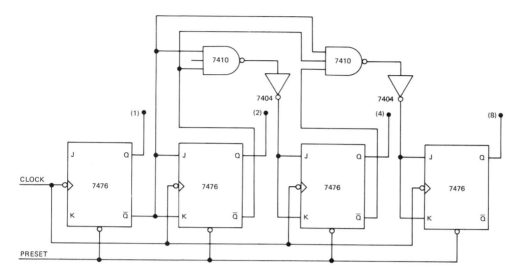

Note: The down-counter arrangement can be reset to 1111 at any time by driving the preset line logic-low. It counts down to 0000 and then automatically recycles, starting with 1111. The preset function is asynchronous and independent of the clock pulses.

Fig. 4-3. A widely used synchronous down-counter arrangement.

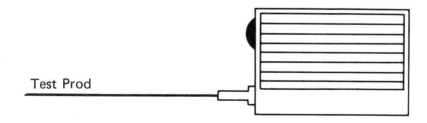

Test Prod

Technical Note: A miniature high-gain audio amplifier provides digital activity indication when its "hot" input lead is applied at any node that is going from logic-high to logic-low, or vice versa. No ground return lead is used —the return is provided by capacitive coupling from the miniature amplifier to the troubleshooter's hand. (Input impedance to the tester is very high.)

Fig. 4-4. A novel digital activity indicator.

is soldered to the "hot" terminal of a 1/8-inch mini-phone plug, which in turn is inserted into the input jack on the mini-amplifier.

Note that this activity indicator is useful only in the audio-frequency range. In other words, the digital circuit under test should be driven or clocked at a comparatively slow rate. You can use a slow-pulse generator for tests, or the digital circuit can be manually pulsed. No ground lead is used with the activity indicator—an effective ground return is provided by the stray capacitance of the mini-amplifier to the troubleshooter's hand.

> *Experiment*: Touch the test prod of the activity indicator to a V_{CC} terminal. Note that a loud click is produced.

> *Experiment*: Touch the test prod in turn to the Q output terminals of FF1, FF2, FF3, and FF4 in Fig. 4-1. The counter may be driven from a slow-pulse generator. Note that the elapsed time between clicks doubles as you proceed from FF1 to FF2, to FF3, and to FF4.

> *Experiment*: Touch the test prod to the "hot" output terminal of a square-wave (or pulse) generator. Observe that the activity indicator outputs clicks at very low frequencies, and outputs audio tones at higher frequencies. Note that there is no audible output when the generator frequency exceeds your high-frequency limit of hearing.

SYNCHRONOUS COUNTER WITH RIPPLE CARRY

Troubleshooters should recognize the distinction between a synchronous counter with ripple carry (Fig. 4-5) and the synchronous counter with look-ahead carry (Fig. 4-2). Observe in Fig. 4-5 that when the readout is 0111, the control logic level must pass through both of the AND gates before it reaches the last flip-flop input. This control path adds two gate propagation delays to the time that is required to set up (t_{setup}) the last flip-flop input before arrival of the clock edge.

The chief advantage of the synchronous counter with ripple carry is that only a single extra two-input AND gate is required for each FF that is added to the chain. This contributes to circuit simplicity, but each of the added AND gates introduces an additional propagation delay between all of the prior outputs and JK inputs to the FF.

By the same token, the chief advantage of the synchronous counter is that only one gate propagation delay is involved to set up any FF in the chain. However, for each FF that is added to the chain, the corresponding AND gate must be provided with one more input. In turn, a trade-off is involved in circuit complexity.

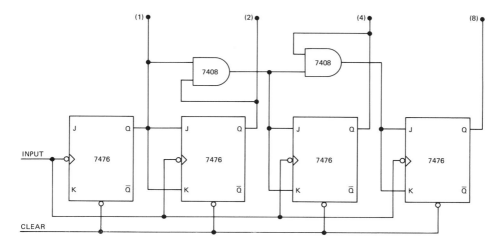

Note: This synchronous counter with ripple carry normally checks out the same as the previously described synchronous counter. Note, however, that ripple carry has the effect of reducing the maximum operating speed of the counter. In other words, the ripple-carry counter will start to exhibit erratic counting action at a trigger input speed that is well within the capability of the synchronous counter.

Fig. 4-5. Typical synchronous counter with ripple carry.

Any particular counter has a rated maximum operating speed. Inasmuch as a synchronous counter with ripple carry introduces more propagation delay between the JK input of an FF and all prior outputs than does a "true" synchronous counter, an input frequency limit will be reached at which the control output will not arrive at the next FF input soon enough to be recognized as a valid data input.

> *Experiment*: Using a 0.05 μF capacitor charged to V_{CC}, pulse the input of the counter shown in Fig. 4-5. Observe the response at the Q output of the first FF. Repeat the test half a dozen times. Do you obtain the expected response each time?
> Next, connect an SPST slide switch between the counter input and ground. Throw the switch closed and open half a dozen times. Do you obtain the expected response each time?
> Then, replace the slide switch with a mercury switch. Throw the switch closed and open half a dozen times. Do you obtain the expected response each time?
> Which method of manual pulsing is most reliable?

PROGRAMMABLE DOWN-COUNTER

Observe next the widely used type of programmable down-counter depicted in Fig. 4-6. It is instructive to assemble this configuration on an experimenter socket, and to make the following tests:

1. Set the program-enable line logic-high.
2. Set the program A line logic-high.
3. Set the program B line logic-low.
4. Set the program C line logic-low.
5. Set the program D line logic-high.

The number nine (1001) has now been programmed into the counter. Next, make the following tests:

1. Set the program-enable line logic-low.
2. Clock the counter manually and observe the (8)(4)(2)(1) Q outputs.
3. The counter normally counts down from 1001.
4. To gain familiarity with this important configuration, repeat the foregoing tests for several other programmed numbers.

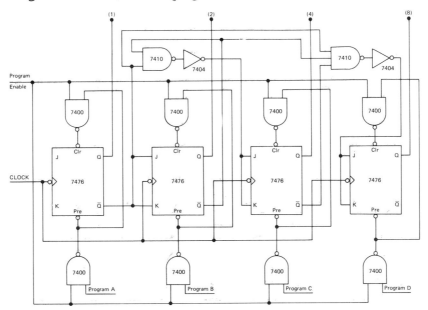

Fig. 4-6. A widely used type of programmable down-counter.

BASIC FREQUENCY COUNTER

Digital troubleshooters encounter various types of frequency counters. A basic divide-by-12 frequency counter is exemplified in Fig. 4-7. This type of counter is employed in digital clocks, for example. The divide-by-12 action is provided by a JK FF configuration which first divides by two and then divides by six. Note the reset circuit; when both R_0 inputs are logic-high, all FF's are driven to 0.

Observe that FF-A divides by two, while FF-B, -C, and -D divide by six. In practice, the counter may first divide by two, and then divide by six, or, it may first divide by six, and then divide by two. This counter circuit is a bit "tricky" inasmuch as it does not count up to binary 6, but counts in binary ($Q_D Q_C Q_B$) as follows: 0 (000), 1 (001), 2 (010), 4 (100), 6 (101), and 6 (110)—note that binary 3 does not appear in this counting sequence. Nevertheless, six pulses are required to obtain one complete output pulse at Q_D, or, the configuration effectively divides by six.

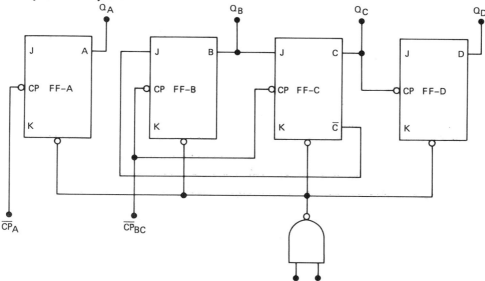

Practical Note: The troubleshooter should recognize that a specialized counting sequence is used in this arrangement, which could be a source of confusion to the neophyte. In other words, the normal counting sequence is: 0000, 0001, 0010, 0011, 0100, 0101, 1000, 1001, 1010, 1011, 1100, 1101. This unconventional counting sequence is employed to minimize hardware.

Fig. 4-7. A basic divide-by-12 frequency counter.

If we use FF-A for the input, and use output Q_A as the clock for the divide-by-six section, the configuration provides divide-by-12 operation. Note that this arrangement does not count from 0 to 11 in binary sequence inasmuch as binary six and seven do not appear in this counting sequence. Nevertheless, binary 1011 normally outputs after 11 input pulses are applied.

Next, observe the gated counter arrangement depicted in Fig. 4-8. The AND gate (termed the main gate), is switched on or off as required by a precision time base. A counter functions as a divider if only one bit is used as the output. Note that a frequency counter configuration often has an input section that divides the input frequency before actual counting takes place. This initial frequency division is called prescaling.

Useful familiarization with prescaling can be easily obtained by constructing the 7492 divide-by-12 counter arrangement shown in Fig. 4-9. To check out the circuit action, start by initializing the clock logic-high; clear the counter by switching the clear line from logic-high to logic-low. Then, switch the clock line from high to low to high, and so on. In normal operation, the output changes state on every twelfth clock pulse.

Main Gate Demonstration

A helpful main-gate demonstration is depicted in Fig. 4-10. Observe that the prescaler output goes logic-high when the main gate is logic-high, and vice versa. Since the input frequency is 100 kilo-Hertz in this example, the output frequency is 8.3 kHz, approximately. In turn, the probe at the main scaler outputs glows continuously while the main gate is logic-high.

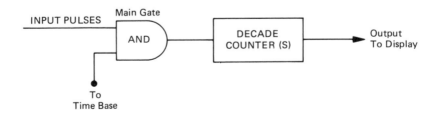

Note: If n denotes the number of Hertz for a signal that occurs during a time period t, the average frequency of the signal over interval t is equal to n/t Hz. Thus, if t = 1 sec in the arrangement shown above, the output from the counter is equal to the signal frequency in Hz. (Each input pulse corresponds to one complete excursion of the signal.)

Fig. 4-8. Fundamental frequency counter arrangement.

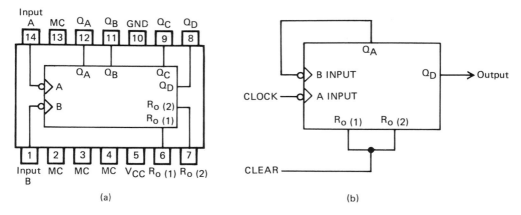

Technical Note: A prescaler is a configuration that produces an output signal related to the input signal by a fractional scale factor such as $1/2$, $1/8$, $1/10$, and so on. A familiar example of a digital prescaler is a decade frequency divider which has an output frequency equal to one-tenth of the input frequency.

Fig. 4-9. Prescaler circuit for a frequency counter. (a) Pinout for the 7492 divide-by-12 counter; (b) prescaler circuit connections.

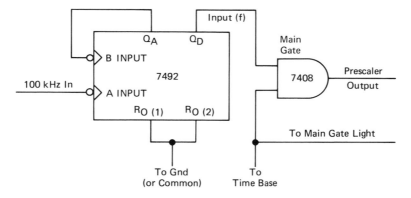

Note: This prescaler demonstration arrangement can be driven from a square-wave or pulse generator. The prescaler output may be indicated by a logic probe. The time-base function can be simulated by manually switching the time-base line logic-low/logic-high/logic-low. Observe that the input signal (f) is indicated at the prescaler output when the main gate is logic-high. The state of the main gate is indicated by an LED; this is called the main gate light in frequency counter circuits.

Fig. 4-10. Arrangement for main gate demonstration.

A helpful follow-up demonstration can be made by reducing the input frequency to 12 Hertz. If a logic probe is also connected at the input to the prescaler, it will flicker at a 12-Hz rate; whereas, the probe at the prescaler output will flash on and off at one-second intervals. (The main gate must be logic-high, or the probe at the prescaler output will remain dark.)

SHORT-CIRCUIT LOCALIZATION WITH SERVICE-TYPE DVM

Most malfunctions in counter circuitry are caused by open circuits or short circuits. As noted previously, a fault may occur inside of an IC, or it may occur in the external circuitry. In either case, the voltage to ground falls to practically zero in the case of a short circuit to ground. A special type of test is required to localize the short circuit.

First, consider a short circuit that occurs somewhere along a PC conductor, as depicted in Fig. 4-11. The troubleshooter's question is whether the short circuit is located at one end of the PC conductor, or whether it is located somewhere between the ends of the conductor. A DVM is connected at each end of the conductor, as shown in the diagram. The V_{CC} supply voltage is turned off.

To localize the short circuit, a test current considerably greater than the normal circuit operating current is injected, as shown in the diagram. A test current in the range from 150 to 200 mA is adequate to provide useful IR drop indications with most service-type DVM's. The test current is experimentally injected at various points along the PC conductor, and DVM indications are evaluated as follows:

1. If the DVM indicates a positive IR drop when current is injected at A, but indicates a negative IR drop when current is injected at B, the troubleshooter concludes that the short circuit is located between A and B.

2. When the test current is injected at B, the DVM will indicate zero.

3. On the other hand, if the DVM indicates a positive IR drop when current is injected at A, or B, or C, the troubleshooter concludes that the short circuit is located between C and the right-hand end of the PC conductor.

4. In case there is a short circuit inside the IC package at the right-hand end of the conductor, the DVM will indicate zero when the test current is injected at the right-hand end of the conductor.

5. Again, if the DVM indicates a negative IR drop when current is injected at A, or B, or C, the troubleshooter concludes that the short circuit is located between A and the left-hand end of the PC conductor.

6. In the event that there is a short circuit inside the IC package at the left-hand end of the conductor, the DVM will indicate zero when the test current is injected at the left-hand end of the conductor.

(a)

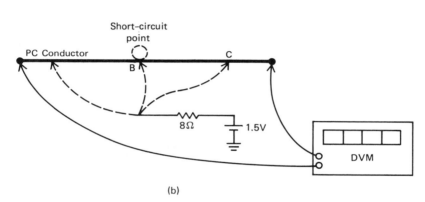

(b)

Note: The DVM indicates the IR drop along the PC conductor. A 1.5V battery
in series with an 8-ohm resistor injects approximately 180 mA into the
PC conductor, which produces measurable IR drops.

Short-circuit localization is made by injecting the test current at various
points along the PC conductor. When the test current is injected at A,
the DVM indicates a positive IR drop. When the test current is injected
at C, the DVM indicates a negative IR drop. When the test current is
injected at B, the DVM indicates zero voltage drop. This is the short-circuit point.

Fig. 4-11. Short-circuit localization with service-type DVM.

As a practical note, any dc voltmeter can be used for short-circuit localization, if you inject a sufficiently high value of test current. However, it is good
practice to use only enough test current to obtain clearly readable indications
on your meter.

Troubleshooters can be guided by the rough rule-of-thumb that a printed-circuit conductor has 0.01 ohm of resistance per inch. Accordingly, a current flow
of 100 mA will produce a voltage drop of 1 mV per inch along the PC conductor. If the PC conductor is comparatively short, you may need to use a current
flow of several hundred mA to localize a short circuit with a service-type DVM.

5

Troubleshooting
Encoders and Decoders

Localizing Short Circuits to V_{CC}• Two-to-Four Line Decoder • Marginal Pulse Voltages • BCD-to-Decimal Decoder • Four-to-Two Line Encoder • Two-to-Four Line Decoder and Four-to-Two Line Encoder • Gray Code • XS3 Code • Troubleshooting Short-Circuited PC Conductors • Circuit Internal Resistance

---

LOCALIZING SHORT CIRCUITS TO V_{CC}

Digital troubleshooters expect to occasionally encounter short circuits from a node to V_{CC}; the PC conductor is "stuck high" at approximately 5V, and the problem is to localize the point at which the conductor is short-circuited to V_{CC}. The short circuit may occur at any point along the PC conductor, or it may occur at one end of the conductor, inside of an IC package.

A service-type DVM can be used to localize a short circuit to V_{CC} as shown in Fig. 5-1. The DVM is connected between the ends of the "stuck high" conductor and indicates any IR voltage drop that may occur along the conductor. Test-current flow is provided by probing the "stuck high" conductor with a grounded 25-ohm resistor. This load resistor produces approximately 200 mA of current flow.

Observe in Fig. 5-1 that when a short circuit to V_{CC} occurs along the "stuck high" conductor as depicted, the DVM will indicate a positive voltage when the load resistor is applied at A. On the other hand, the DVM will indicate a negative voltage when the load resistor is applied at C. In turn, the troubleshooter concludes that the short circuit will be found somewhere between A and C. When the load resistor is applied at B, the DVM indicates zero voltage.

Ne..t, suppose that the short circuit to V_{CC} occurs at the lefthand end of the "stuck high" conductor in Fig. 5-1. In this situation, the DVM indicates a positive voltage when the load resistor is applied at A, or B, or C. Again, suppose that the short circuit to V_{CC} occurs at the righthand end of the conductor. In such a case, the DVM indicates a negative voltage when the load resistor is applied at A, or B, or C.

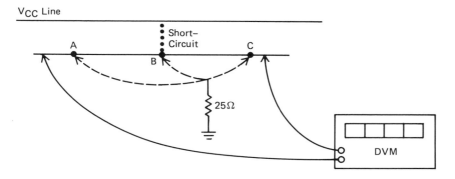

Technical Note: When a node becomes short-circuited to V_{CC}, the node is "stuck high" at approximately 5V above ground. The short circuit may be along a PC conductor, or at either end of the conductor, inside an IC package.

This localization test provides short-circuit current to ground, with associated IR checks along the "stuck-high" conductor. In this example, an IR drop will be measured when the load resistor is applied at A or C; however, there will be zero voltage indication when the load resistor is applied at B.

Fig. 5-1. Localizing a short circuit to V_{CC}.

TWO-TO-FOUR LINE DECODER

Troubleshooters are often concerned with decoder circuitry, and need to understand the circuit action that normally occurs. A decoder is a circuit or device that responds to application of unique input states or conditions and produces a unique output for that group of states or conditions. For example, binary coded decimal (BCD) to decimal decoders are in wide use. Four input lines are employed, and the circuit action produces a logic-high pulse on one of the ten output lines, in accordance with the input states and conditions.

Note that an encoder circuit is basically similar to a decoder circuit, except that it performs an opposite function. In other words, an encoder accepts one or more signals in uncoded form and outputs a coded signal that can be processed by a following logic circuit. It is instructive to assemble and check out a two-to-four line decoder, as follows:

The experimental two-to-four line decoder depicted in Fig. 5-2 employs two 7404 inverters and four 7408 AND gates. Logic states on the output lines 0, 1, 2, 3, and 4 are determined by permutations of logic states on input lines A and

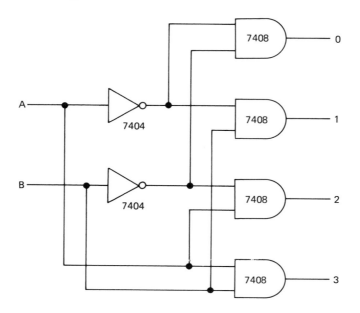

Note: The output states may be checked with a logic probe. Note that "floating" inputs are effectively logic-high, so that the inputs to the decoder are logic-high if A and B are not connected to V_{CC} or to ground. In this case, output line 3 will normally be logic-high. Or, if both inputs are grounded, output line 0 will normally be logic-high. Observe also that if inputs A and B are "floating," the output state does not change if the input lines are short-circuited together.

Fig. 5-2. Experimental two-to-four line decoder.

B. Observe that if A is logic-high and B is logic-low, output line 2 is logic-low and the other outputs are logic-low. On the other hand, if A is logic-low and B is logic-high, output line 1 is logic-high and the other outputs are logic-low.

Note that there are four possible input states in Fig. 5-2, and there is the corresponding possibility of driving any one output line logic-high. (It is not possible to have all outputs logic-low in this arrangement.) Note also that a three-input decoder can have eight unique outputs, a four-input decoder can have 16 unique outputs, and so on. Typical trouble symptoms in decoder circuits are an input line or output line "stuck low" or "stuck high."

To briefly recap, a "stuck low" symptom may be caused by a short circuit to ground; a "stuck high" symptom may be caused by a short-circuit to V_{CC}. If an inverter input becomes open-circuited, its output will be "stuck low." If an AND-gate input becomes open-circuited, its output can be driven logic-high, but cannot be driven logic-low in full accordance with its truth table.

MARGINAL PULSE VOLTAGES

Trouble symptoms can be caused also by marginal pulse voltages. Although we loosely speak of 0V and 5V as logic-low-and logic-high levels, these ideal values are never measured in practice. An input voltage in the range from 0 to 0.8 volt is within low tolerance for TTL circuit operation. Similarly, an input voltage in the range from 2 to 5 volts is within high tolerance.

An output voltage in the range from 0 to 0.4 volt is within low tolerance, and an output voltage in the range from 2.4 to 5 volts is within high tolerance. Pulse voltages through a digital system will normally vary, depending upon the number of branch circuits (loading or fan-out) that are present. If a fault imposes abnormal current demand, pulse input and/or output voltages can become marginal and result in erratic counter operation.

As a practical note, "piggy back" digital test equipment necessarily imposes an increased current demand on the V_{CC} power supply. In turn, if operation is already marginal, connection of digital test equipment to the V_{CC} line could aggravate the malfunctioning of the counter. If this source of difficulty is suspected, use a bench-operated power supply to energize the "piggy back" digital test equipment.

BCD TO DECIMAL DECODER

Binary coded decimal (BCD) to decimal decoders such as shown in Fig. 5-3 are in extensive use. It is important to recognize the normal operating characteristics of this type of decoder. Binary coded decimal numbers can be a bit tricky for the beginner, because they can be easily confused with ordinary binary numbers. A BCD number always has four bits; there are ten BCD numbers from 0 through 9. Note the following facts:

1. Binary number 1 is equal to 0001, and BCD number 1 is equal to 0001.
2. Binary number 3 is equal to 0011, and BCD number 3 is equal to 0011.
3. Binary number 13 is equal to 1101, but BCD number 13 is equal to 0001 0011.
4. If BCD 13 were misread as an ordinary binary number, its value would be falsely stated as 19.
5. Two BCD to decimal decoders would be employed to decode the BCD number 13 into its decimal equivalent. One decoder would process units, and the other decoder would process tens.
6. The units decoder would process the 3, and the tens decoder would process the 1.

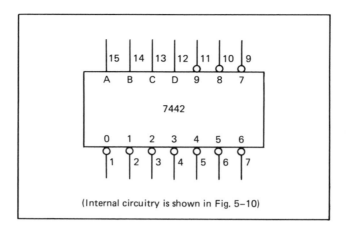

(Internal circuitry is shown in Fig. 5–10)

Note: Pin 8 is Gnd, and pin 16 is V_{cc}. A, B, C, and D are the inputs to the decoder. 0 through 9 are the outputs from the decoder. The outputs are normally logic-high; a unique output state is represented by a logic-low state. Only one output line is activated in response to a particular ABCD input.

Fig. 5-3. Experimental BCD to decimal decoder.

Observe that the largest BCD digit is 1001. In other words, there is no such thing as 1010, or 1011, or 1100 in the BCD number system. If a "forbidden" BCD digit should be inputted by the decoder for any reason, "garbage" would be outputted.

FOUR-TO-TWO LINE ENCODER

Encoders are encountered in various digital systems, and should be recognized in logic circuit diagrams. In the example of Fig. 5-4, a unique output is coded on two lines. The input typically receives a unique data input as from instrument switches and in turn codes these inputs for use by the instrument's internal circuits.

Observe in the diagram that input line 0 has no connection to the decoder gates, and does not enter into the decoder action. If inputs 1, 2, and 3 are logic-low, output lines A and B are logic-low. If 123=HLL, A is logic-high and B is logic-low. If 123=LHL, A is logic-low and B is logic-high. If 123=HLH, A and B are both logic-high.

Troubleshooters frequently work with keyboard to BCD encoders such as exemplified in Fig. 5-5. Here, ten keyboard switches input to the encoder, which

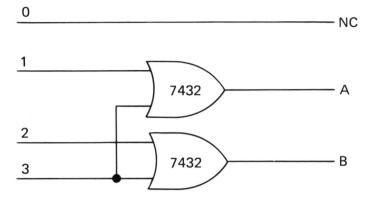

Note: An encoder provides change from one digital code to another. If the codes are widely disparate, the configuration is called a code converter. An encoder commonly converts switch closures into a digital code for transmission over a communication channel.

Fig. 5-4. A simple four-to-two line encoder.

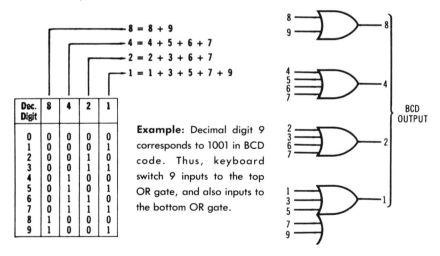

Dec. Digit	8	4	2	1
0	0	0	0	0
1	0	0	0	1
2	0	0	1	0
3	0	0	1	1
4	0	1	0	0
5	0	1	0	1
6	0	1	1	0
7	0	1	1	1
8	1	0	0	0
9	1	0	0	1

8 = 8 + 9
4 = 4 + 5 + 6 + 7
2 = 2 + 3 + 6 + 7
1 = 1 + 3 + 5 + 7 + 9

Example: Decimal digit 9 corresponds to 1001 in BCD code. Thus, keyboard switch 9 inputs to the top OR gate, and also inputs to the bottom OR gate.

Note: Because decimal digit 9 corresponds to 1001 and decimal digit 8 corresponds to 1000 in the BCD code, the top OR gate in the encoder will be activated when either decimal 8 or decimal 9 is to be transmitted. Therefore, keyboard switches 8 and 9 are connected to the inputs of the top OR gate. Similarly, the other keyboard switches are connected to the three remaining OR gates as indicated in the diagram.

Fig. 5-5. Example of a keyboard to BCD encoder.

in turn outputs BCD numbers. Four OR gates are employed. Only one of the input lines is activated for any particular decimal number; however, all four BCD output lines are correspondingly activated.

Observe that this is a units encoder. To transmit the decimal number 13 in BCD code, a tens encoder would also be required. To transmit the decimal number 713 in BCD code a hundreds encoder would have to be included. Note the following relations:

> Decimal number: 713
> BCD equivalent: 0111 0001 0011
> Binary number: 1011001101

You will also encounter elaborated encoders which input from keyboard switches and output the American Standard Code for Information Exchange (ASCII), shown in Fig. 5-6. At this point, we are only concerned with the circumstance that various kinds of encoders are in common use. Details of ASCII and related encoders are not included in this chapter.

TWO-TO-FOUR LINE DECODER AND FOUR-TO-TWO LINE ENCODER

Digital troubleshooters also work on decoder/encoder arrangements, such as depicted in Fig. 5-7. This is a demonstration setup and does not correspond to a specific commercial design. The essential requirement is to recognize that "straight" binary code is not employed throughout digital systems, and that various decoders and encoders will be utilized in some subsections.

GRAY CODE

The Gray code merits particular notice, because it is involved in analog-to-digital (AD) conversion. Input/output devices for digital systems may require interfacing facilities that provide for AD conversion. As an illustration, when a digital computer is used to process weather data, one of the basic variables consists of the changing direction of a weather vane.

This variable, change in direction, is processed by converting a given direction into binary numbers for data entry into the computer. One AD converter arrangement that has been widely used is an electromechanical design, depicted in Fig. 5-8. Light areas in the disk denote conducting material; whereas, dark areas denote insulating material. Rotational positions of the vane are sensed by means of three carbon brushes, each of which is in contact with one of the concentric bands.

	000	001	010	011	100	101	110	111
0000	NULL	① DC_0	b	0	@	P		
0001	SOM	DC_1	!	1	A	Q		
0010	EOA	DC_2	"	2	B	R		
0011	EOM	DC_3	#	3	C	S		
0100	EOT	DC_4 (stop)	$	4	D	T		
0101	WRU	ERR	%	5	E	U		
0110	RU	SYNC	&	6	F	V		
0111	BELL	LEM	'	7	G	W	Unassigned	
1000	FE_0	S_0	(	8	H	X		
1001	HT / SK	S_1	)	9	I	Y		
1010	LF	S_2	*	:	J	Z		
1011	V_{TAB}	S_3	+	;	K	[		
1100	FF	S_4	(comma) ,	<	L	\		ACK
1101	CR	S_5	—	=	M	]		②
1110	SO	S_6	.	>	N	↑		ESC
1111	SI	S_7	/	?	O	←		DEL

Example: | 100 | 0001 | = A

b_7 — — — — — — — b_1

The abbreviations used in the figure mean:

NULL	Null Idle	CR	Carriage return
SOM	Start of message	SO	Shift out
EOA	End of address	SI	Shift in
EOM	End of message	DC_0	Device control ①
			Reserved for data
			Link escape
EOT	End of transmission	DC_1 - DC_3	Device control
WRU	"Who are you?"	ERR	Error
RU	"Are you . . . . ?"	SYNC	Synchronous idle
BELL	Audible signal	LEM	Logical end of media
FE	Format effector	SO_0 - SO_7	Separator (information)
HT	Horizontal tabulation		Word separator (blank,
			normally non-printing)
SK	Skip (punched card)	ACK	Acknowledge
LF	Line feed	②	Unassigned control
V/TAB	Vertical tabulation	ESC	Escape
FF	Form feed	DEL	Delete Idle

Reproduced by special permission of Reston Publishing Co. and Lloyd Rich from Understanding Microprocessors

Fig. 5-6. American Standard Code for Information Exchange (ASCII).

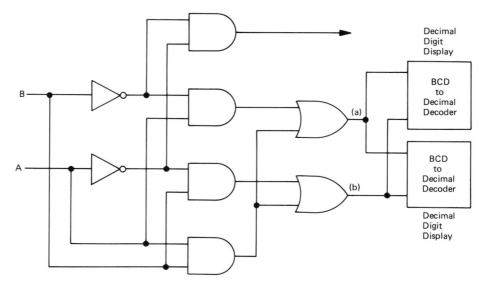

Note: In this demonstration decoder/encoder arrangement, the coded input signal is decoded by the inverters and AND gates, and is then encoded again by the four-to-two line encoder (OR gates), to finally be decoded by the BCD to decimal decoders for activating the decimal digit displays.

Fig. 5-7. A two-to-four line decoder and four-to-two line encoder arrangement.

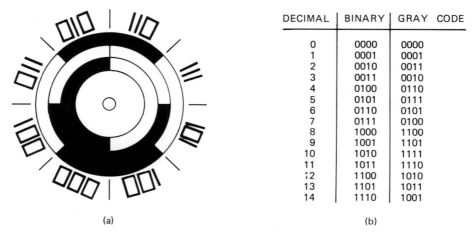

DECIMAL	BINARY	GRAY CODE
0	0000	0000
1	0001	0001
2	0010	0011
3	0011	0010
4	0100	0110
5	0101	0111
6	0110	0101
7	0111	0100
8	1000	1100
9	1001	1101
10	1010	1111
11	1011	1110
12	1100	1010
13	1101	1011
14	1110	1001

(a)   (b)

Fig. 5-8. Electromechanical analog-to-Gray code converter. (a) A three-bit A-to-D disk; (b) four-bit Gray code.

In this example, the converter is provided with eight segments. This three-bit encoder digitizes the shaft position into an equivalent three-bit binary number. You are likely to encounter a more elaborate design with four concentric bands for four-bit encoding. Note that the binary numbers are generally expressed in Gray code, because it is a code that employs consecutive numbers that differ by a single bit. An advantage of this code format is that it eliminates 180° ambiguity.

Note that the maximum error in an analog-to-Gray converter is represented by one segment of rotation. We observe that the reading error can be reduced by using more segments on the disk. As an example, an eight-bit converter (disk with eight segments) provides a shaft resolution of 1.4°. This is a resolution that corresponds to a maximum reading error of approximately 0.4 percent. A Gray-to-binary code converter is exemplified in Fig. 5-9.

XS3 CODE

Troubleshooters will occasionally encounter the Excess-3 (XS3) code, and need to recognize its difference from the BCD code. The two codes are basically similar, except that the XS3 code is obtained by adding 3 to each digit in the BCD code. For example, the first ten XS3 code numbers are:

XS3	BCD	DECIMAL
0011	0000	0
0100	0001	1
0101	0010	2
0110	0011	3
0111	0100	4
1000	0101	5
1001	0110	6
1010	0111	7
1011	1000	8
1100	1001	9

Encoding and decoding to and from the XS3 code is usually accomplished by simply adding 3 to each BCD number when encoding, and subtracting 3 from the XS3 number when decoding. An advantage of the XS3 code is that it is self-complementing. In other words, if all the 0 and 1 bits in an XS3 number are complemented, the 9's complement of the number is obtained.

Another advantage of the XS3 code is that all XS3 numbers have at least one 1 bit in them. This provides the distinction between zero and no information. Note that three IC's have been standardized in the 54/74 family to de-

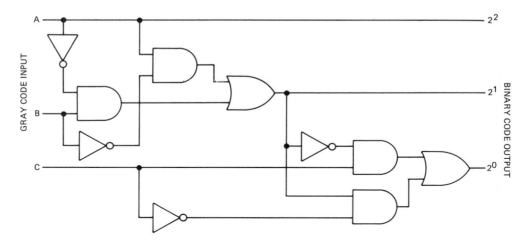

Note: Observe the Gray-to-binary correspondences in Fig. 5-8. For example, Gray 0111 corresponds to binary 0101. (Disregard the MSB's in this example.) When inputs A, B, and C are all logic-high, binary 2^2 goes logic-high via feedthrough; binary 2^1 remains logic-low; binary 2^0 goes logic-high.

Fig. 5-9. Gray-to-binary code converter.

code three number codes: the BCD code, the XS3 code, and the Gray code. These are examples of the hardware that you encounter in practice.

With reference to Fig. 5-10, the connection diagram and the logic symbol for types 5442, 43, and 44 are shown. Each decoder comprises eight inverters and ten four-input NAND gates, as exemplified for the 42 BCD-to-decimal decoder.

TROUBLESHOOTING SHORT-CIRCUITED PC CONDUCTORS

A common troubleshooting problem involves a suspected short circuit between PC conductors, as depicted in Fig. 5-11. In this situation, neither of the conductors is at ground or V_{CC} potential. A practical approach to this fault condition is to switch off V_{CC} and to inject a comparatively large test current at the end of one conductor, and to ground the corresponding end of the other conductor. A positive voltage is applied from the battery, inasmuch as the IC's associated with the conductors will usually "look like" open circuits to the positive voltage.

A service-type DVM may be used to check IR voltage drops along the PC conductors. For example, if there is a short circuit along the path of the conductors, as exemplified in Fig. 5-11, a positive voltage drop will be measured

LOGIC SYMBOL

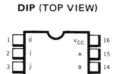

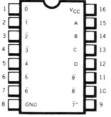

V_{CC} = Pin 16
GND = Pin 8

9352/5442, 7442
9353/5443, 7443
9354/5444, 7444

PIN NAMES

A, B, C, D	BCD Inputs (9352)
A, B, C, D	Excess 3 Inputs (9353)
A, B, C, D	Excess 3 Gray Inputs (9354)
$\overline{0}$ to $\overline{9}$	Decimal Output

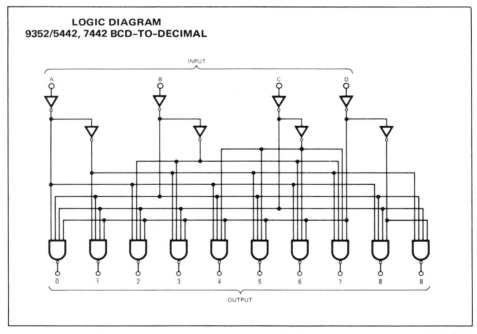

—*Fairchild*

Fig. 5-10. Connection diagram, logic symbol, and representative logic diagram for a commercial BCD/XS3/Gray decoder.

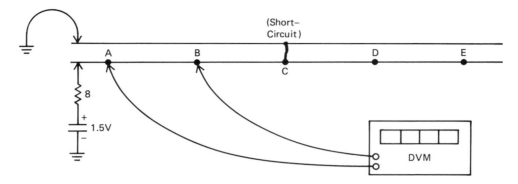

Troubleshooting Note: When a short circuit is suspected between two PC conductors, neither of which is at ground or V_{cc} potential, a positive test voltage may be applied as shown to produce a comparatively large current flow in the PC conductors. Because the applied voltage is positive, devices will ordinarily not conduct. A DVM is used to trace the current flow to the short-circuit point.

Fig. 5-11. Localizing a short circuit between two PC conductors.

between points A and B. A larger voltage drop will be measured between points A and C. On the other hand, no change in voltage will occur when a check is made between points A and D.

Observe that if the meter leads are applied at points C and D, or points C and E, zero volts will be indicated. In turn, the troubleshooter can approximate the short-circuit point. As previously noted, a higher current can be injected if needed to obtain useful meter indications—this depends upon the sensitivity of your DVM.

Next suppose that the short circuit is not along the path of the PC conductors. For example, the short circuit might be inside of an IC package at the lefthand end of the conductors. In such a case, the troubleshooter will find zero voltage drop at any pair of test points along the conductors. His procedure, in turn, is to inject the test current at the righthand ends of the conductors. Now, if the short circuit is actually in the lefthand IC package, voltage drops will be measured at any pair of test points along the conductors.

Similarly, if the short circuit were in the IC package at the right hand of the conductors in Fig. 5-11, the troubleshooter would measure voltage drops at any pair of test points. The same troubleshooting principles apply also to branched nodes, wherein a short circuit occurs in one of the branches. Each branch is regarded as an independent pair of conductors. Localization of a short circuit is accomplished in the same manner as in a simple circuit. Test current may be injected at the ends of any pair of branched conductors.

Circuit Internal Resistance

We have seen that when a short circuit occurs to ground, to V_{CC}, or to another conductor which is at neither ground nor V_{CC} potential, that localization of the short-circuit point involves current-oriented test procedures. The reason for this orientation is that a short-circuit condition is associated with very low internal resistance. In turn, voltage measurements to ground, or to V_{CC} do not provide useful test data.

This is just another way of saying that voltage is a current-resistance product, and that conversely, current is a voltage-resistance ratio. In turn, when the resistance value is very small, the current-resistance ratio is very large. Although the existing circuit current is often too small to provide useful IR test data, comparatively large test currents may be injected into the fault path to obtain easily measurable IR test data.

6

Troubleshooting
Master-Slave Flip-Flops

Construction and Checkout of an RS Master-Slave Flip-Flop • Assembling a Master-Slave RS Flip-Flop • Troubleshooting Cables and Connectors • The "Open-Collector Evil" • Wire-AND, Wire-OR • Commercial Logic Probes • Multiple Inputs and Outputs • RST Flip-Flop Construction • Edge-Triggered, D Master-Slave Flip-Flop Configuration

CONSTRUCTION AND CHECKOUT OF AN RS MASTER-SLAVE FLIP-FLOP

Digital troubleshooters encounter master-slave flip-flops in the majority of digital systems. Therefore, it is necessary to clearly understand how this type of circuitry operates and how to troubleshoot it. Master-slave flip-flops are clocked; however, two-phase clocks are used. The clock waveforms are 180 degrees out of phase with each other.

With reference to Fig. 6-1(a), an RS latch consists of a pair of cross-connected NOR gates. This circuit was previously noted. Next, an RS flip-flop is depicted in Fig. 6-1(b). A single clock waveform is used (typically a square wave). Observe that the AND gates block signal (data) entry while the clock is logic-low. On the other hand, when the clock is logic-high, an R signal or an S signal will pass through to the latch section.

Next, a master-slave RS flip-flop configuration is shown in Fig. 6-2. Observe that it consists of two RS flip-flops connected in series. *Moreover, the first RS flip-flop is clocked 180 degrees out of phase with respect to the second flip-flop.* Therefore:

1. A set (S) or a reset (R) signal can enter the master flip-flop only while Clk 1 is logic-high. In other words, the output states of the master flip-flop can be changed when (and only when) Clk 1 is logic-high.

2. An output signal from the master flip-flop can enter the slave flip-flop

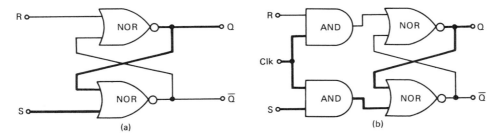

Note: When the RS latch has its R input logic-low, and its S input logic-high, its Q output goes logic-high (3.89V), and its Q̄ output goes logic-low (0.093V). Conversely, when its S input is logic-low, and its R input is logic-high, its Q output goes logic-low, and its Q̄ output goes logic-high. When both of its inputs are logic-low, it "holds" the preceding output states. When both of its inputs are logic-high, the output states are un-predictable—this is a "forbidden" input condition.

When the clocked RS flip-flop has its clock line logic-high, the circuit ac-tion is the same as noted for the RS latch. On the other hand, when the clocked RS flip-flop has its clock line logic-low, there is no response to either logic-high or logic-low R and S inputs.

Fig. 6-1. RS latch configurations. (a) Basic reset-set latch; (b) clocked reset-set latch (flip-flop).

only while Clk 2 is logic-high. In other words, the output states of the slave flip-flop can be changed when (and only when) Clk 2 is logic-high.

3. Since Clk 1 is logic-high while Clk 2 is logic-low (and vice versa), a data signal entered into the master flip-flop will be stored until Clk 2 goes log-ic-high.

4. Clk 2 goes logic-high as soon as Clk 1 goes logic-low, whereupon the data that was briefly stored in the master flip-flop enters the slave flip-flop.

5. Clk 1 then goes logic-high, and a new data signal may enter the master flip-flop. Now, the flip-flop has new data stored in its master section, and old data stored in its slave section.

6. Clk 2 again goes logic-high as soon as Clk 1 goes logic-low, whereupon the old data is "clocked out" of the slave section and the new data is "clocked into" the slave section.

Assembling a Master-Slave RS Flip-Flop

Unless you are quite familiar with master-slave circuitry, it will be very help-ful to assemble the master-slave RS flip-flop arrangement depicted in Fig. 6-2.

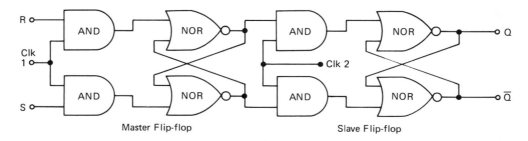

Master Flip-flop   Slave Flip-flop

Note: The master-slave RS flip-flop is driven by a two-phase clock waveform. The troubleshooter may use the slow-pulse generator shown in Fig. 2-7. In this application, the Q output from the slow-pulse generator is connected to the Clk 1 input, and the Q̄ output from the slow-pulse generator is connected to the Clk 2 input. The two clock waveforms have the following time relation:

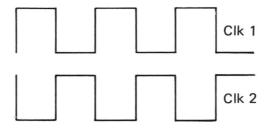

It is suggested that the troubleshooter assemble the master-slave RS flip-flop on an experimenter socket such as the Radio Shack No. 276-174, using the type 7408 quad 2-input AND gate IC, and the 7402 quad 2-input positive NOR gate IC. The Radio Shack numbers are 276-1822, and 276-1811, respectively.

Fig. 6-2. Master-slave RS flip-flop configuration.

Note that this is a *level-triggered* flip-flop; whereas, the configuration shown in Fig. 3-1 was an *edge-triggered* flip-flop. (Fig. 6-3 shows the plan of a plug-in board.)

After you have assembled the master-slave RS flip-flop depicted in Fig. 6-2, use a logic probe to make the following tests:

1. Stop the clock, and check the output of each gate with a logic probe. Observe that the stored data remains unchanged from the instant that the clock was stopped.

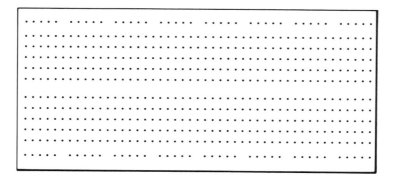

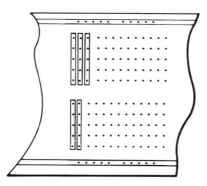

Note: This experimenter's socket board provides 560 holes into which device and component pigtails may be plugged for interconnection. Underneath the socket board, conductors are provided as shown in the partial view. These conductors provide interconnection of each column of five holes, and also provide interconnection of each row of holes along the top and bottom of the socket board.

Fig. 6-3. Plan of an experimenter's plug-in socket.

2. Connect both the R input and the S input to Gnd, and start the clock. Note that the stored data is promptly "clocked out" (Q goes logic-low, and $\bar{Q}$ goes logic-high).

3. The master-slave flip-flop is now unloaded, and it remains unloaded until new data is entered.

4. To enter a new data bit, disconnect the R input from Gnd, and connect it to a logic-high level, such as V_{CC}. Observe that this logic-high level is promptly clocked through the master and slave sections.

TROUBLESHOOTING CABLES AND CONNECTORS

Experienced digital troubleshooters know that "tough dog" jobs can be caused by faults that are so obvious that they are overlooked. For example, a new personal computer operated normally, except that programs from the computer could not be stored in the external memory (a tape recorder). A checkout by ear when the tape was played back through the speaker showed that the pulse recording was very weak.

With reference to Fig. 6-4, the cable interconnecting the keyboard and tape recorder fell under suspicion, inasmuch as the tape recorder operated normally from a microphone input. Acting on a "hunch," the troubleshooter plugged in a replacement cable between the keyboard and tape recorder, whereupon normal operation was restored.

> *Moral:* Don't overlook the obvious—check out the "easy" possibilities first!

THE "OPEN-COLLECTOR EVIL"

A "tough dog" problem confronted by digital troubleshooters, regardless of the test equipment that may be available, is what the troubleshooter "fondly"

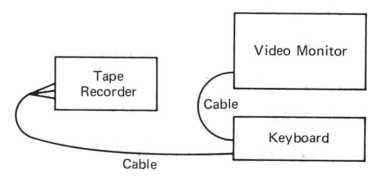

> **Troubleshooting Note:** All cables and connectors in a digital system are potential troublemakers. It is good practice to start by flexing and pulling the cables. Make certain that the connectors are properly mated. For a follow-up check, replace the cables to determine whether normal operation is restored.

Fig. 6-4. Keyboard connects via cables to the monitor and tape recorder, in this example.

calls the "open-collector evil." In other words, there is a subfamily in the TTL IC family termed "open collector" gates. These are circuits whose outputs can be tied together (sometimes designated "wire OR" or "wire AND") so that one circuit's output can constrain the other circuits' outputs to be in a given state, regardless of their inputs.

With reference to Fig. 6-5, gates U1, U2, U3, and U4 are "wire-ORed" together. Under certain conditions, gate A's output can cause gates B's, C's, and D's to be a TTL low, regardless of the B, C, and D input states. The bottom line is that from the troubleshooter's viewpoint, gates U2, U3, and U4 (in this example) are constrained to operate improperly with respect to a conventional truth table. The clue to the difficulty is an asterisk (*) at the output terminal of the gate.

Note carefully that although this configuration is called a wired-AND or a wired-OR arrangement, it is actually neither from the functional viewpoint. In other words, the configuration provides negated-AND action, which is the same as OR-NOT action. Observe that if inverters are included in the A, B, C, and D inputs, that the arrangement will provide AND action. Again, if an inverter is included in the Y output lead, a wired-OR arrangement will provide OR action.

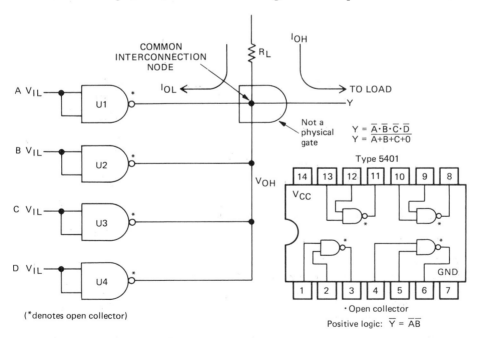

Fig. 6-5. Four open-collector NAND gates operating in wire-AND mode with a common pull-up resistor.

CHART 6-1

WIRE-AND, WIRE-OR
(Open-Collector Circuits)

An open-collector configuration is shown below. Note that the open collectors of the NAND gates have a common interconnection node. Circuit operation is that of a negated AND gate, or of a NOR gate.

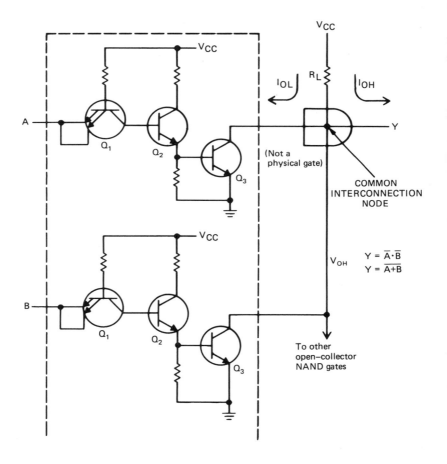

A typical logic diagram for a wire-AND arrangement is shown below. The configuration is variously called an implied-AND, dot-AND, wire-AND, phantom-AND, or wire-OR connection. Whether termed a wire-AND circuit or a wire-OR circuit depends primarily upon the troubleshooter's viewpoint.

This, then, is the "open-collector evil." When a trouble symptom directs suspicion upon open-collector gates, the usual procedure is to replace the gates one at a time until the malfunction disappears. Alternatively, the outputs can be unsoldered and the ICs individually tested. (See also Chart 6-1.)

A wire-AND circuit such as shown in Chart 6-1 may employ open-collector NAND-gate packages as exemplified in Fig. 6-5 with an external pull-up resistor. The arrangement is variously called an implied-AND, dot-AND, wired-AND, wired-OR, or phantom-AND connection. In any case, a "tricky" point for the beginning troubleshooter is that the pull-up resistor is often omitted in logic diagrams (the pull-up resistor is implied, but not explicitly shown).

With reference to Fig. 6-6, either a wired-AND symbol or a wired-OR symbol may be shown in logic diagrams. Whether the diagram employs one symbol or the other depends upon the viewpoint of the circuit designer. Of course, the circuit function is the same, regardless of the symbolism that is used. The fact that a physical gate is not involved is denoted by the dot interconnection inside of the AND or OR symbol.

Moral: To keep from "knocking himself out," the troubleshooter must be alert to the possibility of circuit constraints that prevent gates from obeying their basic truth tables. Such circuit constraints are indicated by asterisks at gate outputs and by dot-AND or dot-OR symbols.

Note in passing that wired-OR circuitry is sometimes used inside of IC's, as exemplified in Fig. 6-7. Wired-AND (wired-OR) circuitry with an external pull-up resistor is more likely to be encountered in digital equipment that has been in use for a considerable time. With the advent of bus structures such as those

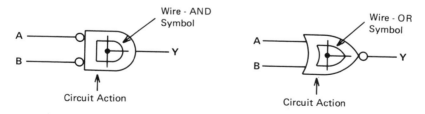

Troubleshooting Note: Although the troubleshooter recognizes that a wired-AND configuration is under consideration, his conventional test instruments may be inadequate—particularly if the wired-AND output is stuck low. When voltage-oriented tests are inadequate, the troubleshooter should follow current-oriented test procedures, as explained subsequently.

Fig. 6-6. Wired-AND and wired-OR symbols (dot-AND and dot-OR symbols), enclosed by their circuit-action symbols.

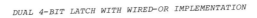

DUAL 4-BIT LATCH WITH WIRED-OR IMPLEMENTATION

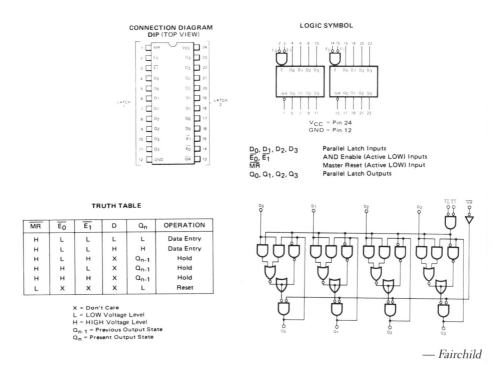

CONNECTION DIAGRAM
DIP (TOP VIEW)

LOGIC SYMBOL

V_{CC} = Pin 24
GND = Pin 12

D_0, D_1, D_2, D_3	Parallel Latch Inputs
$\overline{E_0}$, $\overline{E_1}$	AND Enable (Active LOW) Inputs
$\overline{MR}$	Master Reset (Active LOW) Input
Q_0, Q_1, Q_2, Q_3	Parallel Latch Outputs

TRUTH TABLE

$\overline{MR}$	$\overline{E_0}$	$\overline{E_1}$	D	Q_n	OPERATION
H	L	L	L	L	Data Entry
H	L	L	H	H	Data Entry
H	L	H	X	Q_{n-1}	Hold
H	H	L	X	Q_{n-1}	Hold
H	H	H	X	Q_{n-1}	Hold
L	X	X	X	L	Reset

X = Don't Care
L = LOW Voltage Level
H = HIGH Voltage Level
Q_{n-1} = Previous Output State
Q_n = Present Output State

— *Fairchild*

FUNCTIONAL DESCRIPTION
LATCH OPERATION — Data can be entered into the latch when both of the enable inputs are LOW. As long as this logic condition exists, the output of the latch will follow the input. If either of the enable inputs goes HIGH, the data present in the latch at that time is held in the latch and is no longer affected by data input.

The master reset overrides all other input conditions and forces the outputs of all the latches LOW when a LOW signal is applied to the master reset input.

Fig. 6-7. Example of a four-bit latch IC with internal wired-OR logic circuitry.

utilized in microprocessor-based systems, the wired-AND configuration has become obsolescent. Operationally, the wired-AND configuration has a disadvantage in that its speed is limited in comparison to three-state gates, for example.

COMMERCIAL LOGIC PROBES

Commercial logic probes, such as illustrated in Fig. 6-8, provide comparatively sophisticated digital test facilities. Thus, the Model 545A localizes nodes stuck high or stuck low, intermittent pulse activity, and normal pulse activity. In other words, the probe shows whether the node being probed is logic-high,

Fig. 6-8. View of the Hewlett-Packard logic probe. (Courtesy, Hewlett-Packard.)

logic-low, bad level, open-circuited, or pulsing. The high input impedance of the probe ensures against excessive circuit loading, not just in the logic-high state, but in the logic-low state as well.

The probe pictured in Fig. 6-8 also provides switch-selectable, multifamily operation, with a built-in pulse memory. A single lamp display is utilized. This probe operates from 4 to 18 volts in CMOS applications, or from 4.5- to 15-volt dc supplies in the TTL mode (standard TTL thresholds are maintained). The built-in pulse memory helps to capture intermittent hard-to-see pulses. *To detect a glitch, the probe is connected to a circuit point, the memory is reset, and the troubleshooter then waits for the glitch to appear.* (The memory will capture and retain a random pulse until reset.)

Operation at frequencies up to 80 MHz in TTL, and up to 40 MHz in CMOS, is provided by the illustrated probe. Note that when troubleshooting circuits consist of analog components, the task is one of verifying relatively simple characteristics, such as resistance, capacitance, or turn-on voltages of components with two, or at most, three nodes.

In analog circuits, discrete circuitry is often utilized (although much integrated analog circuitry will also be encountered). Note that although the function of discrete analog circuitry may be complex, each device or component performs a comparatively simple task. In turn, the complex function may often be disregarded, and systematic checkouts of devices and components made with a DVM, for example.

On the other hand, discrete circuitry is the rare exception, and not the rule in current digital-logic configurations. In turn, the digital troubleshooter must concern himself with complex digital signals, and must decide whether these signals are correct for the function that the digital IC normally performs.

Multiple Inputs and Outputs

Verification of normal component operation often requires driving and observing many inputs (for example, as many as ten inputs), while the troubleshooter simultaneously observes several outputs (from two to eight outputs). *Thus, a fundamental difference between discrete circuitry and integrated circuitry is the number of inputs and outputs associated with each component—and the need to drive and observe these inputs and outputs simultaneously.*

RST FLIP-FLOP CONSTRUCTION

The troubleshooter will encounter RST flip-flops in various digital systems, and it is important to understand how they function. RST denotes reset-set toggle, and the basic RS toggle master-slave flip-flop is shown in Fig. 6-9. It is a slight elaboration of the configuration depicted in Fig. 6-2. If you are not familiar with RST flip-flops, it will be very instructive to build this unit and check its operation with a logic probe:

1. With both clock lines disconnected, check the R, S, Q, and $\bar{Q}$ terminals for logic-high and logic-low states with a logic probe.
2. Connect one output from a slow-pulse generator to the Clk 1 terminal, and again check the R, S, Q, and $\bar{Q}$ terminals for their logic states.
3. Also connect the other output from the slow-pulse generator to the Clk 2 terminal, and recheck the R, S, Q, and $\bar{Q}$ terminals for their logic states.

It is important to note that the RST flip-flop is a *level-triggered* configuration; whereas, the toggle latch that was depicted in Fig. 3-4 is an *edge-triggered* arrangement. A level-triggered flip-flop is also called a *one's-catching flip-flop.*

It is not practical to construct an RST flip-flop from simple RS latches, such

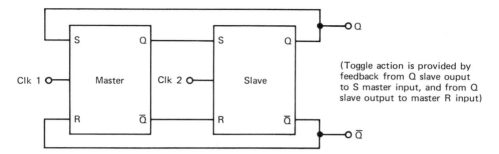

(Toggle action is provided by feedback from Q slave ouput to S master input, and from Q slave output to master R input)

Note: This is the basic RS toggle (RST) flip-flop configuration. Its circuit action is comparable to that of the toggle latch shown in Fig. 2-4. However, the RST flip-flop employs more sophisticated circuitry. Note that a square-wave generator may be used as a clock; the direct output from the generator serves as Clk 1, and when the direct output is passed through an inverter, it serves as Clk 2.

The logic diagram for the master-slave RS flip-flop is shown in Fig. 6-2.

Fig. 6-9. The RS toggle master-slave flip-flop.

as shown in Fig. 6-1. Master-slave flip-flops must be used in RST configurations because of *race problems* that are encountered if simple RS latches are used. In other words, when an AND gate is driven by simultaneously rising and falling waveforms, their timing must be extremely accurate to avoid false spike (glitch) outputs from the AND gates. Since it is not practical to maintain such precise timing, malfunction due to glitches is avoided by using master-slave flip-flops.

EDGE-TRIGGERED, D MASTER-SLAVE FLIP-FLOP CONFIGURATION

Troubleshooters frequently encounter the edge-triggered D flip-flop with NAND implementation, as shown in Fig. 6-10. It is a positive-edge triggered arrangement, and it is helpful to understand its operation, inasmuch as edge-triggering is accomplished by means of propagation delay.

With reference to Fig. 6-11, observe that when the clock is logic-high and the data input is logic-high, Q is logic-high and Q̄ is logic-low.

Next, observe in Fig. 6-12 that if the clock is still logic-high, and the data input goes logic-low, Q remains logic-high and Q̄ remains logic-low.

Then, as shown in Fig. 6-13, when the clock is logic-low and the data input goes logic-high, Q remains logic-high and Q̄ remains logic-low.

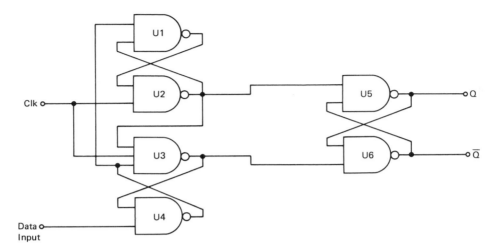

Note: The troubleshooter who is not familiar with edge-triggered flip-flops may construct this arrangement from NAND gate ICs. It may be clocked from a square-wave generator, or from the slow-pulse generator that was previously noted. The data input can be driven from V_{cc} or from ground. Circuit action can be followed with a logic probe.

Fig. 6-10. Edge-triggered, D master-slave flip-flop configuration.

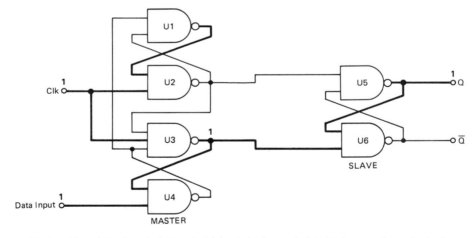

Note: The data line is being held logic-high, and this high state has clocked through to the Q output. As long as the data input is held logic-high, the Q output will continuously remain logic-high. (Although the clock signal goes alternately logic-high and logic-low, the Q output is held at an unchanging logic-high level by the logic-high data input line.)

Fig. 6-11. D Master-slave FF with data logic-high and clock logic-high.

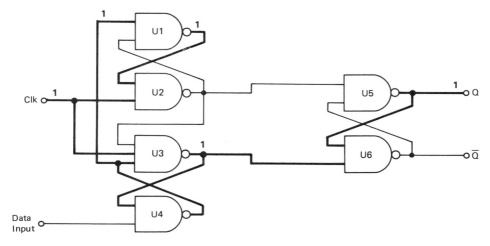

Note: If the data input goes logic-low while the clock is still logic-high, the Q output remains locked in its logic-high state. *This condition results from the fact that the data input is locked out at this time.* In other words, U3–U4 cannot "flip" because one input to U3 is being held logic-low.

Fig. 6-12. Clock is logic-high, data input is logic-low.

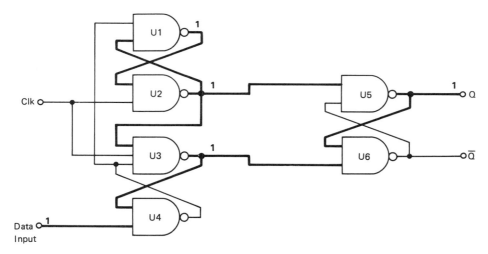

Note: Here, the data input is being held logic-high while the clock goes logic-low. The Q output remains locked in its logic-high state. U3–U4 cannot "flop" because two inputs of U3 are logic-low. U5–U6 cannot "flop" because neither input of U6 can go logic-low at this time.

Fig. 6-13. Clock is logic-low, data input is logic-high.

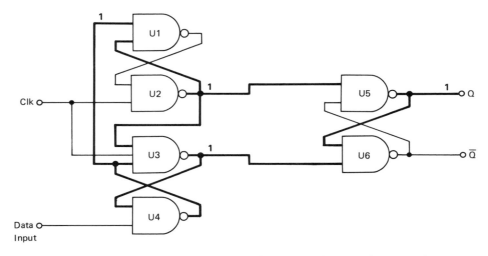

Note: Now, the data input is being held logic-low, while the clock goes logic-low. The Q output remains locked in its logic-high state. U3–U4 cannot "flop" because one input of U3 is logic-low. U5–U6 cannot "flop" because neither input of U6 can go logic-low at this time.

Fig. 6-14. Clock is logic-low, data input is logic-low.

When, as shown in Fig. 6-14, the clock is still logic-low and the data input goes logic-low, Q remains logic-high, and $\bar{Q}$ remains logic-low. The clock input to U3 is logic-low, and the other two inputs to U3 are logic-high. The data input is logic-low. We will see that it is possible to edge-trigger this configuration and thereby make Q go logic-low, and to make $\bar{Q}$ go logic-high. (This possibility exists because of propagation delay.)

Finally, with reference to Fig. 6-15, observe that when the clock goes logic-high, all three inputs to U3 go logic-high simultaneously. Accordingly, the output of U3 is driven logic-low. Consequently, Q goes logic-low and $\bar{Q}$ goes logic-high.

Note carefully that after a brief propagation delay (through U3) both of the inputs to U4 have gone logic-low. Therefore, the data input is now "locked out." In other words, Q remains logic-low and $\bar{Q}$ remains logic-high, no matter whether the data input is driven logic-high. This edge-trigger sampling action is shown in Fig. 6-16.

The propagation time of U3 is approximately 10 ns. Thus, the state of the data line does not affect the RS master-slave flip-flop except during this 10ns sampling interval. This is an important operating feature, because the data line can be used in other data-processing "jobs" over most of the clock cycle. In

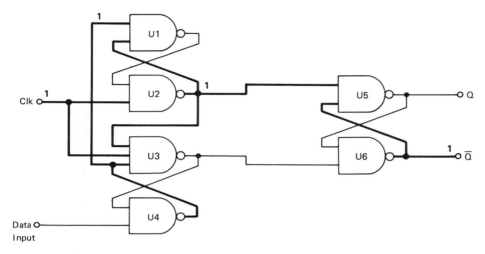

Note: Finally, the clock goes logic-high while the data input is being held log-ic-low. Now, all three inputs of U3 are logic-high, and U3–U4 "flops," with the result that U5–U6 also "flops" and the flip-flop unloads—the Q output goes logic-low. After the very brief propagation delay through U3, both inputs of U4 are logic-low. The data input is locked out because the output of U4 cannot go logic-low at this time. In other words, the flip-flop cannot be loaded unless a rising edge of the clock waveform is present while the data input is being held logic-high. Note that the flip-flop will remain unloaded until such time as a new logic-high data signal may be entered.

Fig. 6-15. Clock is logic-high, data input is logic-low.

turn, digital systems that employ D master-slave flip-flops can provide faster operation with less complex circuitry.

In the case of level-triggered flip-flop, the data line must not change state over one-half of the clock cycle (while the clock is logic-high). This is why a level-triggered flip-flop is also called a "one's catching" flip-flop. It is essential to replace an edge-triggered flip-flop *only with an equivalent edge-triggered flip-flop.* Similarly, it is essential to replace a level-triggered flip-flop *only with an equivalent level-triggered flip-flop.*

Replacement flip-flops must be true equivalents. In other words, a positive edge-triggered flip-flop *cannot be replaced with a negative edge-triggered flip-flop,* or vice versa. Note also that some level-triggered flip-flops have active-low clock inputs, instead of active-high clock inputs. In turn, an active-high flip-flop *cannot be replaced with an active-low flip-flop,* or vice versa. This is just another way of saying that an active-high flip-flop triggers on the logic-high portion of the clock waveform; whereas, an active-low flip-flop triggers on the logic-low portion of the clock waveform.

Digital troubleshooters could soon become "lost in the woods" if they did not recognize the distinction between edge-triggered and level-triggered flip-flops, as well as the distinction between negative-edge triggering and positive-edge triggering. These differences are as significant in circuit action as are active-high and active-low responses. This is just another way of saying that the professional digital troubleshooter cannot be too knowledgeable concerning circuit action.

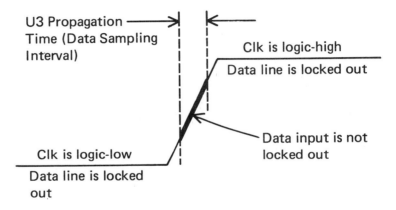

U3 Propagation Time (Data Sampling Interval)

Clk is logic-high
Data line is locked out

Data input is not locked out

Clk is logic-low
Data line is locked out

Note: The data input line is locked out at all times except for a brief "window" on the rising edge of the clock pulse, due to U3 propagation time. The signal on the data input line is sampled during this "window." The data signal might be logic-low, or it might be logic-high. (In the example of Fig. 6-15, the data signal was logic-low.) If the signal on the data input line is logic-high during the "window," the flip-flop will load.

Fig. 6-16. The data input is briefly sampled on the rising edge of the clock pulse.

7

Troubleshooting Multiplexers and Demultiplexers

Device Input and Output Resistances • Paradox? • CMOS Trouble-shooting Precautions • Normal vs. Short-Circuit Current Flow • Multiplexers • Data Selector Operation • Demultiplexers • Data Distributor • Commercial Demultiplexer/Addressable Latch • Trouble-shooting Multiplexers and Demultiplexers

DEVICE INPUT AND OUTPUT RESISTANCES

Digital devices operate in switching circuits and have two-valued input and output resistances. By way of comparison, analog devices generally operate in linear systems and have single-valued input and output resistances. *As shown in Fig. 7-1, a TTL NAND gate has a <u>normal</u> output resistance of 56 ohms, approximately when its output terminal is logic-high; it has a <u>normal</u> output resistance of 94 kilohms, approximately when its output terminal is logic-low.*

However, if the output interconnect develops an open bond inside of the IC, the NAND gate will have an abnormal output resistance of infinity. On the other hand, if the output interconnect develops a short circuit to ground inside of the IC, the NAND gate will have a subnormal output resistance of practically zero. *If the output lead becomes short-circuited to V_{CC}, the output terminal will draw about 38 mA, and the NAND gate will have an abnormal output resistance of 132 ohms, approximately.*

Since the output of a NAND gate is connected to the input of a following device, such as another NAND gate, *the logic-high and logic-low input resistances of a NAND gate are the same as its logic-high and logic-low output resistances.* This perhaps unexpected circumstance is a result of the fact that the second NAND gate functions as an active load for the first NAND gate, and vice versa. (See Fig. 7-2.)

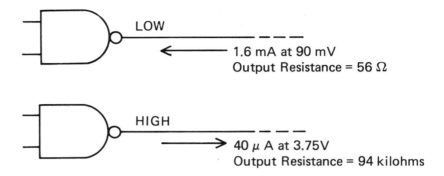

LOW

← 1.6 mA at 90 mV
Output Resistance = 56 Ω

HIGH

→ 40 μ A at 3.75V
Output Resistance = 94 kilohms

Note: Output resistance should not be confused with load resistance. The output resistance of the NAND gate is its voltage/current ratio "looking into" the gate from its output terminal. This is just another way of saying that the output resistance of a NAND gate is not a physical resistor, but the effective resistance of an active circuit.

If the NAND gate is changed into a passive device (by removing its V_{cc} supply), the resistance between its output terminal and ground will be practically infinite, as measured by a lo-pwr ohmmeter.

Fig. 7-1. NAND gate having a **different** output resistance, depending on whether its output terminal is logic-high or logic-low.

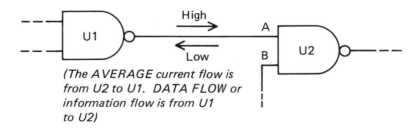

High →

A

U1

← Low

B

U2

(The AVERAGE current flow is from U2 to U1. DATA FLOW or information flow is from U1 to U2)

Note: When the output of U1 is logic-high, it sources 40 μA. When the output of U1 is logic-low, it sinks 1.6 mA. Also, when input A of U2 is logic-high, it sinks 40 μA. When input A of U2 is logic-low, it sources 1.6 mA.

This is just another way of saying that U2 is an active load for U1, and U1 is an active load for U2. An active load becomes a source when its internal voltage exceeds the internal voltage of the former source.

Source/sink U1 is a *controlling* device. Source/sink U2 is a *controlled* device.

Fig. 7-2. Each NAND gate alternates as a source and as a sink.

PARADOX?

Beginning troubleshooters tend to see a paradox in gate action, inasmuch as the node voltage is always positive, whether a gate is sourcing current or sinking current. It *seems* logical to say that if a circuit point is positive with respect to ground, and if the point never becomes negative with respect to ground, that the current flow cannot change direction.

This seeming paradox is quickly resolved by recognizing that the current in Fig. 7-2 is indirectly related to ground potential. In other words, when U2 has a higher internal positive voltage than U1, then electrons will flow from the output of U1 into the input of U2. On the other hand, when U1 has a higher internal positive potential than U2, then electrons will flow from the input of U2 into the output of U1.

CMOS TROUBLESHOOTING PRECAUTIONS

CMOS gates are more easily damaged than are TTL gates. Some CMOS gates (those that are not diode protected) may be damaged by static discharge due to improper handling. Antistatic precautions must be used in this situation; pins should be tied to the V_{SS} terminal until after the IC has been connected into its circuit. Although many CMOS IC's have inputs that are diode-protected against static voltages, such voltages will damage the IC if they exceed the maximum input voltage rating.

CMOS gates have extremely high input and output resistances; this is why they are easily damaged by static electricity, whereas TTL gates have comparatively low input and output resistances. This is just another way of saying that a static discharge produces a high voltage drop at a CMOS input terminal, whereas it produces a near-zero voltage drop at a TTL input terminal.

Troubleshooters should also note that slow-rise or slow-fall pulse input voltages are detrimental to CMOS operation. In other words, a slowly rising or slowly falling input voltage can result in abnormal power consumption. Technically, this means that pulses with rise and fall times of less than 15 μs should be employed. Another practical precaution is to avoid application of any input signal to a CMOS circuit while the power is turned off.

And in the case of TTL gates, all unused CMOS inputs must be grounded (or connected to V_{DD}). Otherwise, malfunction will occur and the chip will draw an abnormal amount of current. CMOS gates are subject to damage by excessive heat. Note also that it is good practice to use a battery-powered soldering gun; if you must use a line-powered soldering gun in CMOS circuitry, be sure to ground the tip with a flexible lead.

Complementary MOSFET (CMOS) gates employ the CMOS inverter as their basic element. A configuration for a three-input CMOS NAND gate is shown in Fig. 7-3. The pull-up MOSFETs are P-channel type; on the other hand, the pull-down MOSFETs are N-channel type. In turn, this is a complementary configuration. If inputs ABC are driven logic-*high* simultaneously, the pull-up MOSFETs cut off, but the pull-down MOSFETs conduct. Consequently, the output terminal has low impedance to ground, and the output state is logic-*low*. This is NAND action. Observe that Q1, Q2, and Q3 are connected in parallel, whereas Q4, Q5, and Q6 are connected in series. Accordingly, if only one of the inputs is driven logic-*low*, the output state will be logic-*high* (NAND action).

A configuration for a three-input CMOS NOR gate is depicted in Fig. 7-4.

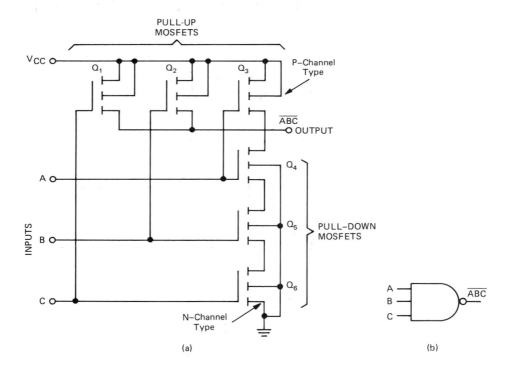

(a)

(b)

Note that if the output from the NAND gate is represented by Y, we may write: $Y = \overline{ABC}$. This is a logical statement, or expression: it is not an equation in the strict sense of the term. This logical statement is read: Y equals A and B and C not.

Fig. 7-3. A CMOS NAND gate. (a) Schematic diagram; (b) logic symbol.

The pull-up MOSFETs are connected in series; the pull-down MOSFETs are connected in parallel. In turn, if one input is driven logic-*high*, the pull-up circuit cuts off and the pull-down circuit conducts. As a result, the output has low impedance to ground and its state is logic-*low*. This is NOR action. If all three inputs are driven logic-*low*, the pull-up MOSFETs conduct and the pull-down MOSFETS cut off. Therefore, V_{DD} is applied to the output terminal, and its state is logic-*high* (NOR action).

Thresholds for CMOS logic depend upon the power-supply voltage. The supply voltage is in the range from 3 to 15 volts, Logic-*high* is 70 percent of the supply voltage, and logic-*low* is 30 percent of the supply voltage.

NORMAL VS. SHORT-CIRCUIT CURRENT FLOW

Troubleshooters need to know the normal vs. short-circuit current values for various families of gates. With reference to Fig. 7-5, observe that CMOS has

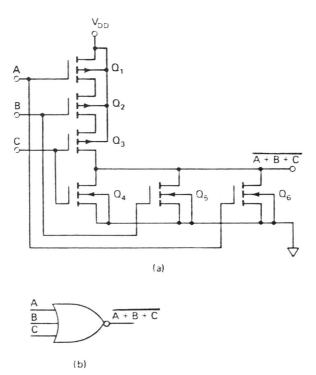

(a)

(b)

Fig. 7-4. A CMOS NOR gate. (a) Schematic diagram; (b) logic symbol.

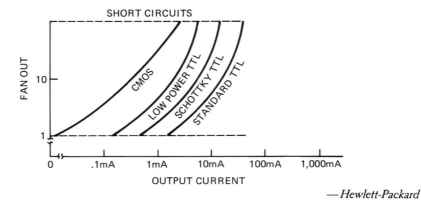

—*Hewlett-Packard*

Troubleshooting Note: A CMOS gate normally draws a very small quiescent current, such as 0.5 nA. On the other hand, if the CMOS gate is short-circuited, it may draw 1 mA. By way of comparison, a standard TTL gate normally draws 1.6 mA; if the TTL gate is short-circuited (output logic-high to ground), the short-circuit current is typically 50 mA.

Fig. 7-5. Normal vs. short-circuit current demands by CMOS and TTL gates.

the smallest current demand in normal operation, although its output current increases excessively in case of a short circuit to ground in the output line. By way of comparison, standard TTL normally draws as much current as a short-circuited CMOS gate.

Note also in Fig. 7-5 that there are two TTL families (low-power TTL and Schottky TTL) which draw less current than standard TTL, although they draw more current than CMOS. Not only does CMOS have a minimum current demand and power dissipation—it is also a high-density device (many more CMOS gates can be formed on a chip than TTL gates). On the other hand, CMOS has an operating disadvantage of comparatively slow speed, compared to TTL. As previously noted, a CMOS gate may operate from a supply voltage of 3V, whereas a TTL gate requires a supply voltage of 5V.

MULTIPLEXERS

Digital troubleshooters are frequently concerned with multiplexers. A multiplexer is any circuit or device in which multiple data lines are selectively channeled into a single output line. In a general sense, multiplexing can be regarded as any mixing of signals from multiple sources into a lesser number of outputs. A multiplexer is an example of a data handling circuit.

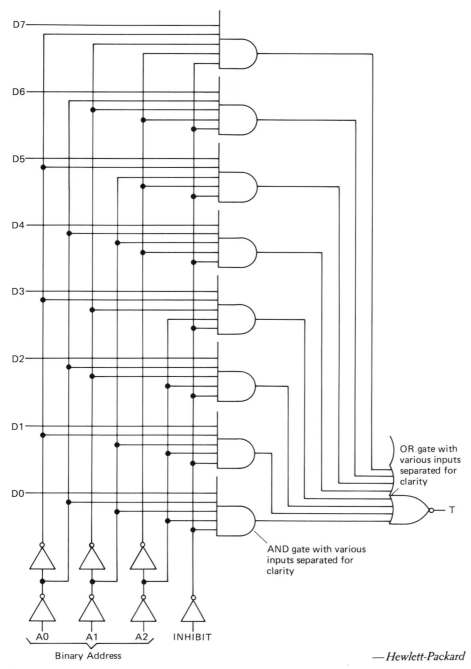

D7

D6

D5

D4

D3

D2

D1

OR gate with
various inputs
separated for
clarity

D0

T

AND gate with various
inputs separated for
clarity

A0 A1 A2 INHIBIT

Binary Address

—Hewlett-Packard

Fig. 7-6. An eight-channel multiplexer circuit controlled by three signals.

A typical eight-channel multiplexer configuration in which the multiplexing (rearranging) is controlled by three signals is depicted in Fig. 7-6. Observe that the logic level present on the selected data input D_0-D_7 is to be placed in a sequence on the output line T; the address inputs A_0, A_1, A_2 are stepped from 000 to 111 in binary code to select each of the inputs at the proper time. As an illustration, $A_0 = 0$, $A_1 = 0$, $A_2 = 0$ would place the bit or logic level present on D_0 on T; again, $A_0 = 1$, $A_1 = 0$, $A_2 = 0$ would select the data on D_1 and so on.

Thus, multiplexing is the process of mixing signals from multiple sources into a lesser number of outputs. This particular choice of mixing eight lines of data into a particular sequence on a single line represents the configuration of one specific integrated circuit. However, the troubleshooter will encounter other common multiplexers that operate to multiplex four or 16 lines onto one output line, or binary word multiplexers that can multiplex three four-bit wide parallel words into a single four-bit wide output.

Data Selector Operation

Note also that the eight-input multiplexer exemplified in Fig. 7-6 can also be operated to select one input and to continuously gate the data from that line through to output T. When the configuration is used in this way, it is called a data selector—but is fundamentally a multiplexer.

A commercial example of a quad two-input multiplexer IC package is shown in Fig. 7-7. The logic diagram for this multiplexer is depicted in Fig. 7-8. You will note the basic similarity between this configuration and the more elaborate circuit depicted in Fig. 7-6. The active-low Enable input in Fig. 7-8 is similar to the Inhibit input in Fig. 7-6. The four (quad) dual inputs of the circuit in Fig. 7-8 are I_0a-I_1a, I_0b-I_1b, I_0c-I_1c, and I_0d-I_1d.

DEMULTIPLEXERS

Troubleshooters are concerned with demultiplexers as often as with multiplexers. A demultiplexer takes data from one source and distributes it according to a specified pattern into several output lines. A typical eight-channel demultiplexer configuration is depicted in Fig. 7-9. Observe that this represents the reverse of the multiplexing arrangement shown in Fig. 7-6.

The data-input line T in Fig. 7-9 receives incoming data, and the binary address on A_0, A_1, and A_2 is sequentially stepped from 000 through 111. In turn, the inputted data appears sequentially on output lines D_0 through D_7. Observe

Type 9322

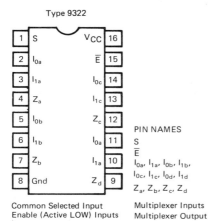

ENABLE	SELECT INPUT	INPUTS		OUTPUT
$\overline{E}$	S	I_{0x}	I_{1x}	Z_x
H	X	X	X	L
L	H	X	L	L
L	H	X	H	H
L	L	L	X	L
L	L	H	X	H

H = HIGH Voltage Level
L = LOW Voltage Level
X = Either HIGH or LOW

PIN NAMES
S
$\overline{E}$
$I_{0a}, I_{1a}, I_{0b}, I_{1b},$
$I_{0c}, I_{1c}, I_{0d}, I_{1d}$
Z_a, Z_b, Z_c, Z_d

Common Selected Input
Enable (Active LOW) Inputs

Multiplexer Inputs
Multiplexer Output

Package Pinout

Truth Table

Fig. 7-7. A quad two-input multiplexer IC package pinout.

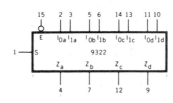

LOGIC SYMBOL

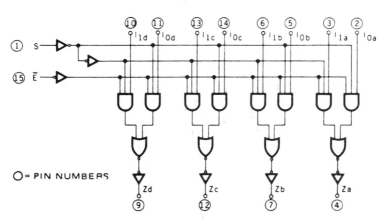

O = PIN NUMBERS

—*Fairchild*

Fig. 7-8. Logic diagram for the quad two-input multiplexer.

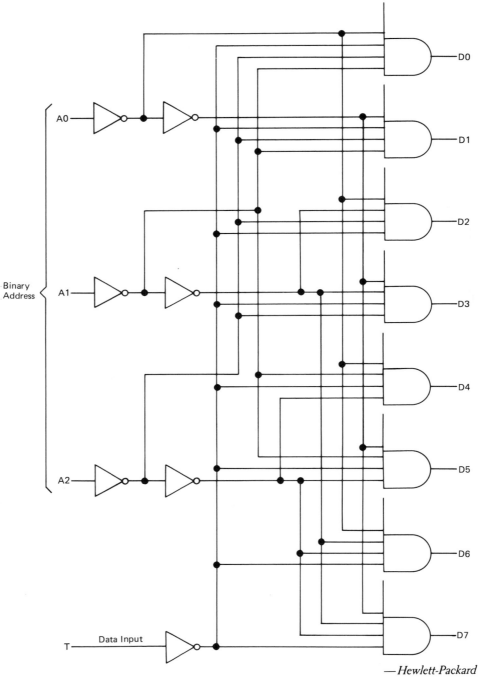

Fig. 7-9. A typical eight-channel demultiplexer configuration.

that if the binary address is 000, the inputted data proceeds to output line D_0. Or, the demultiplexing action is the reverse of multiplexing action.

Data Distributor

Technically, instead of being demultiplexed, the data on the single input line of the circuit in Fig. 7-9 can be gated (from A_0, A_1, and A_2 address lines) through any one of the output gates continuously. After some interval of time, the address may be changed to gate the data into another output line. In this manner, data can be distributed to various destinations. When operated in this manner, the demultiplexer is called a data distributor.

Troubleshooters should be alert for still another operating mode of the basic demultiplexer. In other words, the circuit is sometimes operated as a decoder. For example, if the input line T is held at a logic-high level continuously, the outputs will always represent the binary count determined by the logic levels on A_0, A_1, and A_2. In other words, the particular output line that is logic-high represents the decoded binary input. In this application, the input line T functions as the Enable control. (A demultiplexer with four address line inputs and 16 outputs then becomes a four-line-to-16-line decoder.)

Commercial Demultiplexer/Addressable Latch

Commercial demultiplexers may be listed as decoders or as addressable latches. An example is shown in Fig. 7-10. This is an eight-bit addressable latch which is designed for general-purpose storage applications in digital systems. It is a multifunctional device capable of storing single-line data in eight addressable latches, and being a one-of-eight decoder and demultiplexer with active-high outputs.

This addressable latch also incorporates an active-low common Clear for resetting all latches, as well as an active-low Enable.

As a multifunctional device, this addressable latch has four modes of operation as indicated in Fig. 7-10. In the addressable-latch mode, data on the data line (D) is written into the addressed latch. The addressed latch will follow the data input with all nonaddressed latches remaining in their previous states. In the memory mode, all latches remain in their previous states and are unaffected by the data or address inputs.

In the one-of-eight decoding or demultiplexing mode, the addressed output will follow the state of the D input with all other outputs in the logic-low state. In the Clear mode, all outputs are logic-low and are unaffected by the address and data inputs. When the device is operated as an addressable latch, changing

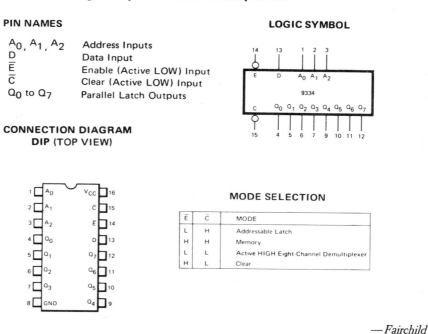

PIN NAMES

A_0, A_1, A_2 Address Inputs
D   Data Input
$\overline{E}$ Enable (Active LOW) Input
$\overline{C}$ Clear (Active LOW) Input
Q_0 to Q_7 Parallel Latch Outputs

CONNECTION DIAGRAM
DIP (TOP VIEW)

LOGIC SYMBOL

MODE SELECTION

$\overline{E}$	$\overline{C}$	MODE
L	H	Addressable Latch
H	H	Memory
L	L	Active HIGH Eight-Channel Demultiplexer
H	L	Clear

—Fairchild

Fig. 7-10. Example of a commercial addressable latch that also operates as a demultiplexer or a decoder.

more than one bit of the address could impose a transient wrong address. Therefore, this should be done only while in the Memory mode.

TROUBLESHOOTING MULTIPLEXERS AND DEMULTIPLEXERS

Although multiplexers and demultiplexers sometimes appear more formidable than counters, for example, they are no more difficult to troubleshoot, provided that their normal circuit action is recognized. Thus, a multiplexer such as depicted in Fig. 7-7 has a truth table which can be used as a guide to check out the device with a logic probe and pulser.

Again, an addressable latch such as shown in Fig. 7-10 has a truth table (Fig. 7-11) which is the basic troubleshooting guide for checking out the latch. One point that should be kept in mind is that the truth table for a multiplexer or a demultiplexer is almost always valid, regardless of the network into which it is connected. In other words, constraints are not usually imposed by any circuit upon the device.

TRUTH TABLE

$\bar{C}$	$\bar{E}$	D	A_0	A_1	A_2	Q_0	Q_1	Q_2	Q_3	Q_4	Q_5	Q_6	Q_7	MODE
									PRESENT OUTPUT STATES					
L	H	X	X	X	X	L	L	L	L	L	L	L	L	CLEAR
L	L	L	L	L	L	L	L	L	L	L	L	L	L	DEMULTIPLEX
L	L	H	L	L	L	H	L	L	L	L	L	L	L	
L	L	L	H	L	L	L	L	L	L	L	L	L	L	
L	L	H	H	L	L	L	H	L	L	L	L	L	L	
.	.	.	.			.	.		.					
.	.	.	.			.	.							
L	L	H	H	H	H	L	L	L	L	L	L	L	H	
H	H	X	X	X	X	Q_{N-1} —————————————————————⟶								MEMORY
H	L	L	L	L	L	L	Q_{N-1}	Q_{N-1}	Q_{N-1} ——————————⟶					ADDRESSABLE
H	L	H	L	L	L	H	Q_{N-1}	Q_{N-1} ——————————————⟶						LATCH
H	L	L	H	L	L	Q_{N-1}	L	Q_{N-1} ——————————————⟶						
H	L	H	H	L	L	Q_{N-1}	H	Q_{N-1} ——————————————⟶						
.	.	.	.				.							
.	.	.	.				.							
H	L	L	H	H	H	Q_{N-1} ——————————————————⟶						Q_{N-1}	L	
H	L	H	H	H	H	Q_{N-1} ——————————————————⟶						Q_{N-1}	H	

X = Don't Care Condition
L = LOW Voltage Level
H = HIGH Voltage Level
Q_{n-1} = Previous Output State

Fig. 7-11. Truth table for the addressable latch shown in Fig. 7-10.

However, it should be kept in mind that this is not an invariable rule. In other words, there is a commercial 1-out-of-10 decoder that is provided with open-collector outputs. An external pull-up resistor is used. In demultiplexer application, this device may be used in a wire-OR configuration. In turn, the troubleshooting procedure becomes "tricky," as noted in Chapter 6.

The bottom line is that if a demultiplexer violates its basic truth table in some respect, it is good practice for the troubleshooter to inspect the output circuitry, on the off-chance that a wire-OR arrangement may have been utilized.

8

Troubleshooting Comparators and Parity Generator / Checkers

Commercial Logic Pulser • Digital Comparators • Five-Bit Comparator • Polarity Comparator • "False Alarm" in Piezo-Buzzer Quick Test • Parity Generator/Checker Operation • Two-Bit Even Parity Generator • Two-Bit Even Parity Generator/Checker • Commercial Eight-Bit Parity Generator/Checker • Parity Trees • Expandable Gates • Three-State Buffers

COMMERCIAL LOGIC PULSER

A commercial logic pulser such as illustrated in Fig. 8-1 is useful in troubleshooting any type of logic circuitry. It accommodates TTL or CMOS implementations, with automatic polarity output, automatic pulse width, automatic pulse amplitude, and provides six push-button programmable output modes. This latter feature makes the pulser particularly useful in troubleshooting counter circuitry, for example.

DIGITAL COMPARATORS

Troubleshooters encounter various types of digital comparators. These devices are in the category of arithmetic operators. It is essential to recognize the standard configurations and to understand their circuit action. Consider first the equality checker depicted in Fig. 8-2. It compares two digital words (two nibbles) and determines whether they are equal.

Each bit in a nibble is compared to the corresponding bit in another nibble by an XOR gate. Outputs from the XOR gates will all be 0's if the two digital words are equal. On the other hand, there will be at least one 1 output from an XOR gate if the two digital words are unequal. In turn, the output from the

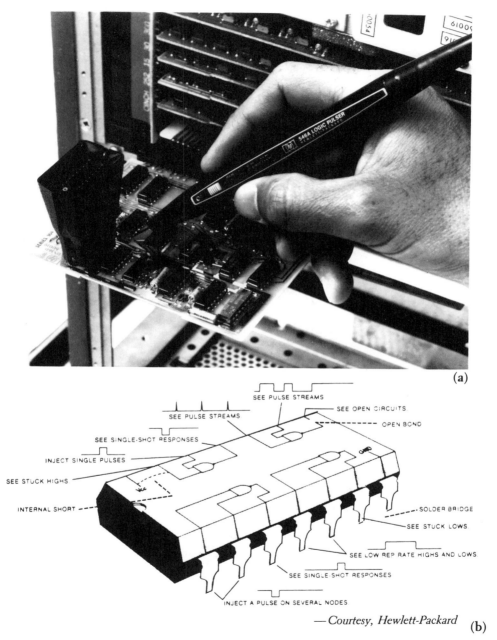

(a)

(b)

—*Courtesy, Hewlett-Packard*

Fig. 8-1. A professional logic pulser. (a) Appearance of pulser; (b) examples of troubleshooting checks.

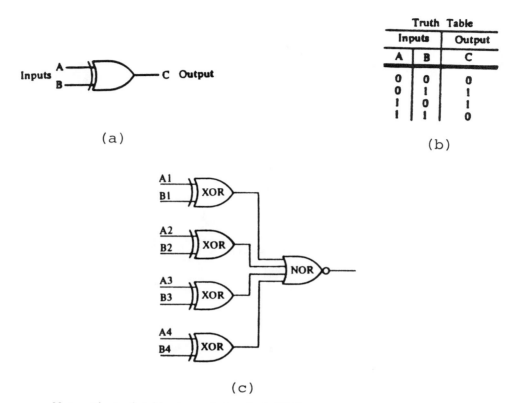

Truth Table

Inputs		Output
A	B	C
0	0	0
0	1	1
1	0	1
1	1	0

(a)

(b)

(c)

Note: The truth table shows that a single XOR gate operates as a comparator (equality checker) for two bits. In other words, if the two bits are 1's, the XOR output is 0; if the two bits are 0's, the XOR output is 0; but if one bit is a 1 and the other bit is a 0, the XOR output is a 1. Thus, a logic-low output indicates equality, and a logic-high output indicates inequality, in this example.

Fig. 8-2. A simple equality checker, or comparator. (a) XOR gate; (b) truth table; (c) XOR gates and NOR gate provide equality checking action.

NOR gate will be 0 if the two digital words are unequal; the output will be 1 if the two words are equal.

Commercial Example

A commercial example of a four-bit quad exclusive-NOR comparator is shown in Fig. 8-3 (Type 9386). The troubleshooter should particularly observe that this configuration has open-collector outputs. It is a comparatively simple

CONNECTION DIAGRAM

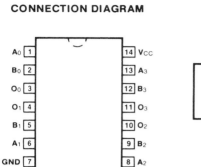

LOGIC SYMBOL
(DIP only)

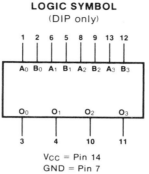

V_{CC} = Pin 14
GND = Pin 7

TRUTH TABLE

INPUTS		OUTPUT
A_n	B_n	O_n
L	L	H
H	L	L
L	H	L
H	H	H

Note: An eight-bit digital word, such as 10011101, is called a *byte*. A four-bit digital word, such as 1001, is called a *nibble*. Any group of 1s and/or 0s is called a *digital word*, or *bit pattern*. A 1 or a 0 is called a *binary number, binary digit*, or *bit*.

LOGIC DIAGRAM

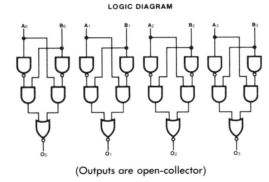

(Outputs are open-collector)

—*Fairchild*

Fig. 8-3. Example of a commercial four-bit quad exclusive-NOR comparator.

device which determines only equality or inequality. Single one-bit comparisons may be made with each gate, or multiple bit comparisons may be made by connecting the outputs of the four gates together.

Five-Bit Comparator

Greater capability, both bit-wise and function-wise, is provided by the five-bit comparator depicted in Fig. 8-4 (Type 9324). It indicates whether one digital word is equal to, greater than, or less than another. Three outputs are provided for this purpose. Observe that an active-low Enable input is included, whereby the comparator can be switched into or out of the input lines.

PIN NAMES

$\bar{E}$	Enable (Active LOW) Input
A_0, A_1, A_2, A_3, A_4	Word A Parallel Inputs
B_0, B_1, B_2, B_3, B_4	Word B Parallel Inputs
$A < B$	A Less Than B Output
$A > B$	A Greater Than B Output
$A = B$	A Equal to B Output

Package Pinout

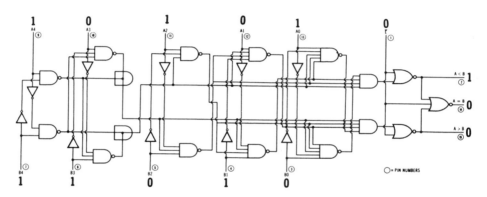

Logic Diagram

$\bar{E}$	Ay	By	$A < B$	$A > B$	$A = B$
H	X	X	L	L	L
L	Word A = Word B		L	L	H
L	Word A > Word B		L	H .	L
L	Word B > Word A		H	L	L

H = HIGH Voltage Level
L = LOW Voltage Level
X = Either HIGH or LOW Voltage Level

Truth Table

Operating Note: Since 10101 is less than 11010 in this example, the "A less than B" output goes logic-high, and the "A equals B" and "A greater than B" outputs remain logic-low.

Fig. 8-4. A commercial five-bit comparator.

Polarity Comparator

Another basic type of comparator that is widely used in digital systems is called a polarity or sign comparator. An example is shown in Fig. 8-5. The comparator indicates whether a pair of input voltages, V1 and V2, have the same polarity or opposite polarities. This polarity relationship is determined by a pair of D flip-flops and two AND-OR gates.

Observe in Fig. 8-5 that if V1 and V2 are both positive, U1 will have both of its inputs positive; A will go logic-high, and the "like polarities" output will go logic-high. Or, if V1 and V2 are both negative, U2 will have both of its inputs positive; B will go logic-high, and the "like polarities" output will go logic-high.

On the other hand, if V1 is positive and V2 is negative, U3 will have both of its inputs positive; C will go logic-high, and the "unlike polarities" output will go logic-high. Again, if V1 is negative and V2 is positive, U4 will have both of its inputs positive; D will go logic-high, and the "unlike polarities" output will go logic-high.

Note also that when U1 has both of its inputs positive, U2 has both of its inputs negative; U3 has one positive input and one negative input; U4 also has one positive input and one negative input. In other words, the same general principle of circuit action governs all combinations of input polarities, and only one AND-gate output can normally go logic-high for a given combination of input polarities.

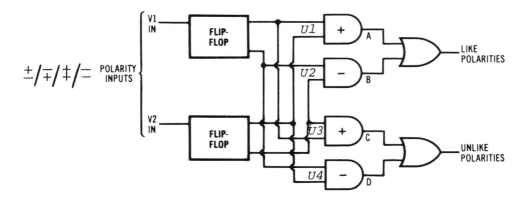

Note: If you are not familiar with the digital ICs used in consumer electronics equipment, refer to pages 113 through 343 in *Encyclopedia of Integrated Circuits*, by Walter H. Buchsbaum, Sc.D.

Fig. 8-5. Example of a polarity (sign) indicator configuration.

"FALSE ALARM" IN PIEZO-BUZZER QUICK CHECK

As previously explained, a very useful quick check for faulty TTL nodes can be made with a piezo buzzer and 3V battery, as depicted in Fig. 8-6. This is the most basic quick checker for TTL digital circuitry comprising AND, OR, XOR, NAND, NOR, and XNOR gates. It is similarly useful in checking out AND-OR, AND-OR-INVERT gates, latches, flip-flops, counters, decoders, multiplexers, and so on.

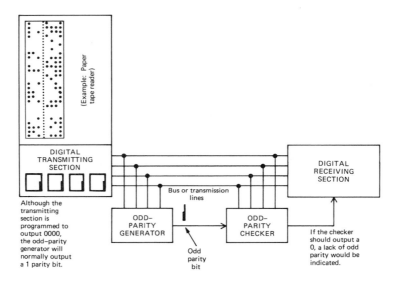

Comparative Even–and Odd–Parity Bits			
Decimal	BCD	Even–Parity Bit	Odd–Parity Bit
0	0000	0	1
1	0001	1	0
2	0010	1	0
3	0011	0	1
4	0100	1	0
5	0101	0	1
6	0110	0	1
7	0111	1	0
8	1000	1	0
9	1001	0	1

Reproduced by special permission of Reston Publishing Co. and Lloyd Rich from Understanding Microprocessors

Fig. 8-6. Example of a four-bit data-transmitting system that includes an odd-parity generator at the transmitting terminal and an odd-parity checker at the receiving terminal.

However, there is a possibility of obtaining a "false alarm" in a few situations. To recap briefly, gates have multi-emitter inputs (with clamping diodes), and totem-pole outputs, as exemplified in Chart 8-1. In turn, when a positive test lead is applied to a gate input or output terminal, practically no current flows, and the piezo buzzer remains silent unless there is a defect associated with the node under test.

As an illustration, if a semiconductor junction is leaky or short-circuited, current will be drawn from the test tip, and the piezo buzzer will sound. Again, if a printed-circuit conductor is short-circuited to ground, or to the V_{CC} line, test current will be drawn and the piezo buzzer will sound. (V_{CC} is always turned off during a piezo-buzzer quick check.)

It was previously noted that a wired-AND or wired-OR configuration could be encountered during in-circuit tests. As seen in Fig. 8-6, this configuration will quick-check "bad" (unless the V_{CC} line is opened during the piezo-buzzer quick check). Accordingly, if a digital IC tests "bad" on a piezo-buzzer in-circuit quick check, the troubleshooter should look at the PC board (or the schematic) to see if a wired-AND or wired-OR node may be present.

In case a wired-AND or wired-OR node happens to be under test, the troubleshooter may open the V_{CC} line by any suitable means, and then repeat the quick check. For example, a plug-in circuit board can be unplugged to open the V_{CC} line. Or, a V_{CC} line switch might be provided. In a "tough dog" situation, you can slit the V_{CC} line with a razor blade, and then repair the "open" with a drop of solder after the quick check is completed.

PARITY GENERATOR/CHECKER OPERATION

Troubleshooters encounter various forms of parity generator/checkers; unless their circuit action is recognized, confusion can result in evaluating data-transfer sequences. Parity denotes the addition of an extra bit to a group of bits for developments of an even or odd number of logic-high's in the bit group, depending on the type of parity that is employed (even parity or odd parity). Use of a parity bit to detect errors in data transmission is based on two assumptions:

1. The probability of error in data transmission is comparatively small (except in malfunction situations).
2. When a data-transmission error occurs, there is a high probability that it will be a single bit error.

With reference to Fig. 8-6, parity is generated and checked to determine whether a data word transmitted from one source is received correctly at the

CHART 8-1

Wired-AND Circuit Can Give a "False Alarm" Indication in a Piezo-Buzzer Quick Check

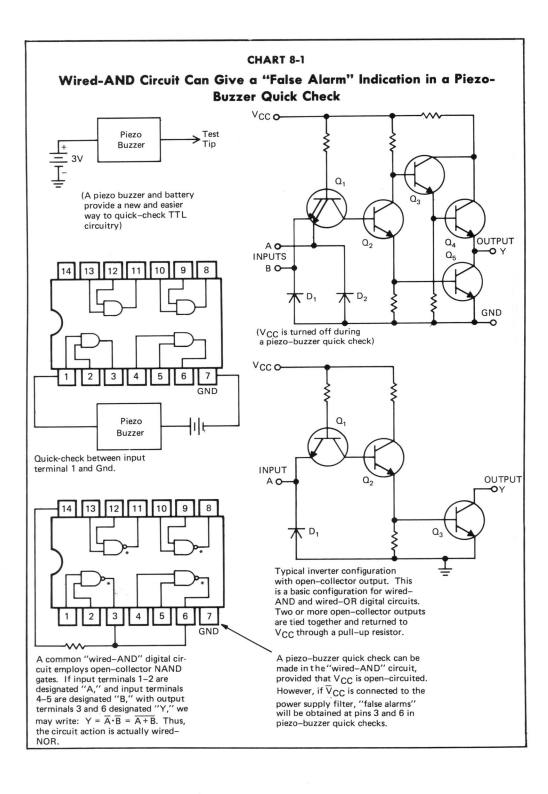

(A piezo buzzer and battery provide a new and easier way to quick-check TTL circuitry)

Quick-check between input terminal 1 and Gnd.

(V_{CC} is turned off during a piezo–buzzer quick check)

Typical inverter configuration with open–collector output. This is a basic configuration for wired–AND and wired–OR digital circuits. Two or more open–collector outputs are tied together and returned to V_{CC} through a pull–up resistor.

A common "wired–AND" digital circuit employs open-collector NAND gates. If input terminals 1–2 are designated "A," and input terminals 4–5 are designated "B," with output terminals 3 and 6 designated "Y," we may write: $Y = \overline{A} \cdot \overline{B} = \overline{A + B}$. Thus, the circuit action is actually wired-NOR.

A piezo–buzzer quick check can be made in the "wired–AND" circuit, provided that V_{CC} is open–circuited. However, if $\overline{V}_{CC}$ is connected to the power supply filter, "false alarms" will be obtained at pins 3 and 6 in piezo-buzzer quick checks.

destination. If an error is detected, the information can be retransmitted. In the cited example, a photoreader reads information from a paper tape and transmits the data to a computer. Odd parity is exemplified.

Two-Bit Even-Parity Generator

When even parity is used, the parity bit is logic-high if an odd number of logic-highs are present on the data lines. The parity bit will be logic-low if an even number of logic-highs are present on the data lines. (The total number of logic-highs is always even.) An XOR gate (Fig. 8-7) functions as a two-bit even-parity generator.

Observe that when an even number of logic-highs occur, the XOR-gate output is logic-low (the parity bit is logic-low). On the other hand, when an odd number of logic-high's occur, the XOR-gate output is logic-high (the parity bit is logic-high).

A pair of XOR gates (Fig. 8-7) functions as a two-bit even-parity checker. This is a three-input XOR-gate configuration. Observe that when all three inputs are logic-low, the Y output is logic-low; when all three inputs are logic-high, the Y output is logic-high. The parity error output (Y output) goes logic-high if the number of logic-input bits is odd.

Two-Bit Even-Parity Generator/Checker

An experimental two-bit even-parity generator/checker can be constructed as shown in Fig. 8-7. It comprises three XOR gates, a pair of JK flip-flops, and an AND gate. Data input (1) allows an error to be experimentally inserted in the data transition. As long as (1) is logic-high, no parity error occurs. On the other hand, a parity error occurs when (1) is logic-low.

Commercial Eight-Bit Parity Generator/Checker

A widely used commercial eight-bit parity generator/checker IC package is depicted in Fig. 8-8. This configuration provides for odd-parity input or even-parity input; it also provides for sum-odd output and sum-even output. For this purpose, odd-input and even-input control terminals are brought out to pins 3 and 4. Note that if these control terminals are both logic-low, or both logic-high, the sum of 1s at 0 through 7 is irrelevant.

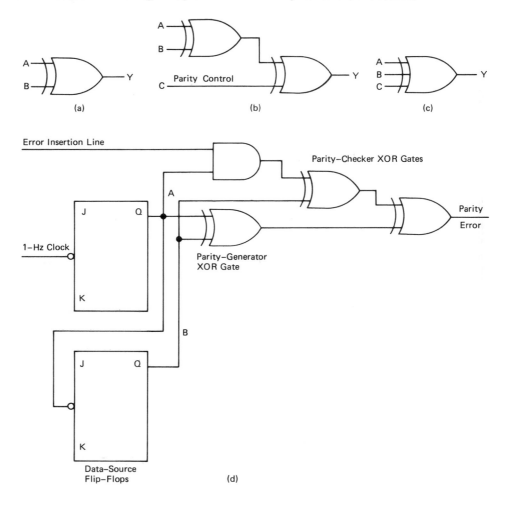

Fig. 8-7. Parity circuits. (a) XOR gate functions as a two-bit even-parity generator; (b) a pair of XOR gates function as a two-bit even-parity checker; (c) circuit may show an XOR gate with three inputs; (d) experimental two-bit even-parity generator-checker.

Parity Trees

The groups of XOR (or XNOR) gates used in parity generator/checkers are called parity trees. Thus, a dual four-bit XNOR parity tree is exemplified in

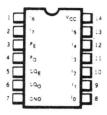

Package Pinout
Type 93180

PIN NAMES

I_0 to I_7	Parity Inputs
P_0	Odd Parity Input
P_E	Even Parity Input
ΣQ_0	Sum Odd Outputs
ΣQ_E	Sum Even Outputs

(a)

INPUTS			OUTPUTS	
Σ OF 1's AT 0 THRU 7	EVEN	ODD	Σ EVEN	Σ ODD
EVEN	H	L	H	L
ODD	H	L	L	H
EVEN	L	H	L	H
ODD	L	H	H	L
X	H	H	L	L
X	L	L	H	H

X = irrelevant

Truth Table

(b)

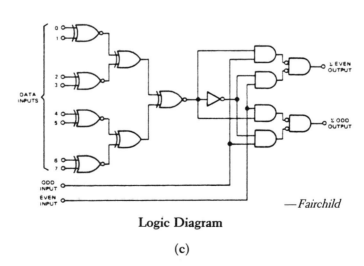

Logic Diagram

—Fairchild

(c)

Fig. 8-8. Example of a commercial eight-bit parity generator/checker. (a) Package pinout; (b) truth table; (c) logic diagram.

Fig. 8-9(a), and an eight-bit XNOR parity tree is shown in Fig. 8-9(b). A parity error indicates that during the course of the previous block transfer of data, a parity error was detected, or one or more bits were not picked up or were dropped out from either the timing track or the mark track.

Note that block transfer denotes the conveyance of a consecutive binary word group from a source to a destination. A track is a series of binary cells that are configured so that data may be read or written from one cell at a time in a serial manner; for example, a track is the portion of a moving-storage medium such as a tape or disk which is accessible to a given reading station.

A timing track is a specified path on magnetic tape or disk media on which an extended series of pulses is recorded; the timing track develops a clock signal for recognition of rows of data by counting, or by the positions of the pulses or marks in the track. A mark is a pulse which indicates a specific event, such as the end of tape indication.

EXPANDABLE GATES

Troubleshooters need to recognize expandable-gate configurations and to understand the associated circuit action. With reference to Fig. 8-10, an expand-

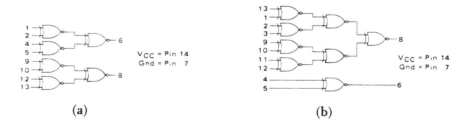

(a)   (b)

Troubleshooting Note: Various errors other than parity errors are of practical concern. Errors are distinguished from mistakes, in that mistakes occur in programming, whereas errors occur in numerical methods; errors are also distinguished from malfunctions inasmuch as malfunctions arise from physical fault conditions. If an error is detected from the results of a program, the troubleshooter may obtain a print-out for step-by-step tracing of program operation on stipulated data. A machine error is a deviation from correct data as a result of equipment failure. A propagated error is a deviation from correct data that occurred in a previous operation and that has spread, causing errors in subsequent data processing operations.

Fig. 8-9. Examples of commercial parity trees. (a) A dual four-bit parity tree; (b) an eight-bit parity tree.

Expandable Gate

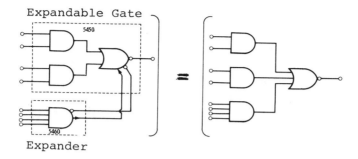

Expander

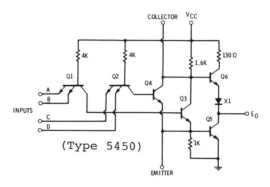

(Type 5450)

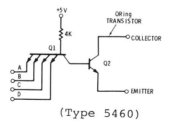

(Type 5460)

—*Fairchild*

Fig. 8-10. Example of a commercial expandable two-wide two-input AND-OR-INVERT gate.

able gate can be compared in basic respects to a conventional gate, except that the number of inputs can be increased, if desired, by adding a logic block. Expandable gates are used when a comparatively large number of inputs are required to be connected to an AND gate, or to an AND-OR-INVERT gate.

As seen in the diagram, a typical expander comprises a conventional AND input section followed by an open-collector output section. In turn, the expandable gate consists of conventional circuitry with the provision of terminals into the collector and emitter branches of the driver section. Accordingly, the expander can drive the output section of the expandable gate as if the expander were an integral portion of the expandable gate.

An important consideration from the troubleshooter's viewpoint is that the expander (in this example) does not drive an emitter input on the expandable gate. Observe that the expander drives the base of Q5 and the base of Q6. Because of this departure from conventional TTL circuitry, some types of quick checks will give "false alarms" when checking out an expandable-gate configuration.

For example, a piezo-buzzer quick check will give a "false alarm" when testing the output terminals of the expander (emitter and collector input terminals of the expandable gate). This erroneous test result stems from the fact that these are base-input terminals which conduct when a positive test voltage is applied.

The bottom line is that when a piezo-buzzer quick check gives a "bad" indication in expandable-gate circuitry, the troubleshooter should check the schematic diagram to determine whether base drive may be employed. In such a case, a logic pulser and probe should be used to check circuit operation. The pulser and probe are dynamic ac testers, and their indications are independent of junction characteristics associated with the test points.

THREE-STATE BUFFERS

Another incidental circuit device that troubleshooters need to recognize is the three-state buffer, exemplified in Fig. 8-11. This is an elaborated buffer with a control input whereby application of the control signal "opens" the buffer output terminal. This arrangement is very extensively used in bus-oriented digital systems.

From the troubleshooter's viewpoint, this is another of the "tricky" devices that can give a "false alarm" in a piezo-buzzer quick check. In other words, the control input to the three-state buffer does not necessarily connect to the cathode of an NPN junction. Some three-state buffer configurations have a control input that connects to a resistive circuit inside of the IC. This type of three-state buffer will give a "false-alarm" in a piezo-buzzer quick check.

Types of Devices

It is helpful to note that although there are numerous varieties of digital devices, that there is a comparatively limited number of types. Thus, the troubleshooter encounters gates, inverters, latches, flip-flops, multiplexers, decoders and demultiplexers, registers, monostables, drivers, arithmetic operators, and memo-

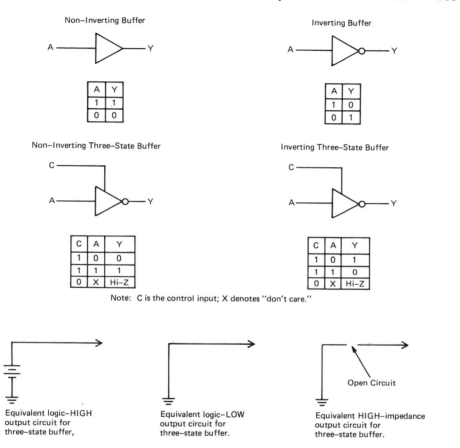

Note: C is the control input; X denotes "don't care."

Fig. 8-11. A three-state buffer or inverter has a control input in addition to a signal input.

ries. These are the basic types of digital devices. Each type branches into a large number of varieties; thus, gates are subdivided into AND, NAND, OR, NOR, AND-OR, AND-OR-Invert, XOR, XNOR, and various specialized varieties such as majority-logic gates.

Gates are further subdivided into totem-pole output and open-collector output varieties, and into combination output arrangements such as XOR/XNOR functions. Gates are also subdivided into TTL and CMOS families. TTL gates are subdivided into standard and Schottky-clamped varieties, with a subvariety called low-power Schottky. High-speed TTL and low-power TTL represent further subvarieties. In general, the troubleshooter must be alert to the ratings of particular devices, and to make certain that any replacement device is suitable for the application.

9

Shift - Register Troubleshooting

Shift-Register Circuit Action • Serial-Parallel Shift Register • Troubleshooting Shift Registers; Logic Comparator • Single-Shot Pulse Indication • Comparator Capabilities • Commercial Example of Shift Register • Serial-In, Parallel-Out Shift Register (Ring Counter or Timing Slot Generator) • Scanner-Monitor Operation and Troubleshooting • Note on "Stuck-At" Trouble Symptom.

SHIFT-REGISTER CIRCUIT ACTION

Apprentice troubleshooters tend to be "spooked" when confronted by shift-register circuitry. However, shift-register circuit action is not difficult to understand after becoming familiar with toggle flip-flops and basic counters. A shift register is a series of flip-flops (Fig. 9-1) configured with the output from one flip-flop connected to the input of the next, and with a common clock to each of the flip-flops for synchronization of data transfer.

Shift registers are classified in accordance with three basic characteristics: their method of data handling (serial-in/serial-out, serial-in/parallel-out, parallel-in/serial out), their direction of data movement (shift right, shift left, bidirectional), and their bit length. A subclass termed recirculating shift registers are also of practical importance.

An experimental serial-in, parallel-out shift-register arrangement is shown in Fig. 9-2. This configuration is intended for static operation; in other words, the clock line is manually pulsed to demonstrate shift-register action. Note in passing that although D flip-flops are used in this circuit, JK flip-flops can also be configured for shift-register operation. The Q outputs of the FFs may be checked with a logic probe.

To observe shift-register action, start by connecting the clear line, data line, and clock line to ground (logic-low). Driving the clear line logic-low clears the shift register (all Q outputs will normally be 0). Next, drive the clear line and the data line logic-high. This removes the clear input so that data can be en-

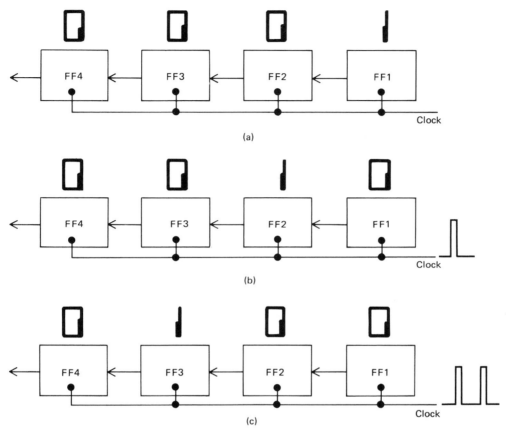

Fig. 9-1. Shift register is operated by clock pulses. (a) Binary number entered into shift register; (b) first clock pulse shifts binary number one position to left; (c) second clock pulse shifts binary number one more position to left.

tered into the shift register. Driving the data line logic-high places a 1 on the D input of FF1.

Now, drive the clock line logic-high and then return it to logic-low. Changing the clock line from logic-low to logic-high and back to logic-low supplies a positive clock edge to all four clock inputs. (Note that the 7474 is a positive-edge triggered device.) We will observe that the foregoing change in clock levels has caused the 1 on the D input of FF1 to shift to the Q output of FF1.

Note that an up arrow (↑) denotes a transition from logic-low to logic-high and back to logic-low in digital-logic notation. Conversely, a down arrow (↓) denotes a change from logic-high to logic-low and back to logic-high.

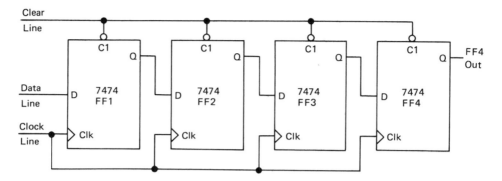

Technical Note: A shift register employs circuitry that resembles counter circuitry in some respects. On the other hand, shift-register function is fundamentally different from counter function. A counter (also called an accumulator) changes state upon receipt of a new input signal—in the absence of a new input signal, a counter "holds" its states unchanged. On the other hand, a shift register changes state on each clock pulse—the contents of the register will be shifted from one flip-flop to the next. After a suitable number of clock pulses have passed, the contents of the shift register will be clocked out of the last flip-flop.

Fig. 9-2. Experimental serial-in, parallel-out shift register.

Next, repeat the forgoing operation—drive the clock line logic-high and then return it to logic-low. This supplies a positive clock edge to all four clock inputs. We will observe that this change in clock levels has shifted a second logic-high into FF1, and that the Q outputs of FF1 and FF2 are now both logic-high.

The next step in the demonstration is to set the data line logic-low. This places a 0 on the D input of FF1. Now, drive the clock line (↑). Observe that the 0 on the D input of FF1 has shifted to the Q output of FF1, the 1 on the D input of FF2 has shifted to the Q output of FF2, and the 1 on the D input of FF3 has shifted to the Q output of FF3.

Finally, if you continue to drive the clock line (↑), the data will be shifted out of the register, and the Q outputs will then be 0000. This is basic shift-register action. The temporary storage function of a shift register facilitates data processing in arithmetical operations, for example.

Serial-Parallel Shift Register

A serial-parallel shift-register arrangement is depicted in Fig. 9-3. The flip-flop Set inputs are utilized for parallel loading (parallel data input). Parallel

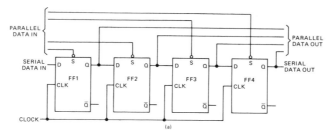

(a)

Note: FF1 is the LSB flip-flop, and FF4 is the MSB flip-flop. Therefore, the FF sequence is "backwards" with respect to standard binary-number notation—the FF readout is from right to left, in this example. Observe that this is a left-shift configuration, inasmuch as left shift denotes a shift from a less-significant position to a more-significant position. Observe, also, that a left shift has the arithmetical effect of multiplying the register contents by 2.

Note: When data bits flow in series, the data is said to have a serial format. On the other hand, when data bits flow in parallel, the data is said to have a parallel format. It follows from this shift-register diagram that the same data may have a serial format in one section of a digital system, and then change into a parallel format in another section of the system.

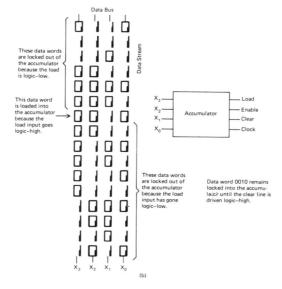

(b)

Fig. 9-3. A serial-parallel, shift-register configuration. (a) Logic diagram; (b) example of parallel data format.

loading is also called broadside loading. Observe that this configuration provides for serial input and serial output; it also provides for serial input and parallel output. It further provides for parallel input and serial output.

TROUBLESHOOTING SHIFT REGISTERS; LOGIC COMPARATOR

While stimulus-response testing (Fig. 9-4) is the mainstay of electronic troubleshooting, the digital nature of the signals in the circuit under test allows for an even faster means of verifying proper component operation. *This is component comparison testing.* By stimulating a known good device with the same signals that are used to stimulate the device under test, and comparing the response of the two components, the troubleshooter can quickly determine whether the device under test is operating properly.

This is the function of the logic comparator (Fig. 9-5). The comparator "steals" the input signals, stimulating the device under test to simultaneously stimulate a known good device. *Any difference in their responses is indicated by an "on" LED which also indicates the output which failed the comparison test.*

Single-Shot Pulse Indication

Note that this comparator contains pulse-stretching circuitry which allows dynamic, single-shot, or intermittent errors to be detected and displayed, as well as static errors. Pulses as narrow as 200 ns are detected and displayed as a 0.1-second blink on the LED display. *Consequently, the most difficult type of possible error—intermittent failures—will be easily detected and displayed.*

In turn, the logic comparator removes the burden of analyzing long, complex digital signals from the troubleshooter's shoulders by automatically determining whether the signal is a good logic-high or logic-low level, and if that level is correct according to the truth table of the circuit under test. Consequently, the logic comparator can greatly reduce the time required in digital troubleshooting procedures.

Comparator Capabilities

Before reviewing what the logic comparator will test, it is important to understand how it works. Through a reference board ("card") the inputs of a reference IC are connected to the inputs of the test IC (Point A in Fig. 9-6(a)). Thus, the reference IC is exercised by the same test signals that stimulate the test IC. The outputs of the test and reference ICs are compared (Point B in Fig. 9-6(a)), and any differences greater than 200 ns are indicated as a failure.

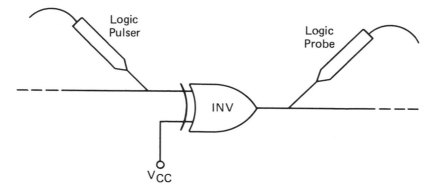

Note: In a stimulus-response test with a logic pulser and probe, the input of the inverter is pulsed to its opposite prevailing state (whichever this might be). In turn, the output is probed to determine whether it changes state in response to the test pulse.

Fig. 9-4. Example of the stimulus-response testing principle.

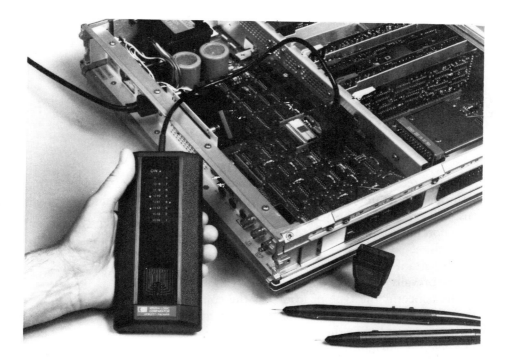

Fig. 9-5. Logic comparator in use. (Courtesy, Hewlett-Packard.)

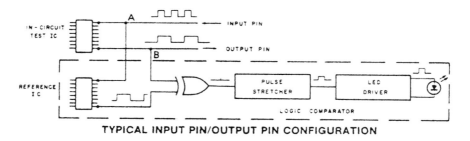

TYPICAL INPUT PIN/OUTPUT PIN CONFIGURATION

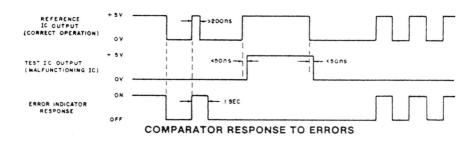

COMPARATOR RESPONSE TO ERRORS

Fig. 9-6(a). Comparator application and response. (Courtesy, Hewlett-Packard.)

Also, the reference IC and the comparator are powered by the circuit under test through the reference board. Hence, the logic comparator observes simultaneously all outputs of the test IC and determines the validity of these signals, based upon both proper voltage levels and proper truth-table response to the input signals.

An important consideration in using the logic comparator is the circuit loading that prevails. Loading considerations can be divided into two parts. The first part concerns the type of load that the comparator presents to the outputs of the IC to which the comparator is connected. The second part concerns the load that is presented to the inputs. These loads are summarized in Fig. 9-6(b).

The logic comparator presents a different load to inputs than it presents to outputs. The table in Fig. 9-6(b) describes, in terms of fan-out loads, the effect of the comparator both on inputs and outputs.

IC Under Test Type	Additional Load to the IC Under Test's Inputs and Outputs Due to Comparator and Reference IC	
	Inputs	*Outputs*
DTL	1.2 DTL loads	.1 DTL load
7400 Series TTL	1.2 7400 Series loads	.1 7400 Series load
Low Power TTL (74L00 Series)	5 low power loads	1 low power load
High Speed/Schottky TTL (74H00 or 74S00 Series)	1.5 7400 Series loads or 1.2 high speed/ Schottky load	.1 7400 Series load or .1 high speed/ Schottky load
NOTE: 1 low power load = .1 7400 Series load.		

Fig. 9-6(b). Comparator loading chart. (Courtesy, Hewlett-Packard.)

COMMERCIAL EXAMPLE OF SHIFT REGISTER

A typical commercial shift register encountered by the troubleshooter is shown in Fig. 9-7. This is a serial-parallel arrangement similar to the basic configuration in Fig. 9-3. Observe that the first FF is configured as a D FF, and that the other FFs operate effectively as D FFs inasmuch as they are supplied complementary inputs.

SERIAL-IN, PARALLEL-OUT SHIFT REGISTER (RING COUNTER OR TIMING SLOT GENERATOR)

With reference to Fig. 9-8, a minor modification of the experimental shift register depicted in Fig. 9-2 provides ring counter (timing slot generator) action. This mode of shift-register operation is utilized extensively in digital equipment. Observe the following circuit actions:

1. When the Clear line is driven logic-low, the first three FFs are cleared, and the fourth FF is preloaded with a 1. The starting readout is this 0001.
2. Preloading the fourth FF places a 1 on the first D input.
3. Set the Clear line logic-high—this releases the Preset and Clear inputs.

Type 9396

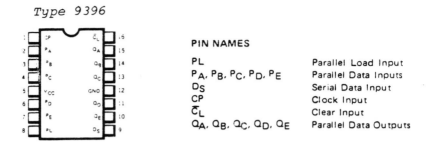

PIN NAMES

PL	Parallel Load Input
P_A, P_B, P_C, P_D, P_E	Parallel Data Inputs
D_S	Serial Data Input
CP	Clock Input
$\bar{C}_L$	Clear Input
Q_A, Q_B, Q_C, Q_D, Q_E	Parallel Data Outputs

Package Pinout

PRESET			SERIAL	CLOCK	OUTPUT	
COMMON	BIT	CLEAR	INPUT			
L	X	L	X	X	L	Clear all output to logical "L".
H	H	H	X	X	H	Preset outputs to 1 input
H	L	H	X	X	L	bit configuration.
L	X	H	H	enable	H	Serial input shift right.
L	X	H	L	enable	L	Serial-to-parallel conversion.

Truth Table

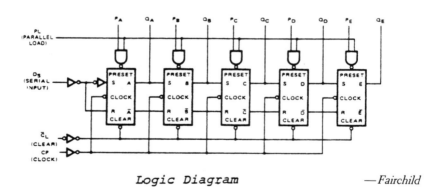

Logic Diagram — *Fairchild*

NOTES:

(a) After loading data, set clear to "H" and preset to "L" clock to give parallel to serial conversion.

(b) Information transferred on rising edge of clock pulse.

(c) Do not enable preset and clear simultaneously.
    Preset — "H" Clear — "L" = undefined output. Dependent upon which enable is removed first.

(d) X Either logical "L" or logical "H".

Fig. 9-7. Commercial example of a five-bit shift register.

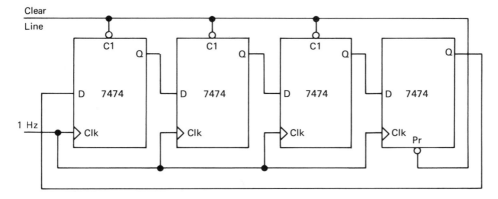

Note: A ring counter or timing-slot generator is also called a recirculating shift register. In other words, any data bit will automatically be recirculated through the register as long as clock pulses are applied. If we stop the clock, the data bit "stands still."

Note also that this is a volatile arrangement—if V_{cc} fails, even for a moment, the stored data bit is lost. However, the register can be cleared and the fourth FF again preloaded to restore operation.

Fig. 9-8. Modification of experimental shift register for ring counting (time-slot generator operation).

4. Observe next that the logic-high 1 at the first FF is transferred through the shift register on each (↑); in other words, the logic-high bit is clocked through the shift register.

5. When the logic-high bit is clocked out of the fourth FF, it is automatically clocked back into the first FF. This is ring-counter or timing-slot generator action.

SCANNER-MONITOR OPERATION AND TROUBLESHOOTING

A scanner-monitor radio provides a familiar example of ring-counter application. The radio automatically samples various channels sequentially for activity. When an active channel is sampled, the tuner locks on that channel until the incoming signal stops. (A small pause interval automatically follows.) After the pause interval, scanning automatically resumes. Scanning action is provided by digital logic, as exemplified in Fig. 9-9. The logic comprises a clock oscillator (slow-pulse generator), counter, and decoder; the decoder is followed by diode switch circuitry.

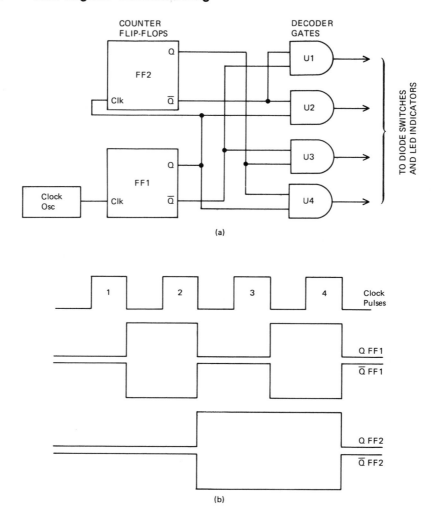

(a)

(b)

Note: This binary counter arrangement with its decoder functions in the same basic manner as a ring counter. A ring counter is a loop configuration in which a bit moves progressively around the loop in response to clock pulses. It is essentially a recirculating shift register wherein one bit has been entered.

Detailed scanner-monitor troubleshooting data is published by Howard W. Sams & Co., Inc.

Fig. 9-9. Logic diagram for a four-channel scanner radio. (a) Configuration; (b) timing diagram.

This four-channel scanner employs a counter with two flip-flops; the counter inputs clock pulses and outputs divide-by-two and divide-by-four waveforms. It is a four-bit ripple-carry counter, also termed a mod-16 (modulus-16 or modulo-16) counter, because it sequences through a total of 16 states. Since each flip-flop sequences through two states, it is also called a 2x2x2x2 counter. Note that when an active channel is sampled, a pulse is generated that stops the clock, so that the counter also stops.

The output waveforms generated by the counter are applied to decoder gates U1 through U4. A decoder is a logic circuit that translates a combination of signals into a single signal which represents the combination. For example, when $\overline{Q}$ FF1 and Q FF2 are simultaneously logic-high, U3 (gate 3) is activated and its output goes logic-high (Fig. 9-10). This is the only gate that is activated at this time. Thus, the four Q signals and the four $\overline{Q}$ signals have been translated into a single signal (gate 3 output) which represents the combination. This is typical decoder action.

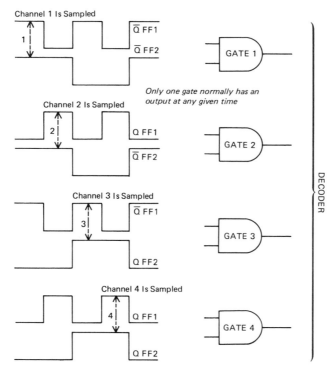

Fig. 9-10. Visualization of decoder operation.

Troubleshooting scanner circuitry is accomplished to best advantage by stopping the clock and "stepping" the counter manually, while checking the circuit waveforms with a logic probe. (The clock input to FF1 (Fig. 9-10) may be manually pulsed by means of a test lead connected through a 1-kilohm resistor to V_{CC}.) In other words, the following test results are normally obtained in this example:

1. When the first clock pulse is applied, one of the AND gates will have both of its inputs logic-high.

2. Assume, for example, that gate 1 has both of its inputs logic-high. Then, the logic probe will normally show that the other three gates do not have both inputs logic-high.

3. When the second clock pulse is applied, in this example, gate 2 will have both of its inputs logic-high. The other three gates will not have both inputs logic-high.

4. When the third clock pulse is applied, gate 3 will have both of its inputs logic-high. The other three gates will not have both inputs logic-high.

5. When the fourth clock pulse is applied, gate 4 will have both of its inputs logic-high. The other three gates will not have both inputs logic-high.

6. When the fifth clock pulse is applied, the foregoing sequence of logic states is normally repeated.

If the foregoing sequence of logic states is not verified, the troubleshooter concludes that there is a fault in the counter circuitry. On the other hand, if the normal operating sequence is verified, the troubleshooter knows that the counter is functioning properly, and that the trouble is located in the following circuitry. For example, an AND gate could be defective, or, a diode switch following the decoder could be defective. In turn, these possibilities are systematically checked out. (See Fig. 9-11.)

NOTE ON "STUCK-AT" TROUBLE SYMPTOM

As indicated in Fig. 9-12, an accidental ground fault to the Reset line can cause a "stuck-at" trouble symptom in a flip-flop. In practice, the reset line may be normally "floating" and logic-high. Accordingly, it is easy for the troubleshooter to overlook a no-connection terminal. However, if this terminal is accidentally short-circuited to ground, the FF becomes "stuck."

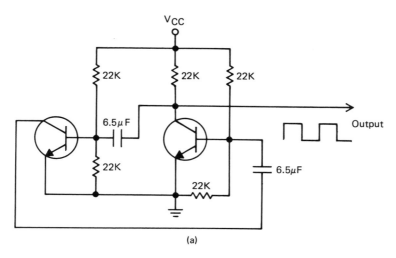

(a)

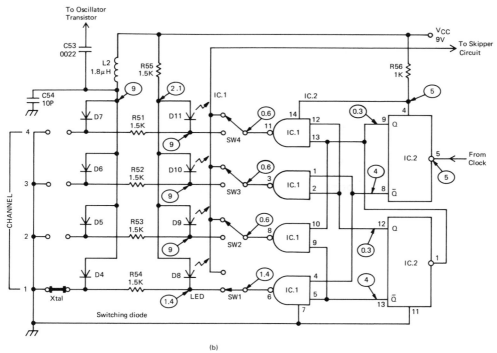

(b)

Fig. 9-11. Scanner-monitor circuitry. (a) Clock (slow pulse) oscillator; (b) diode switching circuitry.

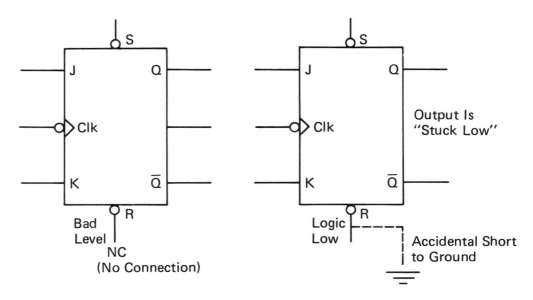

Note: The Reset line is asynchronous, and forces the output state of the flip-flop, independently of the clock. In this example, the Reset is active-low —the flip-flop's output state is forced when the Reset line goes logic-low. In normal operation, the Reset line is maintained logic-high. A floating input will be interpreted as the logic-high state. On the other hand, if the Reset line is accidentally short-circuited to ground, the flip-flop will be forced into maintaining a reset output state, regardless of the data input signal.

Fig. 9-12. Troubleshooting a "stuck" flip-flop.

10

Troubleshooting Binary Adders

Binary Addition • Negative Fan-Out Test • Serial Adder • Parallel Adder • Digital Troubleshooting Procedure • Logic Comparator Test • Testing Sequence • Open Signal Path • Sequential Integrated Circuits • Glitches

BINARY ADDITION

The troubleshooter encounters two basic types of adders, called *serial adders* and *parallel adders*. A serial adder inputs sequential bits and progressively forms their sum; it is called an *accumulator** and is quite similar to a basic binary counter. Its operation was shown in Chart 3-1. This arrangement is alternatively termed an 8421 counter, because its *weighted-code* output has these place values. (Refer back to Fig. 3-9.)

Parallel adders input bits simultaneously. The simplest form of parallel adder is the XOR gate (mod-2 summer) shown in Fig. 10-1. A *half adder* consists of a mod-2 summer with an AND gate (Fig. 10-2). If an augend of 1 and an addend of 1 are inputted simultaneously, the half adder responds by outputting 10, wherein 0 is the sum output and 1 is the carry output.

The next step in parallel-adder configurations is the full adder, depicted in Fig. 10-3. This is the basic building block of all parallel adders. A full adder provides for the inputting of an addend bit, an augend bit, and a carry-in bit; in turn, it outputs a sum bit and a carry-out bit. Full-adder circuit action is described by a pair of logic equations, or by their equivalent truth table. Adder troubleshooting is easily accomplished with a logic pulser and probe.

If a five-channel oscilloscope were connected into the full-adder circuit, the screen display would represent the adder timing diagram, as depicted in Fig. 10-4. The A input signal may be indicated as 0001111; the B input signal may be indicated as 0110011; the C' (carry in) signal may be indicated as 1010101;

---

*Accumulators are usually clocked configurations.

149

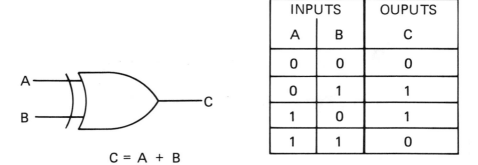

INPUTS		OUPUTS
A	B	C
0	0	0
0	1	1
1	0	1
1	1	0

$$C = A + B$$

Note: An XOR gate is called a *mod-2 summer,* because its full capacity is 2 bits. All parallel adders are configured around mod-2 summers. The logic equation for a mod-2 summer is read "C equals A EXCLUSIVE-OR B."

Fig. 10-1. EXCLUSIVE OR gate and truth table.

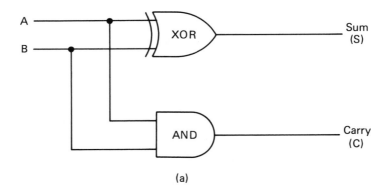

(a)

Truth Table

INPUTS		OUTPUTS	
A	B	S	C
0	0	0	0
0	1	1	0
1	0	1	0
1	1	0	1

(b)

Fig. 10-2. Half adder configuration. (a) Logic diagram; (b) truth table.

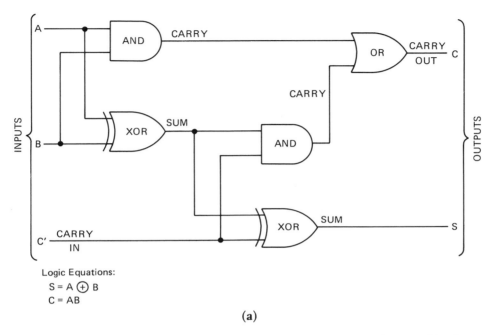

Logic Equations:
$S = A \oplus B$
$C = AB$

(a)

Note: The parallel full adder can input three bits simultaneously (an addend, an augend, and a carry-in). In turn, the full adder outputs a sum bit and a carry-out bit. Thus, a full adder can input 1 and 1 and 1 simultaneously and output 11, or, it calculates $1+1+1=3$.

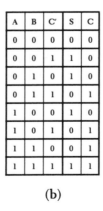

A	B	C′	S	C
0	0	0	0	0
0	0	1	1	0
0	1	0	1	0
0	1	1	0	1
1	0	0	1	0
1	0	1	0	1
1	1	0	0	1
1	1	1	1	1

(b)

Fig. 10-3. Full adder comprises two mod-2 summers, two AND gates, and one OR gate. (a) Configuration; (b) truth table.

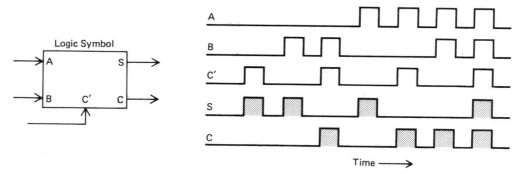

Logic Symbol

Time ⟶

Note: This timing diagram corresponds to the pattern that would be displayed on the screen of a five-channel oscilloscope. However, digital pulses often have waveshapes that are far from ideal. Slowed rise and fall, corner rounding, undershoot, overshoot and ringing are common deviations from the ideal. There are no hard-and-fast rules on tolerable digital-pulse distortion, and the troubleshooter must fall back on his own resources in doubtful cases.

Fig. 10-4. Timing diagram for a full adder.

the S (sum) output signal may be indicated as 1101001; the C (carry out) signal may be indicated as 0010111.

Next, it is helpful to observe the logic flow diagram for a full adder, shown in Fig. 10-5. Since there are two outputs, two logic equations are required to describe the circuit action. It will be seen that the logic equations are an alternate form of truth table, and that the complete action is stated by each.

These equations are read: "S equals A AND B AND C' OR A OR B OR C'," and "C equals A AND B OR A AND C' OR B AND C' OR A AND B AND C'." The signals represented by each horizontal line in the truth table must be simultaneously applied to the adder inputs; otherwise, the circuit will not obey its truth table. The heavy lines in Fig. 10-5 indicate the logic-high states in the circuit for the input conditions: $A = 1$, $B = 0$, $C' = 0$.

The arrangement in Fig. 10-5 is unclocked; it is an asynchronous combinatorial-logic configuration. By way of comparison, we have been observing examples of synchronous sequential configurations in the shift-register section. We will find that more elaborate adder arrangements often employ clocked (synchronous) sequential circuitry. Troubleshooters need to recognize these distinctions, and to understand the circuit actions that are utilized.

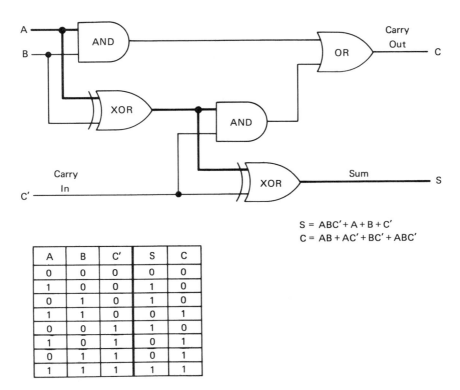

$$S = ABC' + A + B + C'$$
$$C = AB + AC' + BC' + ABC'$$

A	B	C'	S	C
0	0	0	0	0
1	0	0	1	0
0	1	0	1	0
1	1	0	0	1
0	0	1	1	0
1	0	1	0	1
0	1	1	0	1
1	1	1	1	1

Fig. 10-5. A logic flow diagram for a full adder, with logic equations and truth table.

NEGATIVE FAN-OUT TEST

A negative fan-out test is an in-circuit quick-check that determines the result of effectively removing one, two, three, or more unit loads from the output node of a gate, inverter, or other device to determine whether normal operation is restored. Application of the negative fan-out test arrangement shown in Fig. 10-6 is facilitated by an understanding of current flow in digital circuits.

When one gate is added in a driver node, the current demand is increased by one unit load. On the other hand, when one gate is disconnected from a driver node, the current demand is lessened by one unit load. In practical troubleshooting procedures, the question may arise concerning how circuit operation might be affected by removal of one, two, or three (or even more) unit loads from a node.

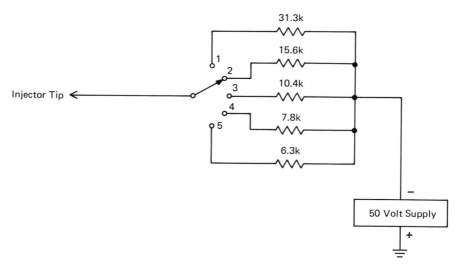

Note: The switch positions from 1 to 5 provide negative fan-outs from one to five unit loads (ULs) when the "constant-current" flow from the injector tip is applied to the output node of a TTL device *in its logic-low state.*

Note: An output node under test must be held logic-low by stopping the clock, or equivalent expedient. (It is meaningless to inject the test current while the output node is logic high.) *Negative fan-out does not remove a load (or loads) in the sense of disconnection—it effectively reduces the load that is imposed on the driver, so that the troubleshooter can quickly determine whether a trouble symptom is being caused by marginal overload.*

Fig. 10-6. Negative fan-out test arrangement.

This question is immediately answered by employment of the negative fan-out test arrangement shown in Fig. 10-6. In other words, this constant-current source is configured in unit-load steps to inject unit-load currents into a node. Thus, the load on the driver is effectively reduced by the number of constant-current unit loads injected by the negative fan-out test arrangement. This topic is further detailed in the next chapter.

SERIAL ADDER

As shown in Fig. 10-7, the basic serial adder is configured around a single full-adder circuit that adds each pair of bits sequentially. These bit pairs are in

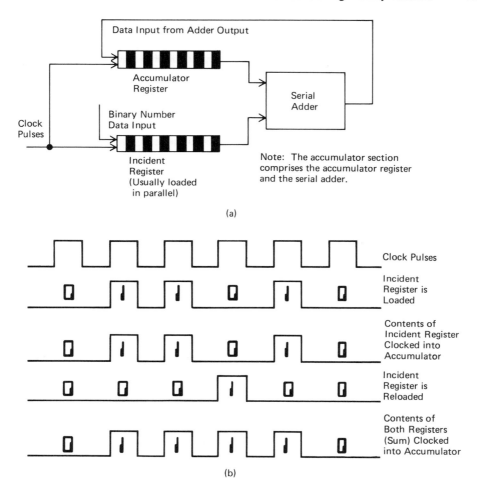

Fig. 10-7. An elementary accumulator configuration in a serial adder arrangement. (a) Skeleton configuration; (b) timing diagram.

temporary storage in the accumulator register and the incident register. The bits to be serially added are usually loaded in parallel into the incident register. The circuitry is arranged so that the sum will be retained in the accumulator. We have seen that an accumulator is essentially a recirculating shift register.

Circuit action proceeds as follows: The binary number representing the augend is loaded into the incident register, and is then automatically clocked into the accumulator. The addend is loaded into the incident register, and the contents of both registers are then automatically clocked into the serial adder. Finally, the sum of the two binary numbers is clocked into the accumulator.

In the example of Fig. 10-7, the incident register is first broadside loaded with the augend 011010 (parallel loading speeds up system operation). The augend is passed through the serial adder (added to 000000) and thereby clocked into the accumulator. Now, the incident register is broadside loaded with the addend 000100.

Next, the contents of both registers are clocked into the serial adder: 0 and 0 are added, and their sum of 0 is clocked into the accumulator; 1 and 0 are added, and their sum of 1 is clocked into the accumulator; 1 and 0 are added, and their sum of 1 is clocked into the accumulator; 0 and 1 are added, and their sum of 1 is clocked into the accumulator; 1 and 0 are added, and their sum of 1 is clocked into the accumulator; 0 and 0 are added, and their sum of 0 is clocked into the accumulator. In turn, the accumulator now contains the sum of the two binary numbers: 011110.

PARALLEL ADDER

Parallel adders employ more than one full adder. For example, the parallel adder depicted in Fig. 10-8 has four full adders. We will find that the adders can also perform subtraction. First, let us follow the adder action. The augend is broadside loaded into the A register; it can be entered when the Load A control line L_A is driven logic-high. The addend is broadside loaded into the B register; it can be entered when Load B control line L_B is driven logic-high.

Ripple carry is employed by the full adders; the Carry Out from one adder is fed to the Carry In terminal of the next adder. To add the contents of the A and B registers, the C_{In} control is held logic-low. In other words, no Carry-In bit is applied to the first adder. When the Enable A and B control line, E_{AB}, is driven logic-high, the contents of the A and B registers are unloaded into the full adders.

Observe that since the C_{In} control was held logic-low, that the outputs from the XOR gates will be the same as their inputs from the B register. With the contents from the A and B registers loaded into the full adders, they proceed to form the sum of these two binary numbers. Any carries that are generated in the addition process ripple through, and the finalized sum appears as $S_3S_2S_1S_0$ at the adder outputs.

This is also a subtracter arrangement. Let us follow the subtracter action. It is necessary to understand that when the 2's complement of a binary number is added to another binary number, the difference between the numbers is obtained. For example, let us subtract 0011 from 1011 by the 2's complement method. (Decimally, we are subtracting 3 from 11.) First, we must form the 2's complement of 0011:

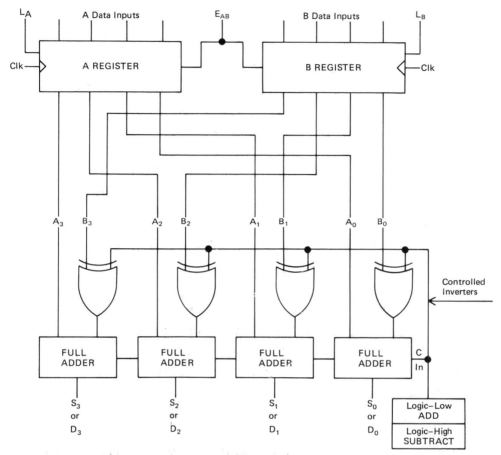

Technical Note: An XOR gate functions as an inverter if one of its inputs is held logic-high. In other words, the XOR gate complements a bit when one input is logic-high. On the other hand, the XOR gate functions as a buffer if one of its inputs is held logic-low. For this reason, it is called a controlled inverter in this application.

Fig. 10-8. Controlled-inverter adder/subtracter with A and B registers.

The 1's complement of a binary number is obtained by complementing the number. In other words, the 1's complement of 0011 is 1100. In turn, the 2's complement is obtained by adding 1 to the 1's complement. Thus, the 2's complement of 0011 is 1101. Now, if we add the minuend 1011 to the 2's complement of the subtrahend, 1101, we obtain 11000. Note carefully that the first 1 is clocked out of the last full adder (is rejected), so that $D_3D_2D_1D_0 = 1000$. Or, decimally, $11 - 3 = 8$.

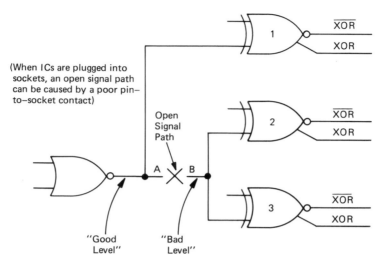

(When ICs are plugged into sockets, an open signal path can be caused by a poor pin–to–socket contact)

Open Signal Path

A ╳ B

"Good Level"   "Bad Level"

Note: A poor solder connection, microscopic crack in a PC conductor, faulty plated-through hole, or equivalent interruption can produce an open signal path in the circuit external to the ICs. *Point B will float to a bad level, while point A is driven by proper TTL or DTL signal levels.* The troubleshooter starts at the input of gate 3 or 4, and proceeds back toward gate 1, and the exact location of the open signal path can be determined using the logic probe.

Fig. 10-9. Example of an open signal path.

The fact that any carry-out from the last full adder in Fig. 10-9 is rejected deserves special mention. This rejection is in accordance with the rules for binary subtraction by means of addition of the 2's complement in the subtrahend. Let us consider another example of subtraction:

To subtract decimal 1 from decimal 2, we subtract binary 0001 from binary 0010. Using the 2's complement addition method, we add 0010 to 1111, and obtain 10001; the first 1 is rejected, leaving 0001 as the answer. It is helpful to consider still another example of subtraction:

To subtract decimal 15 from decimal 15, we subtract binary 1111 from binary 1111. Using the 2's complement addition method, we add 1111 to 0001, and obtain 10000; the first 1 is rejected, leaving 0000 as the answer. Note in passing that the controlled-inverter adder/subtracter can also add negative numbers or subtract negative numbers. However, inasmuch as this is primarily a troubleshooting book, the addition and subtraction of negative numbers will not be detailed in these pages. Interested readers may consult any textbook of binary arithmetic.

DIGITAL TROUBLESHOOTING PROCEDURE

This generalized troubleshooting procedure, provided by the Hewlett-Packard Company, has five steps, as follows:

1. Test all ICs in the digital system, using the logic comparator (or logic probe and pulser), and note the failing nodes.

2. Test for an open output bond, using the logic probe. If an open output bond is indicated, replace the IC driving the failing node.

3. Test for a short to V_{CC} (or Gnd) using the logic pulser and probe. By simultaneously probing and pulsing that bad node, a short to V_{CC} or ground can be detected inasmuch as the pulser is unable to inject a pulse into such a short.

4. Test for a short between two nodes using the logic probe and pulser, or an ohmmeter.

5. If the failure is not found in steps 2 through 4, then the failure is either an open input bond or a failure of the internal circuitry of the IC driving the failing node. In either case, the IC driving the failing node should be replaced.

Logic Comparator Test

In other words, the first step in this troubleshooting procedure is to use the logic comparator to check all <u>testable</u> ICs in the circuit, or in that portion of the circuit which is suspected of malfunctioning, and to thereby note the ICs and pins that the comparator indicates as faulty. In turn, the troubleshooter can better focus attention on those physical areas of the circuit that are malfunctioning.

For those ICs that are not testable with the logic comparator, or for which a reference card does not exist, the logic pulser and logic clip can be used to verify proper IC operation. The logic probe can be used to observe the signal activity on inputs and to view the resulting output signals. From this test data, a decision can be made whether the IC is operating properly, or not.

When more detailed study of the trouble situation is desired, or when signal activity is missing, the logic pulser can be used to inject input signals, and the logic probe can be used to monitor the response. *This technique is especially good when testing digital gates and other combinatorial devices. The logic pulser can be used to cause the inputs to go to a state which will cause a change in the output state.*

Example: A three-input NAND gate which has high, low, low inputs will have a high output. By pulsing the two low inputs high, using the logic pulser and the multistimulus cable, if necessary, the output will pulse low and can be detected by the logic probe. This then indicates that the IC is operating properly. *The logic pulser is also valuable for replacing the clock in a digital circuit, thus allowing the circuit to be single-stepped while the logic probe and clip are used to observe the changes in the circuit's state.*

This first step might be called the "mapping" step, since the effect is to map out the problem areas for further investigation. It is important to do a complete "mapping" of the circuit before proceeding to analyze each of the indicated failures.

Prematurely studying a fault can result in overlooking of faults which cause *multiple failures*, such as shorts between two nodes. In turn, this premature approach often leads to the needless replacement of a good IC, and much wasted time. With a complete trouble-area "map," we can begin to determine the type and cause of the failures. *This is accomplished by systematically eliminating the possible failures of digital circuits discussed above.*

TESTING SEQUENCE

1. The first failure to test for is an open bond in the IC driving the failed node.

2. If the node is not a bad level, then a test for a short to V_{CC} or ground should be made next. This can be easily accomplished with the logic pulser and probe. While the logic pulser is sufficiently powerful to override even a low-impedance TTL output, it is not powerful enough to effect a change in state on a V_{CC} or ground bus. This is just another way of saying that if the logic pulser is used to inject a pulse, while the logic probe is simultaneously used *on the same node* to observe the pulse, a short to V_{CC} or ground can be detected. *The occurrence of a pulse indicates that the node is not shorted, and the absence of a pulse indicates that the node is shorted to V_{CC} (if it is a high), or that the node is shorted to ground (if it is a low).*

3. If the failure is a short, there are two possible causes. The most probable is a fault in the circuit external to the ICs. This type of fault can be detected by careful inspection of the circuit. In turn, solder splashes, whiskers, loose wires, or solder bridges are "cleaned up" as required. *Only if the two nodes which are shorted are common to one IC can the failure*

be internal to that IC. If, after careful inspection, no circuit short can be found, then the IC should be replaced.

4. If the failure is not a short between two nodes, then there are two remaining possibilities. These are: an open input bond, or a failure of the internal circuitry in the IC that the comparator indicates has failed. In either case, this IC should now be replaced. *Thus, by systematically eliminating the IC failures, the cause of the trouble symptom can be located.*

5. A practical step at any point where an IC is replaced is the *retesting* of the circuit with the logic comparator. If the comparator again indicates failure, then more study of the problem must be made, with the knowledge that the failure is not in the IC that has just been replaced.

OPEN SIGNAL PATH

One type of failure that has not been discussed in this algorithm is an open signal path in the circuitry external to the IC (Fig. 10-9). An external open circuit will not be indicated by a logic comparator—in turn, it will not be shown on the trouble-area map. If, after using the logic comparator to test all of the ICs, no nodes are indicated as failing, or, if after finding the cause of the failures indicated by the logic comparator, the circuit is found to be still malfunctioning, then *an open signal path can be suspected.*

Sequential Integrated Circuits

The class of integrated circuits known as *sequential integrated circuits* confronts the digital troubleshooter with many difficult problems. ICs such as memories, shift registers, and flip-flops whose present outputs are dependent on previous inputs are called sequential ICs. Testing these devices with conventional instruments requires the observation and study of relationships among several waveforms.

In some cases, these waveforms are long and complex—and verification of proper IC operation is practically impossible. However, the logic comparator, when properly used, provides a very efficient and simple solution to troubleshooting sequential ICs.

Inasmuch as the operation of a flip-flop or other sequential device depends on the previous input to that device, and since the reference device will not, in general, have had the same "prior" set of inputs as the device under test, it is necessary to "reset" the devices before the comparison procedure is started. This can be accomplished by first clipping the comparator to the device that is to be tested, and causing a reset signal to be applied either by the circuit to be tested or by a logic pulser. (A pulser can be used to inject a reset pulse into the IC's reset input.)

The foregoing procedure ensures that both devices start in the same state and that they will react in the same manner to the sequence of input signals that they receive. The comparator will now flip and not flop when the flip-flop flips. If the test IC is good, the output states of the reference and test IC will always agree, and the comparator will not indicate a fault.

In some cases, the reset lines are connected directly to V_{CC} or to ground and thus are not pulseable. If this situation is encountered, turning the power off and back on sometimes brings both the test IC and the reference IC up to the same state.

With memories and shift registers, the troubleshooter confronts a problem as above described. However, instead of applying a reset pulse to the circuit for establishing a known state, the comparator must merely be attached to the test IC long enough for the reference IC to be loaded with the same data as the test IC. This procedure should require no longer than one complete cycle of the memory or shift-register.

During the time that the reference IC is being loaded with the data, the comparator will display fault indications. If, after a few cycle times, the fault is still indicated, <u>a fault has indeed occurred at the indicated node</u>.

GLITCHES

Glitches are caused by timing errors. For example, if one input to a NAND gate is 1, and the other input is 0, the input signals can normally be complemented without gate malfunction. On the other hand, if the complemented signal arrives with lack of precise simultaneity in state changes, both inputs of the NAND gate will then go logic-high for a brief instant. In turn, a narrow glitch pulse is outputted by the NAND gate.

Glitches can cause malfunctioning in subsequent circuitry, because the glitch represents a spurious pulse. Unless a glitch is extremely narrow, it can be "caught" by a commercial logic probe. Extremely narrow glitches are tracked down to best advantage by means of highly sophisticated scopes. Unusually fast writing speed and high screen intensity are required.

11

Current and Voltage Relations in Digital Circuits

Logic-High Current and Voltage • Phone-Tone Indicator • Digital Current Tracer • Examples • Case History • Changing Negative-Going Square Waves into Positive-Going Square Waves • Clamp Action • Experiment • Device Input Clamps • Output and Input Equivalent Circuits

LOGIC-HIGH CURRENT AND VOLTAGE

When the output from a NAND gate is logic-high, it sinks approximately $40\mu A$ of current from a subsequent NAND gate, as shown in Fig. 11-1. The NAND gate applies about 4V to the input of the driven gate; in turn, the base-emitter junction of the driven gate is reverse-biased. Its equivalent resistance is approximately 100 kilohms. *Note that the diagram in Fig. 1-11 is simplified, in that it does not show the clamp diodes that are connected from each emitter to ground inside of the IC package. These clamp diodes are also reverse-biased, and their junction resistance is effectively in parallel with Q1's base-emitter junction resistance.*

PHONE-TONE COUNT INDICATOR

Troubleshooters sometimes need to keep track of the number of output pulses that have occurred at a test point. A binary counter provides this indication and "memory." In addition, the troubleshooter can proceed faster with his tests if he does not have to repeatedly observe a visual readout. For this purpose, the phone-tone binary counter arrangement shown in Fig. 11-2 will be found most helpful. Everyone is familiar with the "tone-fone" telephone sys-

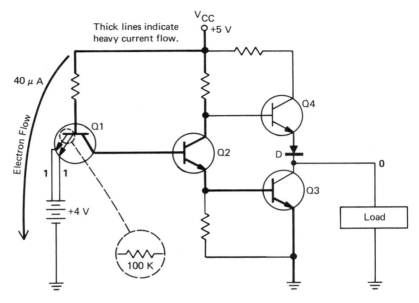

Note: Since Q1, Q2, and Q3 are saturated, the base of Q1 is at ground potential from a practical point of view. The 40 μA is junction leakage current.

Fig. 11-1. TTL NAND gate; logic-*high* inputs produce logic-*low* output.

tem. The configuration in Fig. 11-2 employs four distinctive audio tones for an audible readout up to a total of 15 counts.

DIGITAL CURRENT TRACER

The digital current tracer, illustrated in Fig. 11-3, ranks in importance with the logic probe and logic pulser. This current tracer pinpoints low-impedance faults in digital circuitry by locating current source or sinks. For example, a short-circuit point on a node can be localized while all of the points along the node are stuck-low or stuck-high.

Various similar troubleshooting "dog" problems that cause wasted time and costs can be effectively solved, such as shorted wire-AND/OR configurations. In conventional approaches, ICs are progressively removed until the failed IC is identified by elimination; in this process, circuit boards may also be damaged. A current tracer precisely locates a node fault, even on multilayer boards. In addition, a current tracer can pinpoint hairline solder bridges that often escape notice until a circuit is operated for the first time.

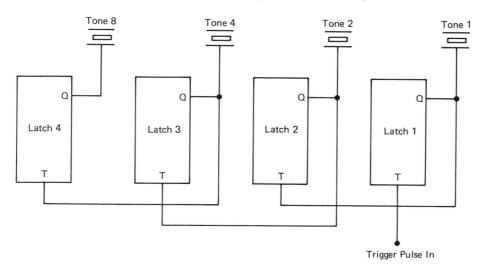

Note: This counter may be constructed from toggle latches, as shown in Fig. 3-1, or equivalent arrangement. The readout tones are provided by piezo buzzers, as depicted in Fig. 4-8. These buzzers should have progressively higher tones, such as do-mi-sol-do (octave higher). A total of 15 audible counts is provided.

If suitable piezo buzzers are not readily available, you can use four transistor RC oscillators with a miniature speaker for sound indication.

Fig. 11-2. **Phone-tone binary counter arrangement.**

The digital current tracer is constructed as a hand-held probe, and is a sophisticated type of tester designed for troubleshooting circuits that carry fast rise-time current pulses. This current tracer senses magnetic fields produced by current change; it displays transitions, single pulses, and pulse trains by a one-light indicator.

This type of current tracer is not voltage-sensitive, and can be used with any logic family in which the current pulses have at least 1 mA amplitude, and have repetition rates less than 10 mHz. (Even in CMOS circuitry, lightly loaded outputs have current pulses with 2 or 3 mA amplitude). See also Fig. 11-4.

Since the digital current tracer responds to current change, it can verify in a bad-node test that the driver is functioning and can trace the current flow to the source or sink that is causing the node to be stuck.

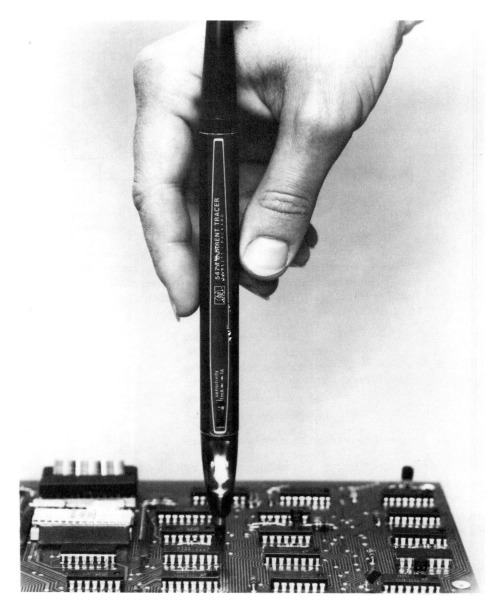

Fig. 11-3. Appearance of a digital current tracer. (Courtesy, Hewlett-Packard.)

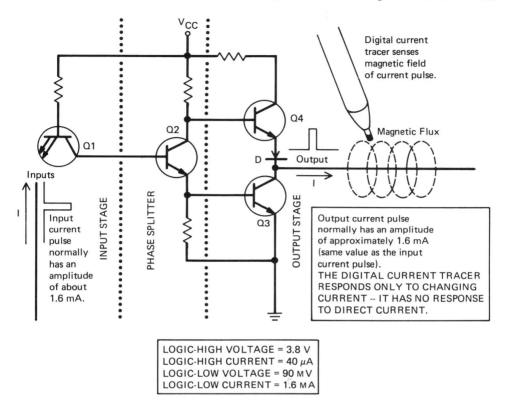

LOGIC-HIGH VOLTAGE = 3.8 V
LOGIC-HIGH CURRENT = 40 μA
LOGIC-LOW VOLTAGE = 90 MV
LOGIC-LOW CURRENT = 1.6 MA

Fig. 11-4. Digital current tracer application.

In application, the dot on the tip of the current tracer is aligned at a reference point, such as the output of a node driver. The sensitivity control is then advanced to obtain indication of ac current activity. In turn, the troubleshooter can proceed to trace the circuit and determine where current is flowing. The indicator lamp changes intensity as the circuit is being probed, and will have the same brightness at the fault point that it had at the reference point.

Knowing both current and voltage data helps the troubleshooter to determine possible faults on a node. For example, when a node is active with AC current, but is unable to change state, the driver is normal—a fault probably exists in the circuitry being driven. The digital current tracer will verify digital current activity, will show the current path, and can pinpoint the fault.

The digital current tracer operates over a wide current range—from 1 mA to 1 A; it provides a bright, easy-to-read indicator lamp at the probe tip, along with a color-coded sensitivity control. In turn, the troubleshooter can easily determine differences in current levels by applying the tracer after setting a reference level. It is also easy to follow current changes in circuits that are operating normally.

To use the digital current tracer, the troubleshooter aligns the dot on its tip at a reference point (usually the output of the node driver). The three-decade current control (Fig. 11-5) is then set to obtain a clear indication of the ac current activity. The troubleshooter can now trace the circuit to determine where the current is flowing. As he probes from point to point (or follows the traces), the indicator lamp changes brightness in accordance with the current intensity.

When the troubleshooter traces current flow to the fault point, the current tracer will most likely indicate the same brightness as at the reference point. The foregoing procedure is useful for pinpointing an undetected solder bridge, a stuck node, or a defective component with an open circuit. *Presence or absence of ac current leads the troubleshooter directly to the fault.*

The digital current tracer employs a shielded inductive pickup, and a wideband, high-gain amplifier to provide the sensitivity required to sense the mag-

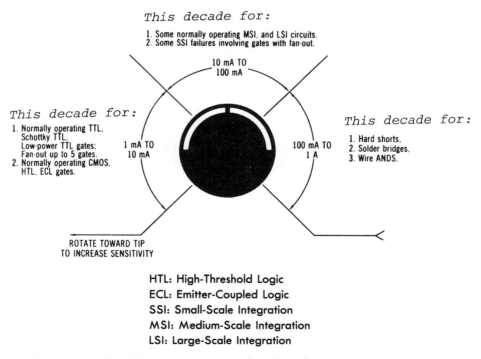

Fig. 11-5. Three-decade current control for digital current tracer. (Courtesy, Hewlett-Packard.)

netic fields associated with current changes along PC board conductors. *The il-lustrated current tracer has sufficient sensitivity to "track" ac current in multilayer board conductors, to trace ac current through the insulation in shorted cables, and to pinpoint faults on computer backplanes and motherboards.*

Examples

With reference to Fig. 11-6, a multiple input fault is shown; there are four inputs from driver U1 to gates U2D, U3A, U4D, and U5A. In this example, gate U5A is short-circuited to ground, causing the node to be stuck logic-low.

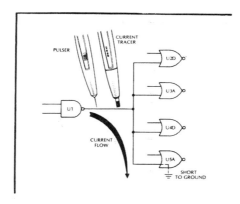

Note: A logic probe is unsuitable in this situation, because the short circuit to ground produces a very low impedance path. Because of this low impedance, the current flow is abnormal. On the other hand, large current changes are accompanied by very small voltage changes. *Therefore, current-oriented tests must be used to track down the fault.*

		CURRENT	
		ACTIVITY	NO ACTIVITY
VOLTAGE	ACTIVITY	NODE NORMAL	OPEN TRACE ON NODE
	NO ACTIVITY	SHORTED OR STUCK INPUT ON NODE	BAD DRIVER ON NODE

Fig. 11-6. Example of a short circuit to ground inside of an IC package. (Courtesy, Hewlett-Packard.)

The short circuit sinks practically all of the current from U1 and from the other inputs. To troubleshoot this malfunction, the following steps are observed:

1. Current pulses are provided by a logic pulser, as shown in the diagram.
2. The reference display for the current tracer is set at the node driver output.
3. Then, the main current path is traced while the indicator lamp is observed.
4. Along the main current path, the indicator lamp continues to glow; on the other hand, the lamp goes dark when the tracer tip is removed from the main current path.

Another example: With reference to Fig. 11-7, a solder-bridge fault is shown. The solder "whisker" or bridge between U1 and U2 causes both of the nodes to operate incorrectly. However, there is current activity in the circuit, and the short circuit can be quickly pinpointed with the digital current tracer. In other words, the current path is between the output terminals of U1 and U2. When the current tracer is moved past the solder bridge toward U3 or U4, the indicator lamp goes dark. Thereby, the short-circuit point is identified.

A reference current setting on the digital current tracer for one node will not necessarily be correct for another node, due to variability in circuit connections

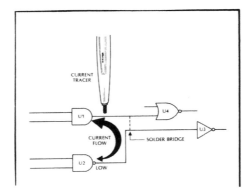

> **Note:** In this example, pulse activity was present at the outputs of U1 and U2 inasmuch as the gates were being driven by prior circuitry. In case the troubleshooter needs to track down a solder bridge along a node in which pulse activity is absent, a logic pulser should be used to provide a source of changing current. (See Fig. 11-6.)

Fig. 11-7. Pinpointing a solder bridge with the digital current tracer. (Courtesy, Hewlett-Packard.)

or to differences in fan-out. The current tracer's sensitivity control permits the troubleshooter to "see" as small as 300μA. There is practically no upper limit on current value—any current greater than 50 mA will produce equal light output.

> If the troubleshooter "loses" a current path as he moves along a conductor, he should check whether the conductor width increases (with resulting current "fan-out," which reduces the magnetic field intensity). If so, the sensitivity of the current tracer may be increased. Another possibility is that the conductor proceeds via a plated-through hole in the circuit board. In turn, the tip of the current tracer is farther from the conductor—the sensitivity of indication should be increased as required.

In another typical situation, the current path "branches" and proceeds to several different locations via several different paths. The current-tracer sensitivity should be increased accordingly. *Note that V_{CC} and ground lines tend to be very "noisy," and have high-amplitude current spikes—although these large current changes are accompanied by very small voltage changes. For this reason, it is recommended that the troubleshooter avoid current tracing along V_{CC} and ground lines, whenever possible. (It is usually feasible to "go around" the noisy lines, or to approach the problem indirectly.)*

Case History

The basic D latch was depicted in Fig. 1-5. With reference to Fig. 11-8, two D flip-flops in a configuration had identical input conditions. However, one flip-flop operated normally, whereas the other flip-flop did not change state. The trouble was pinpointed as follows:

1. With the D input energized by a logic pulser, it was observed that the Q and Q̄ outputs of the "stuck" flip-flop showed no response when checked with a logic probe.

2. Pulsing and probing the Reset line simultaneously showed that the Reset line could not be driven logic-high; this suggested that the line was shorted to ground.

3. Application of the logic pulser and current tracer showed that the conductors near the Reset line drew current; however, the flip-flop was not responding to these current pulses.

4. Further investigation with the pulser and current tracer showed that there was a hairline solder bridge between the Reset line and ground.

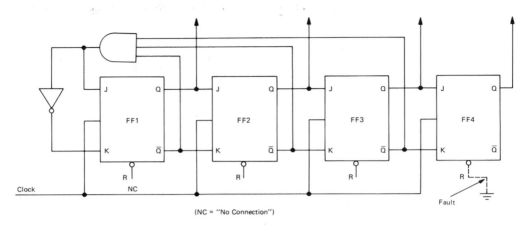

(NC = "No Connection")

Note: The Reset line is asynchronous, and forces the output state of the flip-flop, independently of the clock. In this example, the Reset is active-low —the flip-flop's output state is forced when the Reset line goes logic-low. In normal operation, the Reset line is maintained logic-high. A floating input will be interpreted as the logic-high state. On the other hand, if the Reset line is accidentally short-circuited to ground, the flip-flop will be forced into maintaining a reset output state, regardless of the data input signal.

Fig. 11-8. Troubleshooting a "stuck" flip-flop.

CHANGING NEGATIVE-GOING SQUARE WAVES INTO POSITIVE-GOING SQUARE WAVES

Troubleshooters sometimes use a square-wave generator as a source of clock pulses. It should be observed that some square-wave generators output a positive-going waveform, whereas other square-wave generators output a negative-going waveform. Still other generators output a waveform with equal positive and negative excursions. *If a TTL input is driven by a negative-going square wave, no response will be obtained—a TTL input must be driven by a positive-going square wave.*

To change a negative-going square wave into a positive-going square wave, an inverting amplifier may be used. For example, an op amp with unity gain will invert the polarity of the input waveform. *However, this complication in test facilities should be regarded as a "last resort," and the troubleshooter should make an attempt to obtain a square-wave generator with positive-going output.*

Some square-wave generators are provided with a "fixed TTL output," *designed for clock-substitution tests* in digital systems. An occasional square-wave generator is designed with a built-in series blocking capacitor; in turn, the output waveform has equal positive and negative excursions. *This "ac output" will drive TTL devices, although the troubleshooter should recognize that it is a "nonstandard drive."*

Clamp Action

> *Experiment*: Let us briefly review clamp action with regard to square waves at this point. If a series capacitor is connected in the output of a square-wave generator that provides a *negative-going* waveform, the capacitor removes the negative DC component. In turn, the output waveform is an "ac waveform" with equal positive and negative excursions. (See Fig. 11-9.)
>
> Next, if a diode is shunted from the output of the capacitor to ground, with polarity as indicated, clamp action is obtained—the output waveform is now a positive-going square wave. In other words, the original negative-going square wave has been changed into a positive-going square wave.

It should not be supposed that the clamp circuit in Fig. 11-9 provides the same driving action as an inverting amplifier, such as an op amp. The distinc-

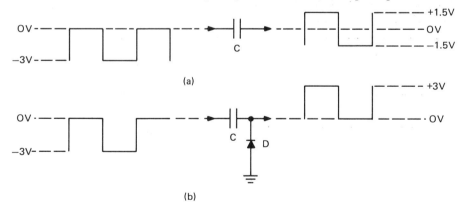

(a)

(b)

Note: A 1 μF capacitor and a 1N34A germanium diode may be used in this arrangement. As a practical note, some square-wave generators output a high surge voltage when first turned on. To avoid possible damage to the diode, the generator may be disconnected from the clamp while it is being switched on.

Fig. 11-9. Example of clamp action. (a) Series capacitor removes dc component from negative-going square wave; (b) series capacitor and clamp diode changes negative-going square wave into positive-going square wave.

tion between them is that the clamp does not have the same output impedance for positive voltages and for negative voltages. In other words, the clamp has a very low resistance to ground for negative voltages, but is virtually an open circuit for positive voltages.

Device Input Clamps

Observe next that *most* TTL devices have built-in clamp diodes, as shown in Fig. 11-10. These clamps are provided to reduce the possibility of false triggering by digital waveforms that are substantially distorted by negative overshoot and ringing. *Note that these clamps have the same circuit action with respect to an "ac input waveform" as the diode in Fig. 11-9(b). In other words, a built-in clamp diode effectively clamps the square-wave negative peaks to ground, when driven from a coupling capacitor.*

As previously noted, a node has a typical internal resistance of 150 ohms in normal operation. The significance of this internal resistance in our present top-

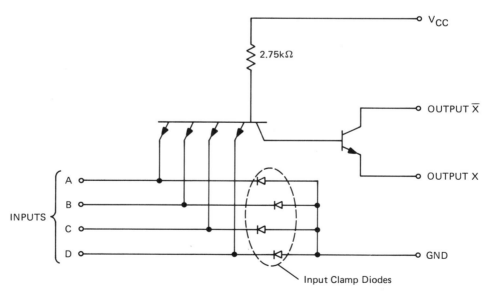

Note: The majority of TTL devices encountered by the troubleshooter will have built-in clamp diodes, as exemplified above. These clamp diodes are provided in order to "clean up" distorted input waveforms that may have negative-going overshoot and ringing excursions. Thereby, the possibility of false triggering due to digital pulse distortion is reduced.

Fig. 11-10. Example of a TTL device with built-in clamps.

ic is seen in Fig. 11-11. Here, input A is coupled to a signal source via capacitor, C. This input node has practically infinite resistance to ground, and it has a resting dc level of approximately 1.6V (in the "bad region").

Next, if a 150-ohm resistor is connected across the DVM terminals, the input node has 150 ohms resistance to ground, and its resting dc level is reduced to about 0.14V (in the logic-low region). *To recall a basic point, TTL inputs "should always be connected to something," and not allowed to float. When a TTL input is driven from a source with a series coupling capacitor, the input is floating insofar as dc voltage relations are concerned.*

Output and Input Equivalent Circuits

The troubleshooter will find it helpful to note the normal output and input equivalent circuits for a typical TTL device in its logic-high and and logic-low

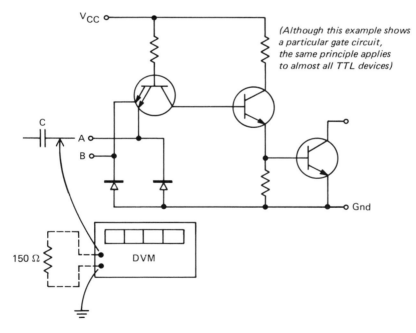

Note: Input A floats at about +1.6V with respect to ground. However, when a 150-ohm resistor is connected from input A to ground, the voltage falls to approximately +0.14V.

Fig. 11-11. When driven via a series coupling capacitor, a TTL input is floating, insofar as dc voltage relations are concerned.

states. Each equivalent circuit comprises a positive dc-voltage source in series with the internal resistance. (See Fig. 11-12.) Thus, a TTL device presents a two-valued load, and represents a two-valued source. These two-valued loads are active loads.

This can occasionally be a "tricky" point for the apprentice troubleshooter, inasmuch as input circuits and output circuits are generally regarded as having a fixed input resistance that remains unchanged as the voltage level varies. Digital circuitry, however, is switching circuitry, and the general rule is that input and output circuits will have two-valued resistances. Thus, a digital input circuit typically has a 100-kilohm resistance or a 93-ohm resistance, depending upon the input voltage level.

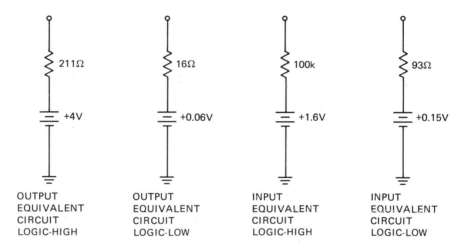

| OUTPUT EQUIVALENT CIRCUIT LOGIC-HIGH | OUTPUT EQUIVALENT CIRCUIT LOGIC-LOW | INPUT EQUIVALENT CIRCUIT LOGIC-HIGH | INPUT EQUIVALENT CIRCUIT LOGIC-LOW |

Note: These are the output and input equivalent circuits for a typical TTL device with unloaded output. The logic-high input equivalent circuit is for floating input. The logic-low input equivalent circuit is for the forced logic-low input state resulting from a shunt of 150 ohms from the input terminal to ground.

Fig. 11-12. Output and input equivalent circuits for the logic-high and logic-low states of a typical TTL device.

12

Troubleshooting
Three-State Buses
(Wire-ANDS)

*Three-State Buses • Experiment • Bus Schedule • Checking the
Direction of Data Flow • Memory Address Register • Floating Output • Bus Driver • Stuck Low/Stuck High • Open Circuits • Bus System Troubleshooting*

THREE-STATE BUSES

Three-state buses are a further development of the wire-AND arrangement
that was previously noted. Nearly all microprocessor systems are bus-organized,
as depicted in Fig. 12-1. This is an example of basic microcomputer architecture. *Architecture* denotes the organizational structure of a computing system.
It is primarily concerned with the central processing unit (CPU) or
microprocessor.

With reference to Fig. 12-1, an elementary microprocessor organization comprises an arithmetic-logic unit (ALU), memory, control, and input/output sections. *All sections are interconnected by buses which are subdivided into address,
data, and control buses. Clock and power-supply lines are also provided. In the
most fundamental view, an ALU is a binary adder.*

As indicated by the dotted bus in Fig. 12-1, direct memory access denotes a
path of direct access to main storage (such as a floppy disc unit) for data transfer without involving the CPU. A DMA function may also denote an arrangement that allows an input/output (I/O) device to take control of the CPU for
one or more memory cycles to write data into memory or to read data from
memory.

A minimal microprocessor arrangement has four principal buses, as seen in
Fig. 12-2:

1. One bus connects the input section to the microprocessor.

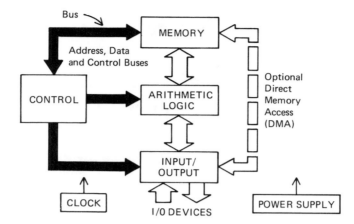

Note: An important advantage of a bus-organized microprocessor system is that any part of the system is immediately accessible to any other part of the system.

Fig. 12-1. An elementary microprocessor organization. (Courtesy, Hewlett-Packard.)

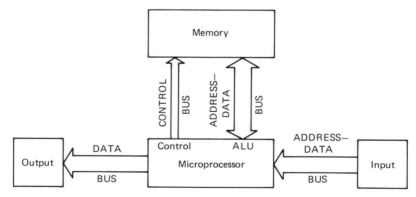

Note: An *address* is an expression, usually a binary number, which designates a particular storage location in a memory.

Data denotes elements of information, usually in binary form, which can be processed or produced by a computer.

Control circuits carry out instructions by interpreting an instruction and applying proper commands to the ALU and other circuits. An example of an *input peripheral* is a keyboard.

An example of an *output peripheral* is a video monitor.

Fig. 12-2. Minimal microprocessor system has four principal buses.

2. Another bus connects the microprocessor to the output section.
3. A bidirectional bus connects the memory and microprocessor.
4. A one-way bus connects the microprocessor to the memory for transmitting control signals.

A control bus may be symbolized by a thinner arrow than a data bus or an address/data bus. *However, a control bus usually contains more wires (or conductors) than an address/data bus.*

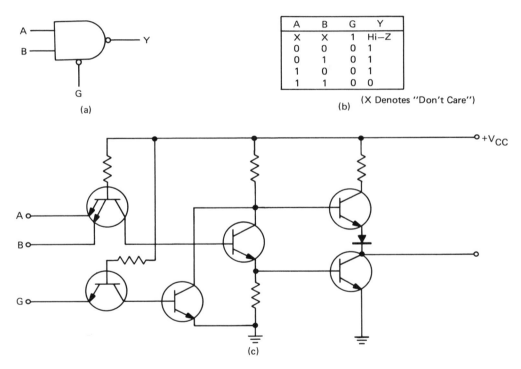

A	B	G	Y
X	X	1	Hi–Z
0	0	0	1
0	1	0	1
1	0	0	1
1	1	0	0

(b) (X Denotes "Don't Care")

(a)

(c)

Note: If inputs A and B are tied together, the three-state NAND gate operates as a three-state inverter. If G is logic-low, a logic-high input produces a logic-low output; or, if G is logic-low and the input is logic-low, the output goes logic-high. If G is logic-high, the output is "open" and does not respond to the input logic state.

Fig. 12-3. Example of a three-state NAND gate. (a) Logic symbol; (b) truth table; (c) schematic diagram.

Experiment

The troubleshooter will find it helpful to become familiar with the operation of three-state devices, such as the three-state NAND gate depicted in Fig. 12-3. Obtain a three-state NAND-gate IC package and proceed as follows:

1. Connect input G to a logic-high source, such as a 3-volt battery.
2. Connect output Y to a dc voltmeter, and a 150-ohm load resistor.
3. Connect inputs A and B at random to the logic-high source and to Gnd (logic-low source), *Observe that output Y is unresponsive to input logic states.*
4. Connect input G to ground; with A logic-high and B logic-low, note that Y goes logic-high; with A logic-low and B logic-high, note that Y goes logic-high.
5. With input G connected to ground, and with A and B both logic-low, note that Y goes logic-high; with both A and B logic-high, note that Y goes logic-low.

BUS SCHEDULE

Observe the register configuration for determination of a bus schedule exemplified in Fig. 12-4. This is a four-bit, two-way (bidirectional) bus. Each bus wire, or conductor, transmits one bit at a time; the data is transmitted in parallel (simultaneously) along the conductors. *Bus activity is chiefly concerned with transmission of data from one register along the bus to another register (for reception) somewhere up or down the bus.*

Register 1 in Fig. 12-4 has been stipulated as the data origin, and register 2 has been stipulated as the data destination. *As previously noted, a register serves for temporary data storage.* Since register 1 is the origin of the data, it has been previously loaded with a nibble (four-bit digital word). *To unload the data from register 1 into the data bus, the 1/R input of the register is driven logic-high.*

At the same time that the 1/R input is driven logic-high, and in order to load the data into register 2, the 2/W input of the register is also driven logic-high. Thereby, the contents of register 1 are transferred into register 2. Note that the contents of register 1 will <u>not</u> be erased until such time as new data may be loaded into register 1.

The control inputs to the four registers in Fig. 12-4 are activated by a control bus (not shown). Eight different control lines are utilized in this example, plus a clock line. (The clock line is common to all four registers.) Also, a power line (not shown) is connected to each register. Accordingly, the control bus in this example has more lines than the data bus.

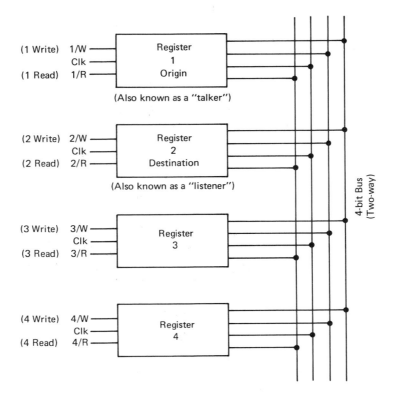

(1 Write) 1/W
Clk
(1 Read) 1/R
Register 1 Origin
(Also known as a "talker")

(2 Write) 2/W
Clk
(2 Read) 2/R
Register 2 Destination
(Also known as a "listener")

(3 Write) 3/W
Clk
(3 Read) 3/R
Register 3

(4 Write) 4/W
Clk
(4 Read) 4/R
Register 4

4-bit Bus (Two-way)

Note: Each register comprises four flip-flops. The flip-flops are clocked, and each register is loaded (or unloaded) in parallel. (Flip-flops are loaded or unloaded simultaneously.) A register stores a nibble until such time as its Read line may be driven logic-high. The register cannot be reloaded until its Write line is driven logic-high.

Fig. 12-4. Register configuration for determination of a bus schedule.

Other arrangements that will be encountered by the troubleshooter employ an eight-bit data bus, so that the data is transferred by bytes instead of by nibbles. (A byte consists of two nibbles.) If an eight-bit data bus was used in this example, the same number of control lines would be employed.

Checking the Direction of Data Flow

The troubleshooter is often concerned with the direction of data flow along a bus. For example, with reference to Fig. 12-4, register 1 is functioning as a data origin (talker), and register 2 is functioning as a data destination (listener).

However, during the next phase of operation, register 2 may be functioning as a talker, and register 2 may function as a listener. Again, register 4 may function as a talker, while register 1 functions as a listener. *To quickly check which direction data is flowing along a bus wire (conductor), a sensitive dc voltmeter may be applied at a pair of available points along the conductor.* For example, an op amp may be used with a service-type DVM, as shown in Figs. 3-5, 3-6, and 3-7. The basis of the data-flow direction test is shown in Fig. 12-5. Data

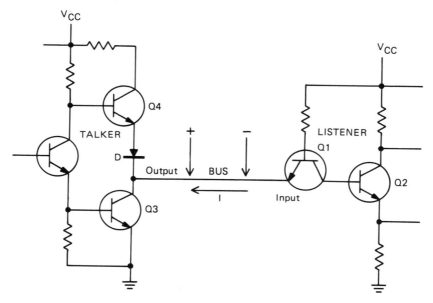

Note that when a sensitive DVM is directly applied to the test points, its polarity indication will be correct. On the other hand, if an op amp is used with the DVM, its polarity indication will be correct only if the negative lead of the DVM is connected to the op-amp output. (The op amp is an inverting amplifier.)

When a service-type DVM is used and the test points are not widely separated, the op amp may need high gain—use a 1k input resistor, instead of 10k.

Note: The *data flow* consists of a succession of current pulses from the listener to the talker. These are dc pulses, and their average value produces an IR voltage drop along the bus wire. At any two points along the bus wire, this IR voltage is more positive at the point nearest to the talker. In turn, the troubleshooter can quickly determine which end of a bus wire is the talker end, and which the listener.

Fig. 12-5. Check of the direction of data flow along a bus conductor.

flows from a totem-pole output to an emitter input. The chief current associated with this data flow is an electron flow from the emitter of Q1 along the bus wire and thence through Q3 to ground. In other words, the direction of data flow is opposite to the direction of electron current flow along the bus wire.

Accordingly, to check the direction of data flow, the troubleshooter applies a sensitive dc voltmeter at a pair of points along the bus wire, and notes which point is positive with respect to the other point. In turn, *the troubleshooter knows that the data is flowing along the bus wire in the direction from the positive point to the negative point.*

MEMORY ADDRESS REGISTER

An example of a memory address register (MAR) connected to a 16×8 read-only memory (ROM) is shown in Fig. 12-6. This memory address register utilizes four of the wires within the eight-wire data bus; the memory uses all eight wires of the bus.

The inputs to the memory address register in Fig. 12-6 are from the least significant wires in the bus $(W_3 W_2 W_1 W_0)$, whereas the outputs from the read-only memory are connected to both the most significant wires and to the least significant wires. *Note that the memory address register cannot be loaded at the same time that the read-only memory is unloaded (enabled). In other words, the memory address register can be loaded only when the least significant wires are available for address transmission.*

This is an example of a *two-state* memory-address register; that is, as soon as data is loaded into the register, the data is also immediately loaded into the read-only memory. The memory in Fig. 12-6 contains on-chip decoding logic for decoding the incoming address word. In turn, a corresponding register in the memory is addressed; thereafter, the addressed data stored in the memory may be unloaded (memory enabled) at any time.

This is just another way of saying that the data addressed in the memory will not be unloaded into the data bus until the enable input of the memory is driven logic-high by the control bus. (This enable pulse cannot be applied until the load input of the memory address register has gone logic-low.) Then, the data addressed in the memory may be unloaded into the eight data-bus wires whenever the data is needed for transmission along the bus to some other register.

Three-state output is utilized in the read-only memory depicted in the Fig. 12-7 example. Note that this is a four-wire, three-state system; each output line from the ROM is connected to a three-state buffer, and the output from each buffer is connected to a data-bus wire.

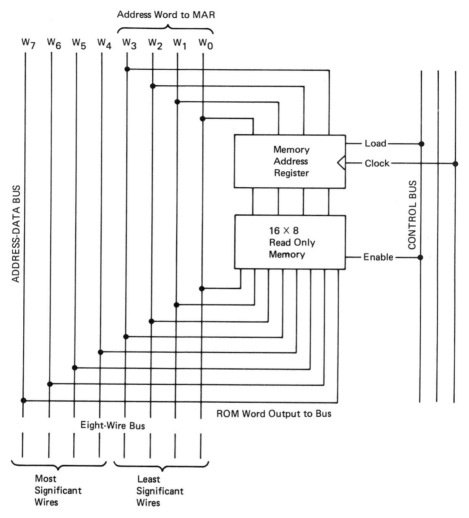

Note: Address word to MAR has its source from another register farther up the bus. ROM word output is entered into another register farther down the bus.

Fig. 12-6. Connections of a memory address register and an eight-bit memory into an eight-wire bus.

    A three-state buffer operates as a switch, in addition to its buffer action. In other words, when the enable input is logic-low, the three-state switches are effectively open, and the ROM outputs are thereby disconnected from the data-bus wires. On the other hand, when the three-state enable line is driven logic-

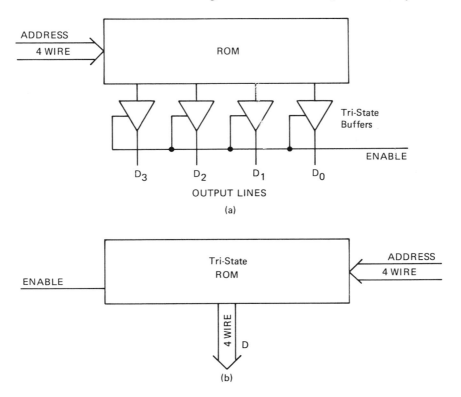

Note: The three-state buffers in this diagram are similar to the three-state inverter described in Fig. 12-3, except that the enable line is active-high, and the output is not inverted.

Fig. 12-7. Arrangement of a three-state ROM. (a) Logic diagram; (b) bus-organization symbol.

high, the three-state switches are effectively closed. In turn, the ROM outputs drive logic-high or logic-low signal levels onto the data bus. These logic levels correspond to the binary word that was addressed in the ROM.

Thus, a three-state buffer derives its name from its circuit action—the buffer output may be logic-high, logic-low, or hi-Z ("floating" or disconnected from the bus wires).

With reference to Fig. 12-8, a three-state driver (or three-state buffer) operates in the same manner as a conventional buffer, except that its enable input provides it with gating action plus output-impedance control. Observe that the control line connects to one emitter terminal of Q1, and also to the base terminal of Q4.

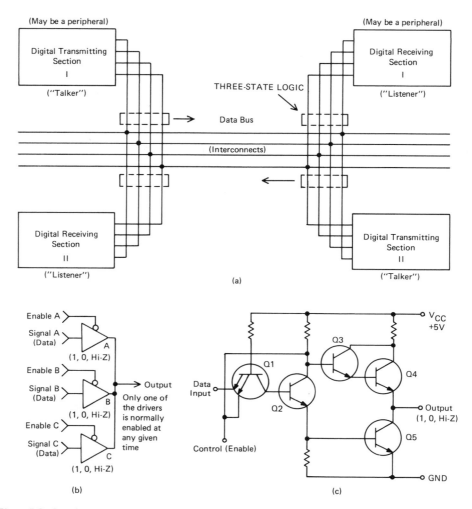

Fig. 12-8. Three-state logic circuitry. (a) Typical interconnect diagram; (b) three-state drivers bused together; (c) internal circuitry of a three-state driver.

The troubleshooter encounters wide application of three-state logic in bus-oriented digital systems, because this architectural feature facilitates transmission of digital data in either direction, as depicted in Fig. 12-8.* *A driver at one end of a bus may be enabled at a certain time, and then turned off, to be followed by enabling of a driver at the other end of the line. Or, a driver in the middle of the line might be enabled.*

---

*Tips on troubleshooting bus structures are tabulated in Fig. 12-10.

In normal operation, only one driver is active on a bus line at any particular time.

Floating Output: As noted above, a three-state driver provides logic-high, logic-low, and floating (open) output states. In its floating state, the driver has very high output impedance (practically an open circuit). This action results from the fact that the enable input (Fig. 12-8) can cut off both of the totem-pole output transistors simultaneously, *which forces the output to float.* Three-state logic is also widely used in logic control circuitry, as exemplified in the RS flip-flop diagram shown in Fig. 12-9.

Three-state drivers are comparatively difficult to troubleshoot. This situation arises because a bus structure can be controlled (constrained) by one faulty device which in turn makes the entire bus faulty. In other words, since all points on the bus are virtually at the same voltage level, the troubleshooter cannot employ meters, oscilloscopes, or other voltage-oriented instruments to determine which component is causing the bus to be stuck.

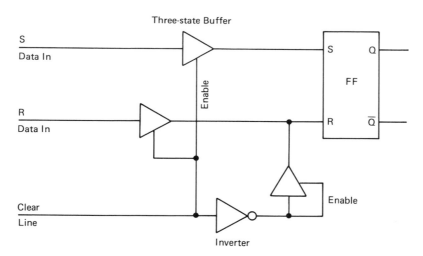

1. While "Clear Line" is held logic-high, data may be applied to the S and R inputs.
2. When "Clear Line" is driven logic-high, the S and R inputs are disconnected from the data lines and the R input is driven logic high—the flip-flop resets, if it was previously set. If not previously set, the flip-flop remains reset.
3. After the flip-flop is cleared, and the "Clear Line" again goes logic-high, new data may be applied to the S and R inputs.

Fig. 12-9. Example of a logic control arrangement comprising a flip-flop with three-state input gating.

One important exception to the foregoing difficulty has been described above. In other words, when a fault causes a reasonable amount of current to flow along a trace or wire, a progressive IR drop occurs which can be tracked from source to sink by means of a sensitive DVM. Moreover, this technique can be extended to data-flow determinations.

As a general rule of thumb, the first decision to make when troubleshooting bus structures is to decide whether the fault is localized in the bus' drivers or listeners. The following pointers will be found helpful:

1. *Bus Driver: Dead or Alive?* Answers to the following questions should be established—

    Do you find pulse activity on the bus drivers' inputs?

    Is the driver enabled?

    Does the driver respond to a stimulus?

    These questions are answerable, using the logic probe and pulser to first determine the state of the circuit, and then to observe whether its state changes when the circuit is pulsed. (Be sure that you can enable or disable the driver without stressing it either physically or electrically.)

    Also check multiple inputs of the drivers to make certain that you have control when you proceed to stimulate the circuit. If you find this impossible to accomplish because of the physical packaging of the circuit, check the bus listeners first.

    Often, use of PC board testers or other troubleshooting equipment will have led you to suspect a particular faulty bus line.

    In turn, the following topics provide tips for making quick checks of stuck lines and to thereby close in on the fault.*

2. *Stuck Low/ Stuck High.* When a bus is stuck in one logic state, it is not necessarily inactive. A bus stuck logic-low, for example, might be shorted to ground at the input to one of the bus listeners. If this were so, the bus driver would still be trying to drive the bus, which refuses to "budge."

    The driver wouldn't be able to alter the bus logic state, in this case, but there would be considerable current flowing on the bus from the driver to the fault. *This current activity is traceable with the H-P 547A current tracer.*

    If the driver is good, but no current pulses are available on the bus for tracing purposes, use an H-P 546A logic pulser at the driver output, and then trace the current flow from the pulser to the fault.

---

*Basic operational relations in a microcomputer are shown in Fig. 12-11.

Type of Bus Driver	Troubleshooting Tips
Wire-AND/OR (Open Collector)	1. Open collectors can sink current, but not source it so a pull-up resistor V_{CC} is connected to the output. 2. Disable driver input(s). 3. Pulse output(s). 4. Faulty driver will draw the most current.
Individual Driver	1. Driver can both source and sink current. 2. Pulse input(s). 3. Probe output(s) for logic state changes, *or* 4. Current Trace output(s) for amplitude and the direction of the current path. 5. Determine if driver is dead or bus is stuck. 6. Replace dead driver, *or* 7. Pulse and Current Trace at output to pinpoint bus fault.
Three-State Driver (With Both Source and Sink Action)	1. Disable driver inputs. 2. Pulse bus output lines. 3. If one output draws current, verify if it is faulty, *or* 1. Enable drivers. 2. Pulse driver inputs individually. 3. If one output fails to indicate current flow, verify if it is open.

Note: When a short circuit between V_{CC} and ground occurs on a PC board, troubleshooters usually employ one or more of the following techniques:

1. Connect a high-current dc supply to the PC board and observe which traces change color.
2. Measure dc microvolt drops across active supply traces and observe where current is flowing.
3. Replace all capacitors on the board.
4. Replace all ICs on the board.

Fig. 12-10. General tips on troubleshooting bus structures. (Courtesy, Hewlett-Packard.)

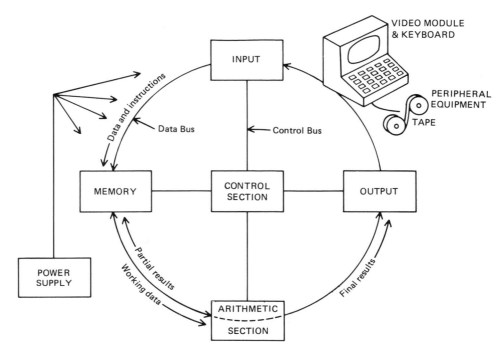

OPERATIONAL INTERRELATIONS IN A MICROCOMPUTER

Fig. 12-11. Example of a data bus and a control bus in a microcomputer.

Use the IC troubleshooters previously described to check bus listeners in the next step after eliminating shorts as a bus problem. If the line wasn't shorted, determine next whether the listeners on the bus respond to inputs.

An open circuit could occur on the bus, or, the bus driver could be faulty. Use the H-P 546A pulser to stimulate lines that lack activity, and then monitor the logic states and current activity on the bus to pinpoint open lines and open listener inputs, using the H-P 545A probe and 547A current tracer.

3. *Open Circuits.* A stuck bus can result from an open circuit at one of three points: the bus driver output, the bus line itself, or a listener input. Usually, these can be pinpointed by pulsing and probing, or by using the current tracer to determine the presence or absence of current at inputs or outputs.

To briefly summarize, a bus system is a network of conductors inside of a digital computer which provide paths for digital signal flow and lines for power-supply current. Note the following definitions:

ADDRESS: An address is a digital word; e.g., a nibble or a byte, which indicates *a specific location in a memory* where digital data are stored, or where digital data are to be stored.

DATA: Data are those basic elements of information (binary pulses) which can be processed or produced by a digital computer.

CONTROL: A control circuit is a subsystem that outputs *instructions* in proper sequence, *decodes* (interprets) each instruction, and applies *operating signals* to the ALU and other subsections in accordance with its interpretation of each instruction.

INSTRUCTION: An instruction consists of digital information that can be suitably coded and inputted as a unit into a digital computer in order to direct the computer to perform one or more operations. All instructions generally contain an *operand*—a digital nibble or byte that is to be processed.

TROUBLESHOOTING BUS SYSTEM CIRCUITRY WITH ELECTROLYTIC CAPACITORS

When a short circuit from V_{CC} to ground occurs in a circuit that includes electrolytic capacitors, the troubleshooter may proceed as follows:

1. Remove power from the circuit.

2. Energize a logic pulser and current tracer from an external 5V supply.

3. *Lift one side of the electrolytics on the supply bus.* This disconnection speeds up troubleshooting time by a factor of ten. (Electrolytics tend to "eat" pulses and thereby create many different current paths.)

4. Pulse across the power-supply pins, or across components in the corners of the PC board. (Use the cables and grabbers supplied with the logic pulser, thereby freeing your hands to move the current tracer around.) Moving the pulsing point from one corner to another and tracing current from the pulsing point assists in fault localization.

5. Inasmuch as you are pulsing into a short circuit, there is a large amount of current available. (Set tracer sensitivity to 1A.)

6. If power enters the board through more than one connector, parallel current paths may occur. In turn, moving the pulsing point around is helpful because the current path can change between the pulsing point and the short-circuit point.

7. When the fault is apparently located, verify it by moving the pulsing point *to* the short circuit point. *In turn, no current paths should be detectable elsewhere on the board.*

8. Finally, remove the suspected component and verify that the V_{CC} to ground short circuit has been eliminated.

EXERCISE IN FUTILITY

Inexperienced troubleshooters should not attempt to disassemble a pocket calculator without complete and detailed instructions. Otherwise a minor fault, such as a poor key contact, will be transformed into a disaster. Comprehensive service information is generally available from the manufacturer.

13

Examples of Generalized Troubleshooting Procedures

Practical Examples of Node and Gate Troubleshooting • Faults Inside of IC Packages • Another Internal Failure • Two PC Boards with Stuck-Low Node • IC or PC Trouble? • Note on IC Swapping and Card Swapping • Logic Clip • Shift Registers Revisited • Propagation Time Measurement • Basic Digital Troubleshooting Rules

PRACTICAL EXAMPLES OF NODE AND GATE TROUBLESHOOTING

Following repair of a malfunctioning PC board (or in production troubleshooting), short circuits due to "whiskers," or solder/copper-gold "bridge faults" may cause ensuing malfunction. A practical example is shown in Fig. 13-1. The short circuit is pinpointed as follows:

1. Use a logic pulser to inject test signals at the driver output at a desired pulse rate.

2. Use a current tracer, adjusted to suitable sensitivity, to track the injected test signal from the node driver output to the short-circuit point.

3. *Indication*: The light on the current tracer will go dark when the "whisker," or other cause of the short circuit is passed.

Another common digital troubleshooting problem is a stuck node. It is necessary to determine whether the driver is dead, or if a short-circuited input may be clamping the node to a fixed level. A practical example is shown in Fig. 13-2. The fault is pinpointed as follows:

1. Use a logic probe and logic pulser to determine the node's logic state,

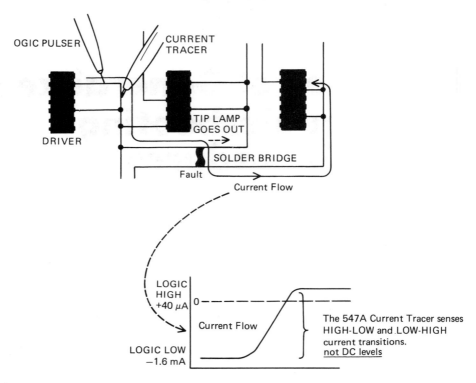

Note: Short circuits may draw excessive current and damage an IC. For example, the 9000 series of TTL devices has an absolute maximum output current rating of 50 mA (logic-low). The absolute maximum temperature rating is +125° C. When several gates are included in the same package, IC damage is particularly likely to occur if more than one output is short-circuited to ground.

Fig. 13-1. Tracking down a solder bridge. (Courtesy, Hewlett-Packard.)

and whether its state can be changed by pulsing. (Short circuits to V_{CC} or to ground cannot be overriden by pulsing.)

2. Use the current tracer with the logic pulser to track the current directly to the faulty input.

3. Adjust the current-tracer reference level as required by turning the sensitivity control until the light barely glows when the pulser is operated in its 100Hz mode.

4. The current tracer will then enable the troubleshooter to run down the fault point.

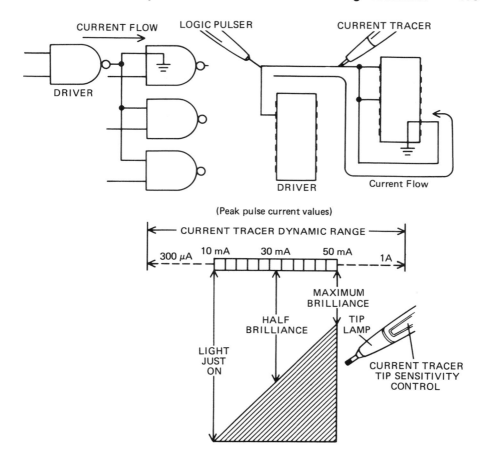

Fig. 13-2. Checking out a stuck node. (Courtesy, Hewlett-Packard.)

Note: Some TTL devices will be damaged if the output is short-circuited to ground for more than 1 second. For example, a NAND gate may normally draw up to 100 mA when its output is short-circuited to ground. In turn, the package is very likely to overheat if the short circuit is sustained.

FAULTS INSIDE IC PACKAGES

Internal short circuits within IC packages can cause puzzling troubleshooting problems unless proper test procedures are observed. A practical example of a grounded input inside of a flip-flop IC package is shown in Fig. 13-3. This fault can be pinpointed as follows:

1. The troubleshooter observed that the node between U1 and U2 was stuck low when checked with a logic probe, although pulse activity was observed at the input of U1 (a driver inverter).

2. When pin 1 of U2 was probed, no pulse activity was found. To follow up, pin 2 was pulsed to determine whether the node would change state.

3. In this case, the node did not change state. To follow up, current was traced from U1 to U2 pin 9.

4. This indicated that the current sink was inside of U2. The malfunction was corrected by replacing U2.

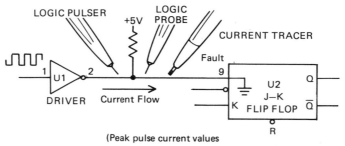

(Peak pulse current values

Settings	Current need for barely lit lamp	Current when lamp set for half-brilliance	Current that will produce a fully bright lamp
1	300 μA	1 mA	≥ 3 mA
2	1 mA	3 mA	≥ 5 mA
3	3 mA	5 mA	≥ 10 mA
4	5 mA	.10 mA	≥ 30 mA
5	10 mA	30 mA	≥ 50 mA
6	30 mA	50 mA	≥ 100 mA
7	50 mA	100 mA	≥ 500 mA
8	300 mA	500 mA	≥ 1 A

When a 10 mA current transition occurs and SENSITIVITY is set for half-brilliance of the tip lamp, the dynamic range of the current tracer is as follows:

DIM LAMP...5 mA
HALF-BRIGHT LAMP..10 mA
FULLY LIT LAMP...≥30 mA

Fig. 13-3. Localization of an internal short circuit.* (Courtesy, Hewlett-Packard.)

---

*This is an example of a J-K flip-flop. However, the same test procedure applies to any type of flip-flop.

Another Internal Failure

Another practical example of failure localization within an IC package is shown in Fig. 13-4. In this case, the shift-register outputs, A, B, C, and D, were found to be stuck logic-low, although pulse activity was normal at the other inputs. The trouble was pinpointed as follows:

1. The logic probe and pulser were applied to make certain that A, B, C, and D were not grounded. (If each pin is probed and pulsed, its state can be changed if it is ungrounded.)

2. Other pins on the IC were probed and checked for normal/abnormal responses.

3. Current was checked at pins A, B, C, and D by pulsing each pin and tracing to determine whether current flow takes place from the pulser to the shift register.

4. In this example, all signal activity was found to be normal except at A, B, C, and D. These pins were stuck logic-low, and did not indicate cur-

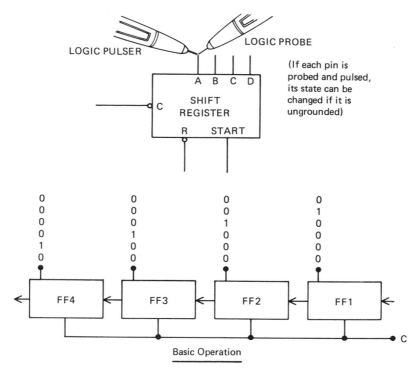

Fig. 13-4. Tracking down a fault inside of an IC package.

rent flow, which suggested an internal failure in the IC, instead of in the circuits connected to the IC.

TWO PC BOARDS WITH STUCK-LOW NODE

Still another practical example of a stuck-low troubleshooting problem is shown in Fig. 13-5. In this case, the troubleshooter determined that pin 13 on U1 was stuck logic-low. This problem was confused by the fact that the node comprising A1U8 pin 13, A2U1 pin 13, and A2U2 pin 4 was spread over two PC boards. The cause of the trouble was pinpointed as follows:

1. The logic comparator was first utilized to find the faulty node. This was identified as pin 13 on A1U8.

2. Probing and pulsing this node indicated that it was stuck logic-low.

3. In turn, probing and current tracing at pin 13 of A1U8 indicated that current was flowing toward PC board A2.

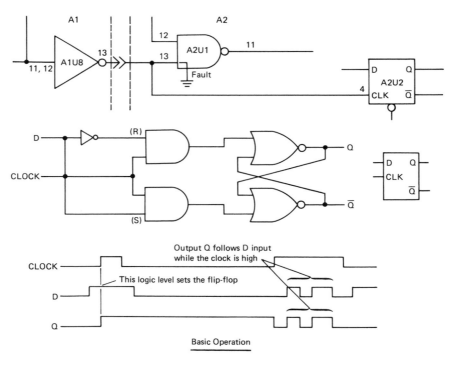

Fig. 13-5. Checking out a stuck-low malfunction. (Courtesy, Hewlett-Packard.)

4. It was observed that A2U1 was sinking current and holding the node log-ic-low. In turn, U2 was not being clocked. *Although the logic comparator localized the failure at pin 13 on A1U8, it required application of the cur-rent tracer to analyze current flow and to verify that A2U1 was the culprit.*

IC or PC Trouble?

One of the common "gremlins" in digital troubleshooting is the needless re-placement of an IC that appears to be faulty on the basis of initial tests, *when the defect is actually external to the IC.* A practical example is shown in Fig. 13-6. Using a logic probe and pulser, U1 tested bad. Although there appeared to be an internal short circuit, the following tests proved otherwise:

1. Pin 12 was pulsed, and it was observed that pin 13 changed state *but in the wrong direction.* (There was no inversion, and pin 13 "followed" pin 12.)

2. Conversely, pin 13 was pulsed, and it was observed that the injected cur-rent appeared at pin 12. *In normal operation, this is an impossible response.*

3. It was concluded that pins 12 and 13 were short-circuited together; a sol-der bridge was finally discovered on the back of the PC board.

A helpful summary of test procedures with logic probes, pulsers, and clips is tabulated in Fig. 13-7.

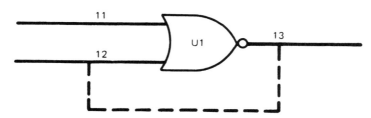

Note: Since a NOR gate is being checked in this example, a key consider-ation is whether the output is *inverted* with respect to the input. Another key consideration (with respect to any gate) is whether a pulse injected at the output terminal appears at the *input* terminal(s). *Although the in-put could be short-circuited to the output inside the IC, this fault is usu-ally in the circuitry external to the IC.*

Fig. 13-6. Distinction of internal defect from external defect. (Courtesy, Hewlett-Packard.)

Fault	Stimulus	Response	Test Method
Shorted Node	Pulser	Current Tracer	• Pulse node • Follow current pulses to short
Stuck Data Bus	Pulser	Current Tracer	• Pulse bus line • Trace current to device holding the bus in a stuck condition
Signal Line Short Circuit	Pulser	Probe Current Tracer	• Pulse and probe test point simultaneously • Short to V_{cc} or ground cannot be overridden by pulsing • Pulse test point, and follow current pulses to the short with tracer
V_{cc}-to-Gnd Short Circuit	Pulser	Current Tracer	• Remove power from test circuit • Disconnect electrolytic bypass capacitors • Pulse across V_{cc} and ground using accessory connectors provided • Trace current to fault
Apparent Open in IC	Pulser	Probe	• Pulse device input • Probe output for response

Fault	Stimulus	Response	Test Method
Solder Bridge	Pulser	Current Tracer	• Pulse suspect line(s) • Trace current pulses to the fault (Light goes out when solder bridge passed)
Sequential Logic	Pulser	Clip	• Circuit clock deactivated • Use Pulser to enter desired number of pulses • Clip onto counter or shift register and verify device's truth table

Fig. 13-7. Summary of test procedures with logic probes, pulsers, and clips. (Courtesy, Hewlett-Packard.)

Note on IC Swapping and Card Swapping

The troubleshooter occasionally encounters digital systems that have ICs plugged into sockets. When this design is employed, the troubleshooting job is easier because preliminary quick checks can be made by swapping similar IC packages back and forth to determine whether the trouble symptom changes. Moreover, substitution tests can be quickly made by plugging new ICs in place of suspected ICs.

Elaborate digital systems that employ many cards (plug-in PC boards) are also encountered occasionally. Sometimes two or more of the cards will have identical circuitry. In such a case, the troubleshooter can swap similar cards back and forth, to determine whether the trouble symptom changes. *Caution: If dissimilar cards are accidentally swapped, the result is likely to "make bad cards out of good ones."*

LOGIC CLIP

Previous mention was made of the logic clip (see Fig. 13-8). The logic clip differs from the logic probe in two basic particulars. A logic clip has a single

Fig. 13-8. Appearance of a logic clip. (Courtesy, Hewlett-Packard.)

threshold in contrast to the two thresholds provided in a logic probe. In turn, the logic clip cannot indicate a bad level; the clip responds to a bad level in the same manner as a TTL gate—it "sees" a logic-high state.

Note also that a logic clip does not have pulse-stretching circuitry—to check for high-frequency or single-shot narrow pulses, the logic probe should be used instead. Because the logic clip has the ability to display signal activity on several pins simultaneously, it will often save considerable time in troubleshooting procedures. For example, in checking out a 7490 decade counter, it is necessary to view at least one input and four outputs simultaneously to determine whether operation is normal.

The logic probe and clip provide a response mode of operation to the troubleshooter that is optimized to digital signals. As previously noted, the mainstay of all digital troubleshooting is stimulus-response testing. In other words, it is necessary to apply a signal and to observe the response in order to determine whether the device is operating normally.

Signal application can be a difficult requirement in circuits that have very low internal resistance. However, the logic pulser provides the necessary drive in all circuits (with the exception of Gnd and V_{CC} buses). Thus, the troubleshooter can jump rapidly from point to point in a circuit, applying pulses and observing responses.

SHIFT REGISTERS REVISITED

A logic clip is useful in checking shift-register operation, inasmuch as a multiplicity of terminals are involved. Sometimes a shift register will exhibit a "stuck at" trouble symptom. This malfunction can be caused by a fault external to the IC, or to a failure inside of the IC. A current tracer is very helpful to distinguish between these two possibilities.

With reference to the case history in Fig. 13-9, a test with a logic probe showed that the "stuck-low" pins were grounded. Next, a current tracer was utilized to determine whether the ground fault was internal or external to the IC. The current tracer tracked the fault up to the input terminals of the IC; in turn, this finding indicated that the fault was internal to the IC.

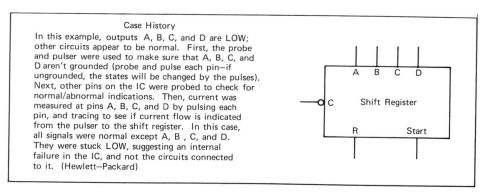

Fig. 13-9. Troubleshooting a ground fault in a shift-register circuit.

PROPAGATION TIME MEASUREMENT

When tracking down glitches, troubleshooters are occasionally concerned with checking propagation time. In other words, if one pulse is slightly delayed with respect to another pulse in some types of gate circuitry, a spurious glitch signal may be generated. In turn, the glitch can produce malfunctioning in subsequent circuitry—the glitch cannot be distinguished from a valid digital pulse.

With respect to Fig. 13-10, observe that the delay time of a flip-flop is typically 20 ns. This is a very short time interval, but it can be easily measured with a high-performance dual-trace scope. In this example, TP denotes a propagation-time error between the channel-A and channel-B signals. The propagation time is measured as follows:

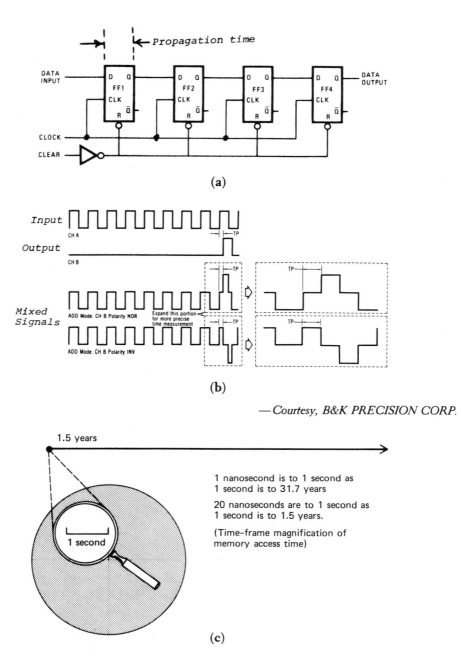

—Courtesy, B&K PRECISION CORP.

Fig. 13-10. Propagation time measurement. (a) A flip-flop has a normal propagation time of approximately 20 ns; (b) a high-performance dual-trace scope provides measurement of propagation time (TP); (c) meaning of the nanosecond unit.

1. Operate the oscilloscope in its Add mode or Subtract mode. In turn, a mixed waveform is displayed and the displacement of leading edges in the component signals clearly indicates the propagation time.

2. Expand the pattern in order to observe the propagation-time interval more precisely.

3. Note the setting of the time base, and calculate the propagation time accordingly.

BASIC DIGITAL TROUBLESHOOTING RULES

When troubleshooting a large digital system with various long lines and peripherals, it is sometimes a temptation to subdivide the job and to assign a crew of troubleshooters to various stations. However, it is good practice to limit the crew to two technicians. In other words, more than two workers on the same system can lead to confusion and lost time.

It was previously noted that obvious trouble possibilities should be investigated first—measure V_{CC}, check all cables and connectors, and make certain that system operating controls are correctly set. (If you find an obvious fault, multiple trouble symptoms may suddenly disappear.)

Play it cool—proceed with deliberate caution and make sure that no trouble symptoms are overlooked. Have adequate digital test equipment at hand. If you cannot "break the case," take a breather and don't get "up tight"—stop for a cup of coffee, and talk it over with your partner.

Analyze and subdivide the digital system. It can happen that the malfunction is being caused by a device that is not in use. It may be helpful to disconnect peripherals and to check out the basic system. If the basic system is okay, reconnect the peripherals one by one.

It is always a temptation to make unjustified assumptions—never assume that a signal must be present, nor that it must be a good signal until it has been checked out. Double-check your partner's test data, in case of doubt. Remember that human nature tends to see what it wants to see.

After you have restored a "tough dog" to normal operation, review your attack on the trouble symptoms. Could you have taken a more effective approach? If you had it to do over again, would you modify your test techniques? A review of this kind can be helpful in sharpening your expertise.

NOTE ON EXCEPTIONS

The troubleshooter becomes progressively aware of exceptions to general rules

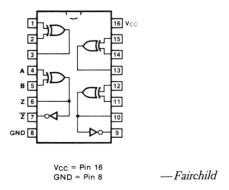

Vcc = Pin 16
GND = Pin 8

—*Fairchild*

Fig. 13-11. Pinout for the 9014 quad 2-input XOR/XNOR gate.

Octal Addition Table

(Decimal)	0	1	2	3	4	5	6	7	8	9	10	11	12	13	14	15	16	17	18
	+	0	1	2	3	4	5	6	7	10	11	12	13	14	15	16	17	20	21	22
0	0	0	1	2	3	4	5	6	7	10	11	12	13	14	15	16	17	20	21	22
1	1	1	2	3	4	5	6	7	10	11	12	13	14	15	16	17	20	21	22	23
2	2	2	3	4	5	6	7	10	11	12	13	14	15	16	17	20	21	22	23	24
3	3	3	4	5	6	7	10	11	12	13	14	15	16	17	20	21	22	23	24	25
4	4	4	5	6	7	10	11	12	13	14	15	16	17	20	21	22	23	24	25	26
5	5	5	6	7	10	11	12	13	14	15	16	17	20	21	22	23	24	25	26	27
6	6	6	7	10	11	12	13	14	15	16	17	20	21	22	23	24	25	26	27	30
7	7	7	10	11	12	13	14	15	16	17	20	21	22	23	24	25	26	27	30	31
8	10	10	11	12	13	14	15	16	17	20	21	22	23	24	25	26	27	30	31	32
9	11	11	12	13	14	15	16	17	20	21	22	23	24	25	26	27	30	31	32	33
10	12	12	13	14	15	16	17	20	21	22	23	24	25	26	27	30	31	32	33	34
11	13	13	14	15	16	17	20	21	22	23	24	25	26	27	30	31	32	33	34	35
12	14	14	15	16	17	20	21	22	23	24	25	26	27	30	31	32	33	34	35	36
13	15	15	16	17	20	21	22	23	24	25	26	27	30	31	32	33	34	35	36	37
14	16	16	17	20	21	22	23	24	25	26	27	30	31	32	33	34	35	36	37	40
15	17	17	20	21	22	23	24	25	26	27	30	31	32	33	34	35	36	37	40	41
16	20	20	21	22	23	24	25	26	27	30	31	32	33	34	35	36	37	40	41	42
17	21	21	22	23	24	25	26	27	30	31	32	33	34	35	36	37	40	41	42	43
18	22	22	23	24	25	26	27	30	31	32	33	34	35	36	37	40	41	42	43	44

Example: Decimal 5 + 4 = Octal 11.

Fig. 13-12. Octal Addition Table.

in digital practice. For example, a gate is defined as a circuit that has two or more inputs and one output, the output being dependent upon the combination of logic signals at the inputs. However, the 9014 quad XOR gate, also known as the quad 2-input XOR/XNOR gate has two outputs.

As depicted in Fig. 13-11, the 9014 consists of four XOR gates; two of the XOR gates have an additional inverted output which provides directly a compare capability (used in code conversion, parity generation/checking, and comparison applications). The Boolean expressions for the gates are: $Z = A\overline{B} + \overline{A}B$; $\overline{Z} = AB + \overline{A}\overline{B}$. Thus, the 9014 violates the standard definition for a gate.

Troubleshooters are chiefly concerned with binary numbers in digital system operation. However, there are exceptions. For example, octal numbers are occasionally processed (Fig. 13-12). Again, hexadecimal numbers are occasionally processed (Fig. 13-13). The tables make it easy to "look up" the sum of a pair of octal numbers, or the sum of a pair of hexadecimal numbers.

Hexadecimal Addition Table

(Decimal)	0	1	2	3	4	5	6	7	8	9	10	11	12	13	14	15	16
	+	0	1	2	3	4	5	6	7	8	9	A	B	C	D	E	F	10
0	0	0	1	2	3	4	5	6	7	8	9	A	B	C	D	E	F	10
1	1	1	2	3	4	5	6	7	8	9	A	B	C	D	E	F	10	11
2	2	2	3	4	5	6	7	8	9	A	B	C	D	E	F	10	11	12
3	3	3	4	5	6	7	8	9	A	B	C	D	E	F	10	11	12	13
4	4	4	5	6	7	8	9	A	B	C	D	E	F	10	11	12	13	14
5	5	5	6	7	8	9	A	B	C	D	E	F	10	11	12	13	14	15
6	6	6	7	8	9	A	B	C	D	E	F	10	11	12	13	14	15	16
7	7	7	8	9	A	B	C	D	E	F	10	11	12	13	14	15	16	17
8	8	8	9	A	B	C	D	E	F	10	11	12	13	14	15	16	17	18
9	9	9	A	B	C	D	E	F	10	11	12	13	14	15	16	17	18	19
10	A	A	B	C	D	E	F	10	11	12	13	14	15	16	17	18	19	1A
11	B	B	C	D	E	F	10	11	12	13	14	15	16	17	18	19	1A	1B
12	C	C	D	E	F	10	11	12	13	14	15	16	17	18	19	1A	1B	1C
13	D	D	E	F	10	11	12	13	14	15	16	17	18	19	1A	1B	1C	1D
14	E	E	F	10	11	12	13	14	15	16	17	18	19	1A	1B	1C	1D	1E
15	F	F	10	11	12	13	14	15	16	17	18	19	1A	1B	1C	1D	1E	1F
16	10	10	11	12	13	14	15	16	17	18	19	1A	1B	1C	1D	1E	1F	20

Example: Decimal 6 + 5 = Hexadecimal B.

Fig. 13-13. Hexadecimal Addition Table.

14

Digital Trouble Symptom Analysis

Requirement for Trouble Symptom Analysis • Example • Decimal/7-Segment Encoder • Four-Bit Toggle Flip-Flop Counter • Timing Diagram with Stuck-High Fault • Multiplexers • Demultiplexers • Parallel Adder • Digital Word Recognizer

REQUIREMENT FOR TROUBLE SYMPTOM ANALYSIS

Although each gate in a digital configuration has a truth table, and although each gate can be checked in-circuit with a logic probe and pulser, this "shotgun method" wastes an excessive amount of time when troubleshooting a complex digital system. *To expedite a troubleshooting job, configurations should first be analyzed with respect to the observed trouble symptoms. Thereby, the trouble-shooter can avoid wasted time in checking out obviously "good" gates.*

Example: With reference to Fig. 14-1, a widely used configuration is shown for a binary coded decimal (BCD) converter. This basic circuit is used, for example, for conversion of binary numbers into decimal numbers for a readout display. In this example, the binary number 0011 is inputted—the decimal number 3 will be outputted in normal operation.

The BCD-to-decimal code converter comprises ten AND gates and four inverters. Binary numbers are inputted in parallel (all four are applied simultaneously). The inputs are weighted 8-4-2-1, as indicated in the diagram. Inverter outputs are weighted $\bar{8}$-$\bar{4}$-$\bar{2}$-$\bar{1}$.

An AND gate in Fig. 14-1 will have a logic-low output unless all four of its inputs are driven logic-high. In the cited example, thick lines are normally driven logic-high, and thin lines are normally driven logic-low.

Consider the trouble symptom analysis that is associated with a decimal readout of 2 (instead of 3) in the example of Fig. 14-1. In this situation, it is evident that all four inputs of gate 2 are logic-high, and that all four inputs of gate 3 are not logic-high. Trouble symptom analysis leads to the following conclusions:

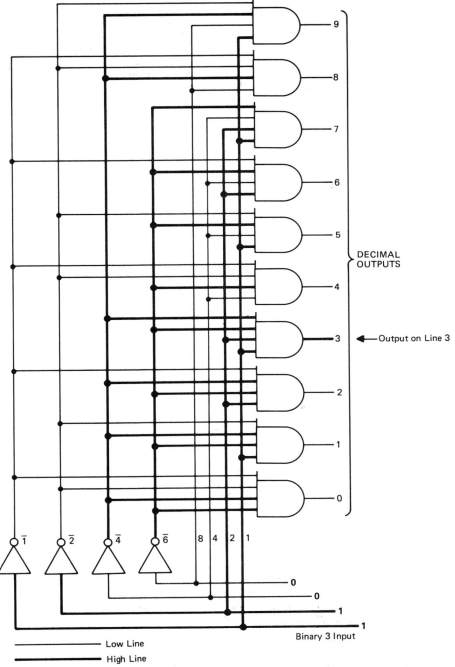

DECIMAL OUTPUTS

Output on Line 3

$\overline{1}$ $\overline{2}$ $\overline{4}$ $\overline{6}$ 8   4   2   1

0

0

1

1

Binary 3 Input

——— Low Line

——— High Line

Fig. 14-1. A BCD-to-decimal code converter generating a 3 output in response to a 0011 input.

1. The weight-1 input line is short-circuited to ground.
2. Both gate 2 and gate 3 are defective.

Since the first possibility has a much higher probability than the second, *the troubleshooter will immediately proceed to check out the weight-1 input line for short circuit to ground.*

Another Example: With reference to Fig. 14-2, a widely used configuration for a decimal-to-binary encoder is shown. This is a diode matrix network; it changes decimal numbers, as from a keyboard, into binary numbers for data processing. In the cited example, the decimal 6 keyswitch has been closed. In turn, the binary number 0110 is normally outputted.

Consider the trouble symptom analysis that is associated with a binary read-out of 0111 (instead of 0110) in the example of Fig. 14-2. In this situation, it is evident that a circuit fault is causing binary output line A to be driven logic-high, when it should be logic-low. Trouble symptom analysis leads to the following conclusions:

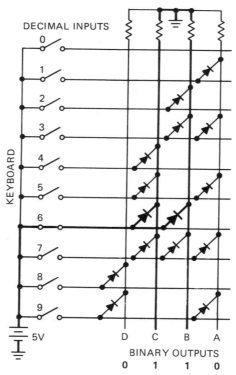

Fig. 14-2. Decimal-to-binary encoder implemented as a diode matrix.

1. If binary output line A remains logic-high when the decimal 6 keyswitch is opened, output line A is short-circuited to V_{CC}.

2. If binary output line A goes logic-low when the decimal 6 keyswitch is opened, the diode 7-C or 7-B is short-circuited and is permitting "sneak current" to enter binary output line A.

Thus, the troubleshooter would not take a "shotgun approach," but would confine his tests to binary output line A and its associated 7-B and 7-C diodes. Of course, individual diodes are accessible in Fig. 14-2 only if the matrix is implemented in discrete-logic form. If the matrix is in IC form, the entire IC must be replaced.

DECIMAL/SEVEN-SEGMENT ENCODER

Another practical example of digital trouble symptom analysis is shown in Fig. 14-3. Here, a widely used type of decimal/seven-segment matrix encoder for driving a readout display is exemplified. Each of the segments in the readout character is illuminated by an LED, which in turn is energized by an output line from the matrix. The matrix encodes decimal digits.

In this example, the decimal digit seven is encoded into an a-b-c output to display a numeral seven in the readout. Encoding is accomplished by diode switches that feed an applied logic-high level to corresponding LED segments.

Consider the trouble symptom analysis that is associated with a readout of 1111111 (instead of 1110000) in the example of Fig. 14-3. In the situation, it is evident that output line 8 is abnormally logic-high. In turn, the troubleshooter concludes that the following possibilities should be checked out:

1. If the abnormal readout 1111111 persists when input line 7 is driven logic-low, line 8 will be found short-circuited to V_{CC}.

2. On the other hand, if the readout returns to 0000000 when input line 7 is driven logic-low, diode 8-a, 8-b, or 8-c will be found short-circuited (thereby permitting entry of "sneak current" into line 8).

FOUR-BIT TOGGLE FLIP-FLOP COUNTER

A widely used four-bit binary counter arrangement that provides a helpful example of digital trouble symptom analysis is shown in Fig. 14-4. This configuration uses J-K flip-flops with the J and K inputs of FF1 maintained logic-high.

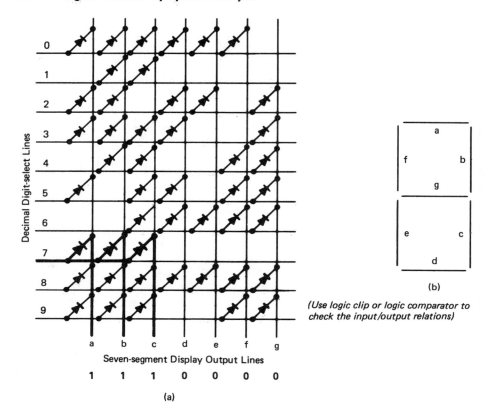

(a)

(Use logic clip or logic comparator to check the input/output relations)

(b)

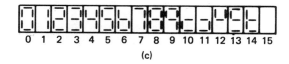

(c)

Fig. 14-3. Decimal/seven-segment diode matrix encoder. (a) Matrix configuration; (b) segment identification; (c) readout characters.

In turn, FF1 toggles on each clock pulse. FF2 toggles on the arrival of a clock pulse, provided that the Q output of FF1 is logic-high.

This counter does not employ ripple carry; instead, AND gates U1 and U2 function as "look ahead" devices, so that there is minimum delay in finalization of the count. For example, suppose that the count is 1111, and that a clock pulse is then applied. Both inputs of U1 are logic-high, and all three inputs of U2 are logic-high. In turn, the outputs of both AND gates are logic-high. Ac-

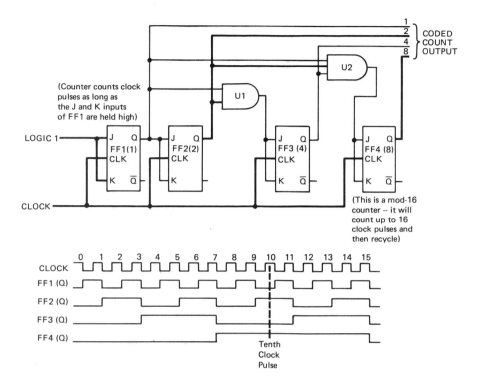

Note: This counter may be easily constructed by the experimenter on a Radio Shack Experimenter Socket 276-174, with two dual J-K flip-flops 276-1803, and a quad two-input AND gate 276-1822. (U2 is configured from two AND gates.) The Clear input on the FF is not asserted, and may be tied to V_{CC}.

Fig. 14-4. A binary counter configuration with timing diagram. (Courtesy, Hewlett-Packard.)

cordingly, when the clock pulse arrives, all four flip-flops immediately "flop" to 0, without waiting for carries to ripple through.

Consider the trouble symptom analysis that is followed in case the readout is 0111 (instead of 0101) on the tenth clock pulse. As seen in Fig. 14-4, the Q output of FF3 should be logic-low on the tenth clock pulse—in this trouble situation, the Q output of FF3 is logic-high. It follows from circuit analysis that the possible causes of malfunction are:

1. The Q output of FF3 may be short-circuited to V_{CC}. In this case, the Q output checks logic-high regardless of the count.

2. The two lower inputs of U2 may be short-circuited together. If so, both of these inputs will always go logic-high or logic-low simultaneously.

To quickly distinguish between these two possibilities, the troubleshooter may turn off the power and measure the resistance from the Q output of FF3 to V_{CC}. If this resistance measures zero, he will conclude that there is a short circuit. On the other hand, if a finite resistance is measured, he proceeds to make further tests.

As explained in the previous chapter, practically infinite resistance will normally be measured between the two lower inputs of U2 in Fig. 14-4. Therefore, if the troubleshooter measures zero resistance between these inputs, the suspicion of a short circuit between the inputs is confirmed. *However, the troubleshooter cannot conclude at this point whether the short circuit is in the external circuit, or inside of U2. Additional tests with the logic pulser and current tracer are necessary to distinguish between these possibilities.*

Timing Diagram with Stuck-High Fault

Consider the timing diagram for the foregoing binary counter configuration with the Q output of FF3 stuck logic-high. This trouble symptom analysis is shown in Fig. 14-5. Observe that the coded count output 4 is always logic-high. In turn, the lower input of AND gate U2 is always logic-high. Timing waveforms for FF1 and FF2 are unaffected by the short to V_{CC}. On the other hand, timing waveforms for FF3 and FF4 are abnormal. Note that when the Q outputs of FF1 and FF2 go logic-low, the Q output of FF4 goes prematurely logic-high inasmuch as the lower input of U2 is stuck logic-high.

Many troubleshooters use dual-trace oscilloscopes, such as illustrated in Fig. 14-6. Although all of the waveforms in a counter timing diagram cannot be displayed simultaneously, any pair of waveforms may be displayed. For example, with reference to Fig. 14-5, FF1(Q) may be displayed with FF2(Q) below it. Then, FF3(Q) may be displayed in place of FF2(Q), and finally, FF4(Q) may be displayed below FF1(Q). Note that in the case of FF3(Q), only a horizontal trace at the logic-high level is displayed, using the dc input function of the oscilloscope.

MULTIPLEXERS

The troubleshooter encounters various types of multiplexers in digital systems. One basic configuration is shown in Fig. 14-7. A multiplexer functions to

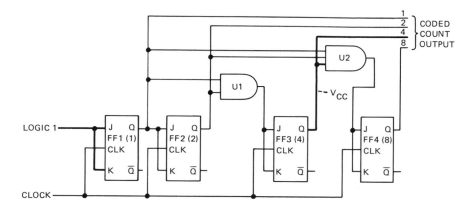

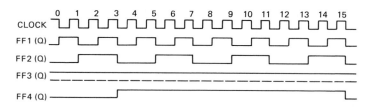

Note: Timing waveforms can be checked to best advantage with a multi-channel oscilloscope. However, the troubleshooter can obtain the same data with a logic probe by manually clocking the counter through a complete cycle of operation.

Fig. 14-5. Timing diagram for binary counter configuration with the Q output of FF3 stuck logic-high.

rearrange the digital data on multiple input lines (D0 through D7), and to output the rearranged data on a single output line (T). In the example of Fig. 14-7, an eight-channel multiplexer is controlled by three binary address lines.

The logic state that is present on any selected input (D0 through D7) is placed in a chosen sequence on the output line T. Observe that this sequence is determined by the particular binary addresses that are clocked into the multiplexer. Thus, the address inputs, $A_0A_1A_2$ (000, 001, 010, 011, etc.), are stepped in binary code to select a particular input at a given time.

As an illustration of multiplexer action, the logic-high lines corresponding to the address 010 are shown as thick lines in Fig. 14-7. If the inhibit line is driven logic-high, it is apparent that a logic-high bit at D2 will be channeled

Model 1477 5" Dual-Trace 15 MHz Triggered Scope

Fig. 14-6. A dual-trace, 15MHz triggered-sweep oscilloscope with ac or dc input facilities. (Courtesy, B&K Precision Dynascan Corp.)

through to output T. Again, an address input, $A_0 = 0$, $A_1 = 0$, and $A_2 = 0$, will channel the logic state that is present at D0 through to output T.

A multiplexer may mix signals from multiple sources in various ways into a smaller number of outputs. (The foregoing example of mixing eight data lines into a particular sequence on a single output line merely represents one widely used mode of operation.)

Other multiplexing modes function to multiplex four input lines into one output line, or to multiplex 16 input lines into one output line. A digital word multiplexer may operate to multiplex three four-bit-wide parallel words into a single four-bit-wide serial output. Observe that if a fixed binary address is applied to a multiplexer, the configuration will continuously channel data from

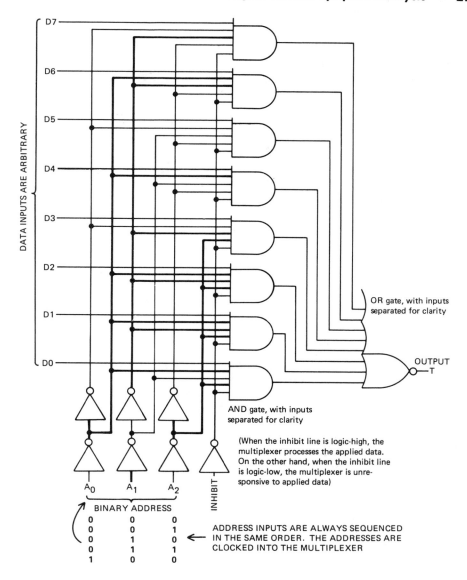

Fig. 14-7. A common configuration for a multiplexer, with example of address input.

one input through to the output line, T. This mode of operation is termed *data selection*, and the multiplexer is being operated as a *data selector*.

Consider the following example of trouble symptom analysis for the multiplexer arrangement shown in Fig. 14-7. If the binary address 010 channels the data from data input D3 into output T (instead of channeling the data from data input D2 into output T), the following possibilities would be checked out:

1. One of the binary address lines may be short-circuited to ground or to V_{CC}. (It is not probable that more than one short circuit would occur.)
2. Two gates may have become defective (not highly probable).
3. Incorrect addresses (data errors) may be inputted.

Observe in Fig. 14-7 that if the output of the first inverter in the A_0 address line becomes short-circuited to ground, its output goes logic-low and the output from the second inverter in the A_0 address line goes logic-high. The result is that data input D2 cannot enter a bit into the multiplexer—but data input D3 can now enter a bit into the multiplexer.

Accordingly, the troubleshooter will proceed to check out binary address line A_0 with a logic probe, pulser, and current tracer to determine whether the malfunction is located in this line. If the suspected short circuit to ground is verified, the current tracer will serve to indicate whether the fault is inside of an IC package or in the external node.

If binary address line A_0 is cleared from suspicion of a short circuit to ground, it could then be theorized that the AND gate in the D2 data input is not passing a bit when it should, and that the AND gate in the D3 data input is passing a bit when it should not. *When this possibility arises, the troubleshooter should immediately measure V_{CC}—an out-of-limits V_{CC} voltage can make two or three gates "look bad," although they will again function normally when V_{CC} is brought within rated tolerance.*

The third possibility of malfunction, incorrect addresses inputted, can occur as a result of malfunction in any section of the prior address circuitry. Therefore, a systematic checkout of the address generating and processing will be required. As a practical note, "tough-dog" address generation and processing problems can be caused by glitches resulting from out-of-tolerance timing relations. Most glitches can be "caught" by a logic probe that is provided with a pulse stretcher and memory.

DEMULTIPLEXERS

A widely used type of demultiplexer is shown in Fig. 14-8. It has the opposite function from that of a multiplexer. As indicated in the diagram, a demultiplexer inputs data from a single source (T), and distributes the data in accordance with a chosen pattern into several input lines.

Observe in Fig. 14-8 that *the address word is applied in parallel to the binary address inputs.* Serial data is inputted at T, and is rearranged on various of the eight output lines D0 through D7. Address words are clocked into the demultiplexer. In this example, $A_0 = 0$, $A_1 = 1$, and $A_2 = 1$. In turn, the logic-high nodes are indicated by thick lines.

If a logic-low bit is now applied at T, it is evident that this data bit will be routed through the circuitry into output line D6. This routing occurs only for the binary address word 011—in the case of binary address word 100, the data bit would be routed through the circuitry into output line D1. Or, in the case of binary address word 010, the data bit would be routed through the circuitry into output line D2.

The troubleshooter will encounter other demultiplexer arrangements that distribute data from a single input line into 2, 4, 6, and other numbers of output lines. *Note that instead of being demultiplexed, the serial data applied at T can be gated by means of the A_0 A_1 A_2 address lines through any one of the output lines continuously. Then, at some later time, the address may be changed and the inputted data continuously gated into another output line.* In this case, the demultiplexer is operating as a *data distributor.*

Note that a demultiplexer may also function as a *decoder.* In other words, if input line T is held logic-high, *the outputs will always represent the binary count corresponding to the logic levels on binary address lines A_0, A_1, A_2.* As an illustration, the logic levels 101 on the binary address lines result in D5 going logic-high—T is now operating as an Enable function.

A demultiplexer with 4 address lines and 16 output lines may be operated as a 4-line-to-16-line decoder.

Consider the following example of trouble symptom analysis for the demultiplexer shown in Fig. 14-8. If there is no output from the demultiplexer, regardless of the logic states of inputs A_0, A_1, A_2 and T, the troubleshooter will investigate these possibilities:

1. The data input, T, may be stuck logic-high, or the T inverter output node may be stuck logic-low.

2. There may be a V_{CC} power failure to the demultiplexer.

3. More than one device may have failed, resulting in the complete lack of output.

Since the first trouble analysis is the most probable from a statistical standpoint, the troubleshooter will start by investigating the T nodes for a stuck-high

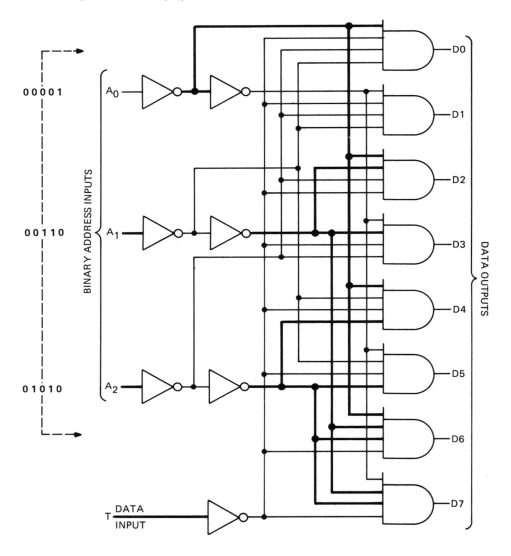

The data input in this example
is ACTIVE-LOW. When T is driven
logic-low by a data bit, output
D6 will go logic-high.

Fig. 14-8. A widely used demultiplexer configuration, with example of address input.

or a stuck-low fault. This suspicion can be quickly verified or cleared by quick-checking with a logic pulser, probe, and current tracer.

The second possibility (V_{CC} power failure) can be checked with a dc voltmeter. Note that the presence of V_{CC} voltage can be established with a logic probe —however, $V_{CC} = 4V$ "looks good" to a logic probe, whereas 4.5V is the absolute minimum V_{CC} rating for typical TTL circuitry.

The third possibility (multiple device failures) is the least probable cause of complete lack of output from the demultiplexer. *Note, however, that V_{CC} REGULATOR TROUBLE can result in the supply voltage exceeding the absolute maximum V_{CC} rating of 5.5V, with consequent damage to some or all of the devices in the demultiplexer.*

PARALLEL ADDER

The troubleshooter encounters many parallel-type adders, as exemplified in Fig. 14-9. Observe that the augend in this example is A_4, A_3, A_2, $A_1 = 1011$, and the addend is B_4, B_3, B_2, $B_1 = 0110$. In turn, the sum at the output of the adder is 10001. The augend is a nibble, and the addend is a nibble. Both nibbles are applied simultaneously at the adder inputs.

Consider the trouble symptom analysis that is incurred in case the sum is incorrectly outputted as 10000 (instead of 10001). This trouble symptom can be caused by the following faults:

1. The LSB (least significant bit) inverter output may be short-circuited to ground.
2. The LSB inverter input may be short-circuited to V_{CC}.
3. There may be an internal failure in the LSB inverter.

The troubleshooter can quickly check out these possibilities with a logic probe, pulser, and current tracer. In the event that less probable faults need to be checked out, the logic states of the devices in the LSB section can be investigated with a logic probe. Note that the four-bit full adder might be fabricated from discrete components, or it might consist of several interconnected ICs, or all of the devices might be included in a single IC. In the latter situation, the troubleshooter is concerned only with whether the fault is in the external circuitry or inside the IC.

DIGITAL WORD RECOGNIZER

When troubleshooting parallel adders and similar data processing circuitry, a

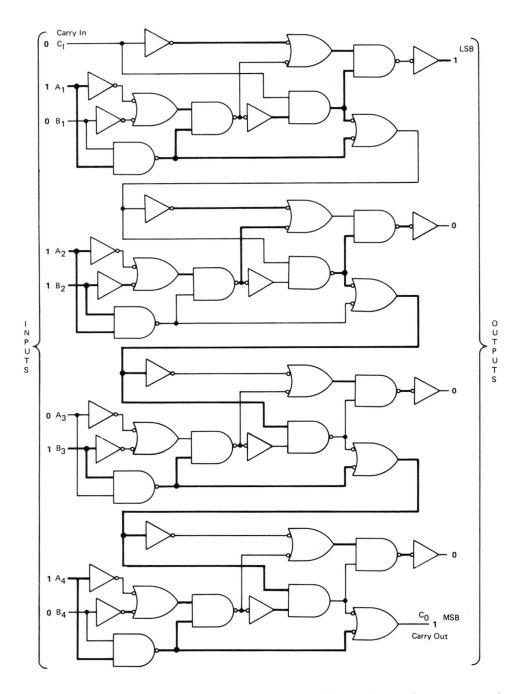

Fig. 14-9. A four-bit full adder; parallel adder with ripple carry, and example of operation.

digital word recognizer may be helpful—and may be indispensable when troubleshooting complex networks. A configuration for a four-bit digital word recognizer is shown in Fig. 14-10. It consists of an AND gate with series input inverters. Each inverter can be short-circuited by throwing an SPST microswitch.

The word recognizer can be programmed for response to any chosen four-bit binary number. For example, if the chosen number is A_3, A_2, A_1, $A_0 = 0000$, all four switches are opened. In turn, the piezo buzzer will sound if the parallel

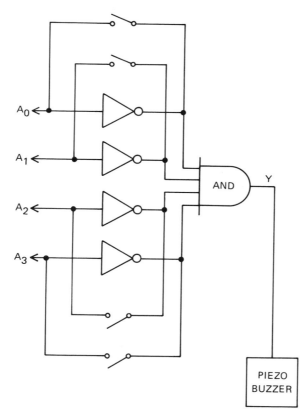

Note: This digital word recognizer arrangment can be "programmed" to respond to any chosen four-bit binary number. When the target number is applied to the inputs, the piezo buzzer will sound. On the other hand, when any other number is applied to the inputs, the piezo buzzer will remain silent.

Fig. 14-10. A four-bit digital word recognizer.

data stream inputs the word 0000 into the recognizer. On the other hand, the piezo buzzer will remain silent if the parallel data stream inputs the word 0010, or 1000, or 0111 into the recognizer.

Next, if the chosen number is A_3, A_2, A_1, $A_0 = 1111$, all four switches are closed. In turn, the piezo buzzer will sound if the parallel data stream inputs the word 1111 into the recognizer. On the other hand, no other combination of bits will be recognized.

Or, if the chosen number is A_3, A_2, A_1, $A_0 = 1001$, and A_3 and A_0 switches are closed, but the A_2 and A_1 switches are opened. Accordingly, the piezo buzzer will sound if the parallel data stream inputs the word 1001 into the recognizer. However, no other combination of bits will be recognized.

If the troubleshooter is concerned with three-bit words, one input of the recognizer is tied to a logic-high point, and the other three inputs are connected into the data bus. Again, if the troubleshooter is concerned with eight-bit words (bytes), an eight-input AND gate is employed with the same input circuitry depicted in Fig. 14-10.

15

Digital Signature Multimeter Familiarization

Overview of the Signature Multimeter • Data Stream Signatures • Pseudorandom Binary Sequence Signal • Cyclic Redundancy Check Code • Troubleshooting Features • Retrofit Notes • Home Computer Troubleshooting • Block Diagram Features • Memory Map Features • Freerunning the Z80 • Freerun Fixture Features • Signature Analysis Test Storage, Access, and Selection • SA Stimulus Routines • Access • Stack Establishment • Troubleshooting Tradeoff Considerations • Test Selection • Flowchart and Assembly Language Code • Hardware and Software for Start, Stop, and Clock • Detecting Start, Stop, and Data with the Clock • RS-232C Port

OVERVIEW OF THE SIGNATURE MULTIMETER

A signature multimeter (Fig. 15-1) is used for component-level troubleshooting of microprocessor-based products. *Its chief function is the detection and display of unique digital signatures associated with the data nodes in a circuit under test. By comparing these actual signatures to the correct ones, a troubleshooter can back-trace to a faulty node.* The SMM illustration in Fig. 15-1 includes timing and multimeter measurements for a total of ten troubleshooting functions, as follows:

1. Normal signature detection and display.
2. Qualified signature detection and display.
3. DC voltage measurement.
4. Differential voltage measurement.
5. Resistance measurement.
6. Frequency measurement.

Fig. 15-1. Signature multimeter is used to troubleshoot microprocessor-based digital circuitry. (Courtesy, Hewlett-Packard.)

7. Totalizing counter.
8. Time interval measurement.
9. Peak voltage measurement.
10. Logic probe function.

DATA STREAM SIGNATURES

A *microprocessor* is the control and processing portion of a microcomputer that is fabricated on (usually) one chip. A *microcomputer* (Fig. 15-2) is a general-purpose computer comprising large-scale integrated components built around the central processing unit (microprocessor). The *data stream* is a sequence of high and low voltages (digital pulses) that represent binary 1's and 0's. As noted in the diagram, a signature multimeter compresses a data stream into a four-character, alphanumeric "funny hex" readout.

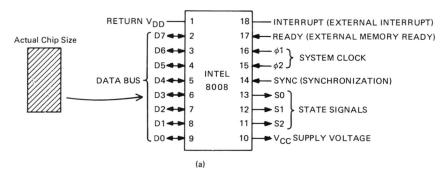

(a)

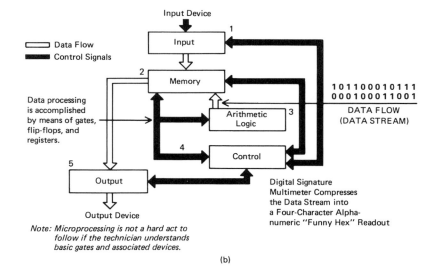

(b)

Fig. 15-2. Microprocessor and microcomputer. (a) Package pinout for the 8008 microprocessor; (b) microcomputer operates with a microprocessor, memory, input, and output devices.

In other words, a signature multimeter displays conventionalized hexadecimal signatures that are present on a circuit node in response to an injected test signal. An example of microprocessor signatures is shown in Fig. 15-3. A hexadecimal signature is obtained by means of data compression—thus, an extensive serial stream of data on a node will be compressed into a four-character hexadecimal signature, such as A22P.

Note in passing that the hexadecimal digits are:
1,2,3,4,5,6,7,8,9,A,B,C,D,E,F

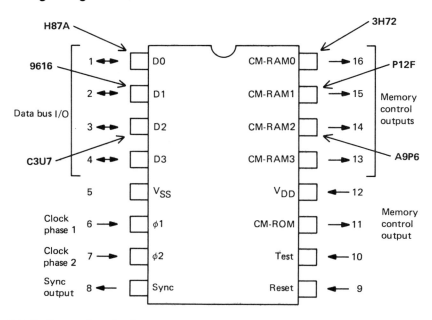

Fig. 15-3. Example of microprocessor signatures.

On the other hand, the "funny hex" digits used in the signature multimeter are:

1,2,3,4,5,6,7,8,9,A,C,F,H,P,U

PSEUDORANDOM BINARY SEQUENCE SIGNAL

A signature multimeter compresses a data stream into a four-character, "funny hex" readout which is fundamentally a pseudorandom binary sequence (PRBS) signal. Note that the PRBS signal does not function to display conventionally meaningful data on a node—*the node signature, although unique, is arbitrary. A node signature has meaning only with respect to the corresponding node signature in a normally functioning circuit.*

Apart from this correspondence (or lack of correspondence), an SMM signature provides no diagnostic information—it is essentially a go/no-go type of analysis. *When the troubleshooter localizes a malfunctioning node on the basis of its SMM signature, he then proceeds to pinpoint the defect by means of logic pulsing, probing, and/or current tracing.* The illustrated SMM includes a built-in logic-probe function.

CYCLIC REDUNDANCY CHECK CODE

SMM operation is based on a cyclic redundancy check (CRC) code, which is a type of check sum. The short, repetitive circuit exercise which is required as a stimulus for signature-analysis testing and troubleshooting may be designed or retrofit into the digital product under test. Retrofit is often greatly simplified by the use of a supplementary microprocessor exerciser (Fig. 15-4).

The PRBS generator comprises 16 flip-flops configured as an XOR feedback shift register. In turn, the outputs of the flip-flops sequence through all of the possible non-zero patterns, and then repeat the sequence. This semi-random selection of bits provides nearly ideal statistical characteristics; nevertheless, the sequences are capable of developing unique signatures *because of their predictability*. Conventional data streams can be overlaid on the PRBS signal, because *feeding any data into a PRBS generator is equivalent to dividing the data by the generator's characteristic polynomial.*

TROUBLESHOOTING FEATURES

A signature multimeter is used to troubleshoot *synchronous* digital circuitry in microprocessor-based products and algorithmic state machines. In *asynchronous* digital circuitry, the time-interval function of the signature multimeter is utilized in checking one-shots and timers; its totalizing function is used for checking interrupt lines, reset lines, and RS-232C interface circuitry. *To analyze a problem associated with a faulty digital node, the peak voltage function of the SMM is used to check logic swings.*

Resistance functions of the SMM are used to trace short circuits, opens, or bad connections. In troubleshooting analog circuitry, the frequency function of the SMM is used to check clocks and dividers. Voltage, differential voltage, and resistance functions are used to check power supplies. Voltage and peak-voltage functions of the SMM can be used to check A/D and D/A converters. Timers are checked using the time-interval function of the SMM.

RETROFIT NOTES

A 6800-based microprocessor product can be retrofitted for signature analysis by the use of an external test stimulus provided by a microprocessor exerciser, as shown in Fig. 15-4. This exerciser provides: a test of the microprocessor's instruction set and interrupts, a free-run test for address and data bus integrity,

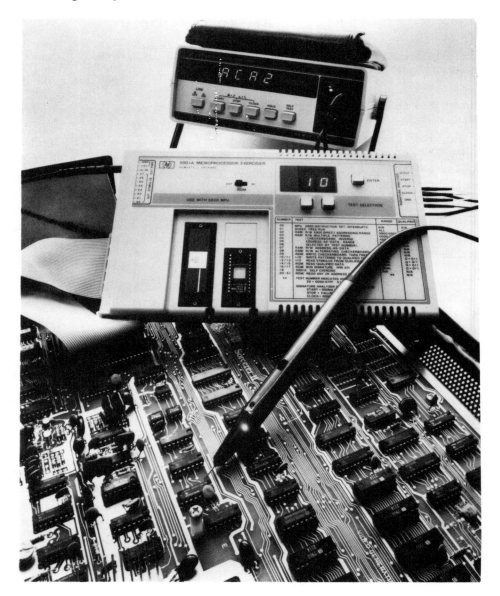

Fig. 15-4. A microprocessor exerciser is often used with a digital signature multimeter. (Courtesy, Hewlett-Packard.)

ROM read tests, RAM read-write tests, output port pattern tests, input port pattern tests, and a self-exercise for operational verification.

HOME COMPUTER TROUBLESHOOTING

This case history, provided by courtesy of Hewlett-Packard, shows how signature analysis was retrofit into a personal computer to allow troubleshooting to the component level with a signature multimeter. Figs. 15-5 and 15-6 show the block diagram and memory map of the standard computer unit, a Z80-based personal computer. The standard computing system incorporates the circuits of the block diagram within a single housing around the keyboard.

In this example, optional equipment is available which expands the capabilities of the computer, but exists as separate items. These are the CRT display, a line printer, a floppy disc, and a S-100 bus expansion module. This example explains how SA has been retrofit into the standard computer unit, but not how it may be implemented in any of the optional peripherals.

BASIC CONSIDERATIONS

The following coverage shows the details of implementing signature analysis into the standard computer unit in terms of hardware, software, and test connections. The illustrations depict retrofitting of signature analysis into the computer, and the accompanying discussion notes the major decisions and tradeoffs that are involved, *and the effects that some of these decisions had on the ease of troubleshooting the computer.*

Note that the signature-analysis stimulus routines for the computer are effective in localizing faults. However, the way in which they were implemented is not necessarily the only way, nor the most efficient way that it could be done.

Block Diagram Features

The personal computer diagrammed in Fig. 15-5 contains a Z80 microprocessor, an operating system contained in Monitor ROM, space for user-created programs in Processor RAM, and a slot on the side of the computer to insert a ROM Pac that contains ROM-based applications programs. Also included is a Video Text Generator that outputs to a CRT for display. It includes memory space for ASCII text characters in Screen RAM, character font in ASCII Font RAM, user-defined graphics font in Graphic RAM, and discrete Video Timing Generator circuits.

The interfaces to the computer diagrammed in Fig. 15-5 consist of two Serial I/O channels for a cassette tape unit and a general-purpose RS-232 link, both supported by a UART, an eight-bit Parallel I/O channel of discrete logic, a

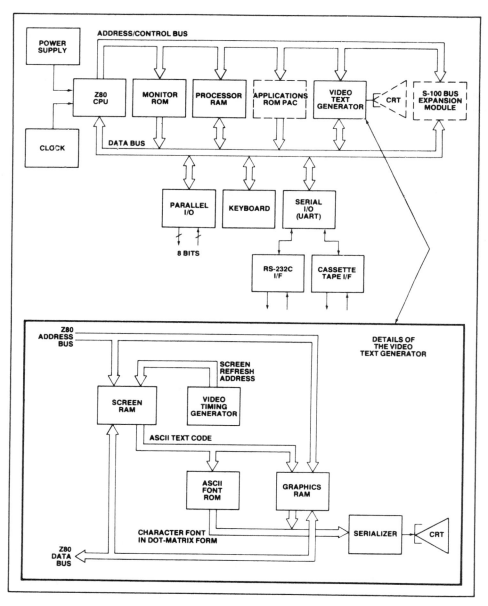

Fig. 15-5. Block diagram of a personal computer with a Z80 microprocessor. (Courtesy, Hewlett-Packard.)

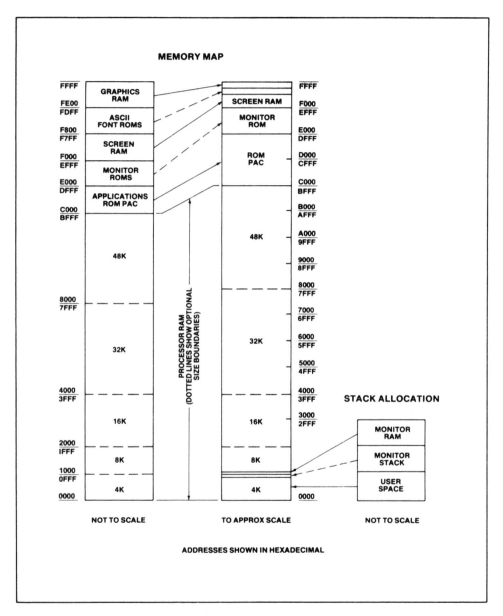

Fig. 15-6. Memory map of the personal computer.

keyboard with associated scan mechanism, and a S-100 Bus Expansion port that is a buffered extension of the Z80 microprocessor bus. Optional equipment is outlined in dashed lines.

Memory Map Features

The memory map diagram in Fig. 15-6 shows the Z80's 64K byte memory space among the circuits of the personal computer. All memory assignments are fixed except for the Processor RAM which can vary from 4K bytes to 48K bytes, depending upon the user's memory requirements. The keyboard, Parallel and Serial I/O devices reside within the input/output space of the Z80, while the S-100 Bus Expansion memory devices automatically map over the Processor RAM as required.

FREERUNNING THE Z80

When the Z80 is placed into the Freerun mode using the Freerun fixture depicted in Fig. 15-7, the Z80's continuous cycling of the address bus stimulates the kernel, or heart, of the computer system. *Signature analysis is then used to isolate kernel circuit failures.* The kernel is defined as those circuits required to be functional so that the microprocessor can execute ROM-based stimulus programs for signature-analysis troubleshooting of circuits beyond the kernel. The kernel circuits comprise:

1. The power supply and Z80's clock.
2. The Z80 microprocessor.
3. The Z80 control lines including gating and buffers.
4. Address and data buses including buffers.
5. Address decode circuits that create the ROM and RAM chip selects.
6. ROMs, including those that contain the signature-analysis programs.

Conventional test equipment, such as voltmeters, frequency counters, or oscilloscopes are used to troubleshoot the Z80's clock and power supply.

CONFIDENCE LEVELS

Although Freerun uses the Z80 to stimulate other circuits of the kernel, Freerun does not check the Z80's ability to execute code. There are several ways to verify this performance with increasing levels of confidence:

1. Since most failures internal to the Z80 show up as incorrect signatures on the address bus during Freerun, the troubleshooter may assume that further testing of the Z80 before it is used to execute the signature-analysis stimulus code is not required.

2. The troubleshooter may assume that if the Z80 can execute any of the signature-analysis routines, it is operating correctly and doesn't need to be tested further.

3. The troubleshooter could add a Z80 instruction set test to the signature-analysis stimulus library. However, since a complete test consumes many bytes of code, and it is difficult to write and because it can't test the Z80's ac parameters, it could be unjustified on the basis of the amount of circuitry that it tests.

Freerun Fixture Features

The fixture depicted in Fig. 15-7 was quickly constructed from available IC sockets, and allowed Freerun to be easily retrofit into the computer. Modifications to the four sockets that make up this fixture break the data bus between the system and the Z80 and apply a NOP instruction to cause it to Freerun.

Socket No. 1 in Fig. 15-7 is a zero-insertion-force socket that allows the Z80 to be removed from the computer and placed into the fixture without damage.

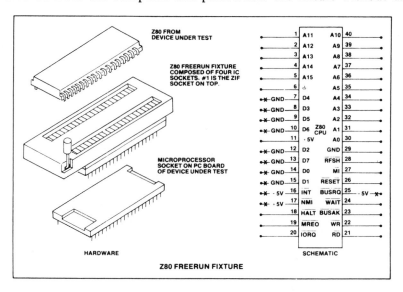

Fig. 15-7. Freerun fixture for troubleshooting the computer. (Courtesy, Hewlett-Packard.)

Socket No. 2 is altered by bending pins on the socket to open the data bus as indicated by the "X" on the schematic. The NOP instruction is applied to the Z80 by wiring the open data bus to ground on socket No. 2. Similar treatment was done to several of the Z80 control pins by opening them and wiring to + 5V dc or ground as required to force them to a known state during Freerun independently of the computer's response.

With reference to Fig. 15-8, Freerun stimulates the fundamental circuits of the computer system so that signature analysis can be used to isolate failures in the kernel, or heart, of the system. The kernel circuits are checked with four setups of the signature analyzer, as shown:

a) The first setup checks the integrity of the address bus and related address decode circuits.

b) The second setup verifies that the code within ROM is correct and that the data bus is free and clear so that instructions can pass from the ROM to the Z80.

c) The third setup is used only when there is an apparent failure in the Z80's control signal outputs.

d) The fourth setup checks the dynamic RAM refresh circuits of the Processor RAM, but not the RAM itself.

The troubleshooter cannot use Freerun to check out the RAM because it powers up in a random state. There is no way to initialize the RAM with the processor because the data bus has been opened up. *All other circuits beyond the kernel can be checked by the troubleshooter using signature-analysis stimulus programs contained in the ROM.*

SIGNATURE ANALYSIS TEST STORAGE, ACCESS, AND SELECTION

Storage: The external-applications ROM Pac provides the most convenient and quick means of storing the signature-analysis test stimulus, as follows:

1. No other ROM needs to be removed, as in most retrofit situations in which ROM substitution is used. The operator simply inserts the signature-analysis ROM Pac into a slot on the computer to run them.

2. A ROM Pac is not as susceptible to damage as a ROM, because the ROM Pac interfaces to the computer with a PC board edge connector instead of fragile IC pins.

3. Production technicians, customer service personnel, and computer distrib-

SIGNATURE ANALYZER		Z80	
INPUT	EDGE	SIGNAL	PIN
START		A15	5
STOP		A15	5
CLOCK		RD	21

ADDRESS BUS SIGNATURE TABLE

ADDRESS	PIN	SIGNATURE	ADDRESS	PIN	SIGNATURE
A15	5	755U	A7	37	52F8
A14	4	3827	A6	36	UPFH
A13	3	3C96	A5	35	OAFA
A12	2	HAP7	A4	34	5H21
A11	1	1293	A3	33	7F7F
A10	40	HPP0	A2	32	CCCC
A9	39	2H70	A1	31	5555
A8	38	HC89	A0	30	UUUU

a. ADDRESS BUS AND DECODERS

SIGNATURE ANALYZER		MONITOR ROM #1		MONITOR ROM #2	
INPUT	EDGE	SIGNAL	PIN	SIGNAL	PIN
START		CHIP SELECT	—	CHIP SELECT	—
STOP		CHIP SELECT	—	CHIP SELECT	—
CLOCK		Z80 RD	21	Z80 RD	21

b. ROM CONTENTS AND DATA BUS

SIGNATURE ANALYZER		Z80	
INPUT	EDGE	SIGNAL	PIN
START		M1	27
STOP		M1	27
CLOCK		Φ	6

c. Z80 CONTROL LINES

SIGNATURE ANALYZER		Z80	
INPUT	EDGE	SIGNAL	PIN
START		A15	5
STOP		A15	5
CLOCK		RFSH	28

d. DYNAMIC RAM REFRESH MULTIPLEXER

Fig. 15-8. Freerun troubleshooting checkout of the computer system. (Courtesy, Hewlett-Packard.)

utors already know how to use the ROM Pac. The signature-analysis tests simply become one of the many applications-ROM-Pacs that are available for the computer.

The disadvantages of storing the signature-analysis tests in the ROM occur because of the method that the computer uses to access the stored programs.

SA Stimulus Routines

With reference to Fig. 15-9, the signature-analysis stimulus routines (SA tests) are stored in a 2Kx8 EPROM within an applications-ROM-Pac that is inserted on the side of the computer. The SA tests are 944 bytes long, of which 534 bytes are the ASCII characters of a test selection menu, 110 bytes are a branch table for test selection, and 300 bytes form the actual SA tests. The program starts at the first address within the applications ROM Pac memory space, address C000H.

Access

When power is first applied to the computer, the Z80 CPU is reset to address 0000H and begins execution there. Since the ROM Pac resides at address C000H, a means is provided to cause the Z80 to jump there and begin execution of the SA tests. However, a ROM Pac is not always inserted into the computer. The program must also recognize the presence or absence of the ROM Pac and jump to the ROM Pac program, if it's there, by means of an operating system stored in the monitor ROMs.

The monitor ROMs reside at memory address E000H, not at address 0000H. (The first address executed by the Z80 at power on is 0000H.) To compensate, a special circuit that resets to zero at power-on temporarily maps the monitor ROMs to location 0000H. The first three locations of the monitor ROMs contain an unconditional jump instruction to location E003H. When the Z80 addresses E003H for the next instruction, the special circuit remaps the monitor ROMs back to their true address space of E000H to EFFFH so that further operating system codes in the monitor ROMs can be executed.

Stack Establishment

The operating system then tries to establish a stack in any available functional RAM so that monitor subroutines can be accessed by the user. The operating system first checks processor RAM to see if enough locations behave like RAM. If the RAM is functional, the operating system establishes a stack and

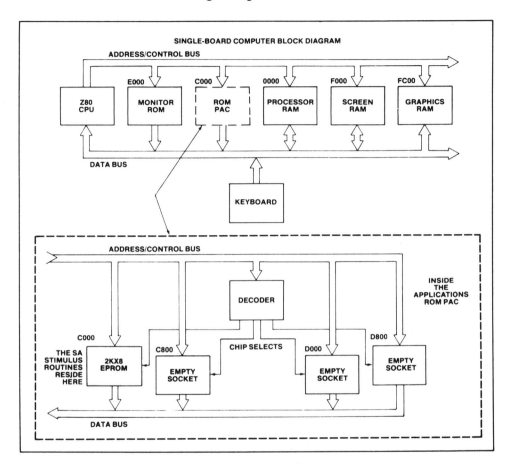

Fig. 15-9. SA stimulus routine storage. (Courtesy, Hewlett-Packard.)

proceeds to do several housekeeping chores to set up the computer for interaction by the user.

If processor RAM is not functioning, the computer will continue to search memory for the next available RAM locations (e.g., Screen or Graphics RAM) until a stack can be established. *If no RAM is functional, the operating system will continue to search forever and will never release control to the user.*

If a stack can be established, the operating system then checks for the presence of a ROM Pac to see if program execution should continue there. The process of determining this requires several subroutines within the operating system that uses the stack. Finally, the operating system sees that the SA ROM Pac has been inserted and jumps to the first location (address C000H) to put up the SA test selection menu. Once the SA tests have been selected and are executing, neither the operating system nor the stack is used.

With reference to Fig. 15-10, the SA tests are automatically accessed by the computer at power-on when an SA applications ROM Pac is inserted. The sys-

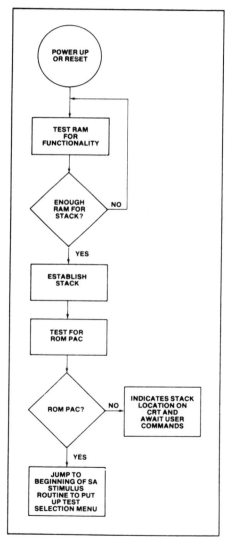

Fig. 15-10. Automatic accessing of the SA tests for troubleshooting the kernel. (Courtesy, Hewlett-Packard.)

tem first goes through a power-up test of RAM to find a place for the operating system's stack to reside. The program then checks for the presence of a ROM Pac by checking the first few locations of ROM Pac memory space for non-zero entries. If the ROM Pac is present, the program then jumps to the first location of the ROM Pac to begin execution. The first steps of the SA tests put up a test selection menu on the CRT, as shown in Fig. 15-11.

This menu is displayed on the CRT to prompt the user to select the number of the desired SA test with one keystroke. *Once the troubleshooter selects a test, it runs continuously and further keyboard entries are ignored.* A reset from the keyboard, such as power-on, stops the test and recalls the menu to the CRT for a new test selection. The details (code, flowcharts, and circuits of tests 0–9) are shown in the remaining sections. Tests A–C are in separate sections with headlines that match the circuit they test and the menu number. For example, the Parallel Port test is found in the section headline "Parallel Port, Test B." Test D is not implemented at this time.

TROUBLESHOOTING TRADEOFF CONSIDERATIONS

Next, consider the troubleshooting tradeoffs that are involved in storing the SA tests in the ROM Pac, versus storing them in a ROM which can be substituted in place of the monitor ROMs. (Substitution is the more common approach to retrofitting SA.) By placing the programs in the ROM Pac, all kernel circuits must be functional in order to run any SA tests. Freerun is used to

```
SIGNATURE ANALYSIS TEST LOOPS

    0----MONITOR ROM #1
    1----MONITOR ROM #2
    2----4K PROCESSOR RAM, ROW #1
    3----4K PROCESSOR RAM, ROW #2
    4----16K PROCESSOR RAM, ROW #1
    5----16K PROCESSOR RAM, ROW #2
    6----16K PROCESSOR RAM, ROW #3
    7----BOTTOM SCREEN RAM
    8----TOP SCREEN RAM
    9----GRAPHICS RAM
    A----STATIC VIDEO PATTERN
    B----PARALLEL PORT
    C----SERIAL RS-232 PORT
    D----S-100 EXPANSION BUS
    SELECT >>_
```

Fig. 15-11. Troubleshooting menu display on CRT. (Courtesy, Hewlett-Packard.)

check them when they aren't functional. *However, this application also contains circuits that the troubleshooter cannot check out with Freerun*—circuits that must also be functional. They are:

1. RAM, so that the operating system can establish a stack. This includes RAM chip selects and support circuits.
2. The special circuit that maps the monitor ROM to location 0000H at power-on.

An *assumption* was made that one of the three sections of RAM (either Processor, Screen, or Graphics RAM) would be functional *so that even bad RAM at one of the locations could be checked out by the troubleshooter with the SA tests,* once a stack was established in another section of RAM and the programs were accessed.

However, it turned out that the foregoing assumption was not good in practice, because of a high percentage of process faults such as solder-splashes, open-circuit traces, and incorrectly installed components. The RAMs, including the dynamic 4K and 16K parts, were not pretested before loading. Their failure rate, combined with the process faults, resulted in the majority of boards having no functional RAM.

Another *assumption* was made about the special circuit of item No. 2. Since the circuit consists of one IC, *it was assumed that the circuit could be checked out easily by the troubleshooter with instruments such as the logic probe.*

If the program had been stored in ROM to be substituted in place of a monitor ROM instead of being placed in the ROM Pac, then RAM would not need to be functional in order to run the SA tests. Remember that the operating system would be replaced with the SA ROM which is then accessed directly at power on (if the mapping circuit is functional). *With this substitution technique, it would be possible for the troubleshooter to check out the RAM even if none was functional.* However, there are some problems with the monitor ROM substitution method in this case because of the retrofit situation:

1. The monitor ROM is masked and an EPROM version could not be directly substituted into the product without cutting traces and rewiring a small section of the board. This was not acceptable. However, a masked ROM version of the SA test was equally unacceptable. (The volume was not judged to be high enough to justify a mask charge because additions to the test repertoire were still planned.) Note that monitor EPROM substitution could have been planned in the design stage by making the circuit easily switched between ROM and EPROM. Or, the SA tests could have been designed into the monitor ROM so that it would always be available in the product without substitution or ROM Pacs.

2. Since the monitor ROMs contain the keyboard and video CRT driver subroutines that allow easy operator interaction with the test selection menu, the drivers would need to be duplicated in the ROM that would substitute the monitor ROM. *It was easier to keep the monitor routines intact so that the SA tests in the ROM Pac could use the drivers as subroutines to put up the menu and allow the keyboard to be used to select the tests. The drivers could have been avoided if a less elaborate test selection method had been designed into the product, such as DIP switches that could be read by the microprocessor.*

SELECTION

The keyboard provides an easy means for the troubleshooter to quickly select a test. It is probably the easiest method when combined with the test selection menu on the CRT. *However, should the keyboard fail, the operator cannot run any SA tests, including any that might help him troubleshoot the keyboard itself.* Here, it was decided that if the keyboard should fail, the operator would unplug the failed unit and exchange it with another one. However, this brings up two problems:

1. It assumes that all logic associated with the keyboard function exists on the keyboard PC board (which is not the case here). The keyboard PC board contains only the key switches and one IC. Several other IC's associated with detecting a key closure are on the main board. The result is that exchanging the keyboard may not correct the problem.

2. *Someone has to troubleshoot the keyboard when it fails, and SA cannot help if the tests are selected by means of the keyboard.* Even Freerun cannot help because the keyboard is treated as an I/O device that is not stimulated by Freerun. It was assumed in this case that the keyboard could be fixed by other means.

FLOWCHART AND ASSEMBLY LANGUAGE CODE

With reference to Fig. 15-12, note the flowchart and Z80 assembly language code that allows program selection. These are the mnemonics particular to the computer's assembler. PRTX is a monitor subroutine which transfers the ASCII characters of the menu from SA ROM to the CRT, starting at "MENU" (address C06CH) to "DEFB" (address C282H). Subroutine KEY-BOARD places a key entry into the accumulator with the zero flag reset.

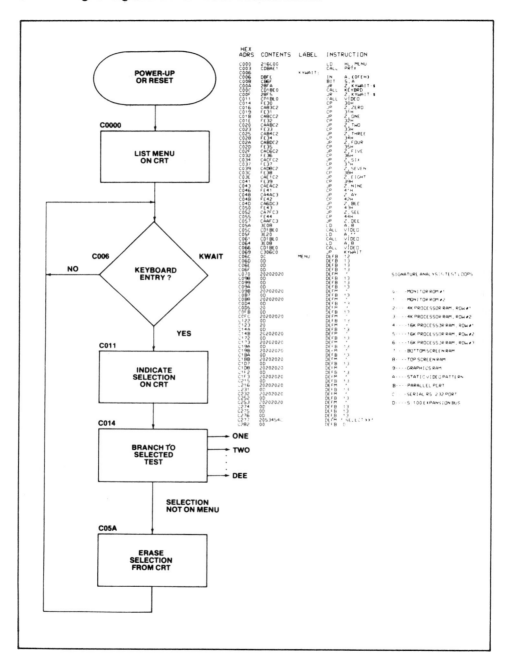

Fig. 15-12. Flowchart and Z80 assembly language code that allows program selection by the troubleshooter.

If no key is depressed, the zero flag is set. VIDEO writes the key entry on the CRT by the menu prompt "SELECT > >." If the entry matches a test number, the program branches to the test with the same label (e.g., 3 branches to "THREE"). Invalid entries are erased from the CRT and the program returns to wait for a new key.

HARDWARE AND SOFTWARE FOR START, STOP, AND CLOCK

For troubleshooting tests 0–9 and B–C, the Start and Stop edges were created by writing code that controlled available hardware. This combination of hardware and software is called program-controlled gating. Figs. 15-13 through 15-16 show the program-controlled gating used in the computer. The Start, Stop, and Clock connections for Freerun and test A are shown in the corresponding sections of this explanation because they are *not* examples of program control gating and do not require any code to be written. Some of the considerations in choosing an I/O register's output as the Start and Stop connections for program control gating in the computer should be noted:

General Guidelines for Creating Start and Stop. Create successive Start and Stop connections that build on the kernel. That is, considering the Start and Stop connections used in Freerun as the first and most basic set, *then the second set should be able to be used by the troubleshooter with the set used in Freerun.* Similarly, the third set should be able to be used by the troubleshooter with the second, and so on. Basic approaches for building a set of Start and Stop connections for the Z80 from Freerun to more complicated circuits are:

First Set: Freerun connections—generally the most significant address bit of the Z80; *used to troubleshoot the next set.*

Second Set: Chip selects and address decodes within the memory space of the processor; stimulated during Freerun *to allow troubleshooting with Start and Stop of the first set.* Also controlled by software *to create the required Start and Stop edges for troubleshooting the next set.*

Start and Stop for this computer fall into the first and third sets. The third set cannot be troubleshot with Freerun, nor is there another test that can be run should Start and Stop fail. *This has caused the troubleshooter to resort to other methods such as shotgunning when the circuits creating start and stop fail.*

Program-Controlled Gating

With reference to Fig. 15-13, for all SA tests (except A), Start and Stop are both connected to bit 0 in the Keyboard Scan Latch addressed as I/O port

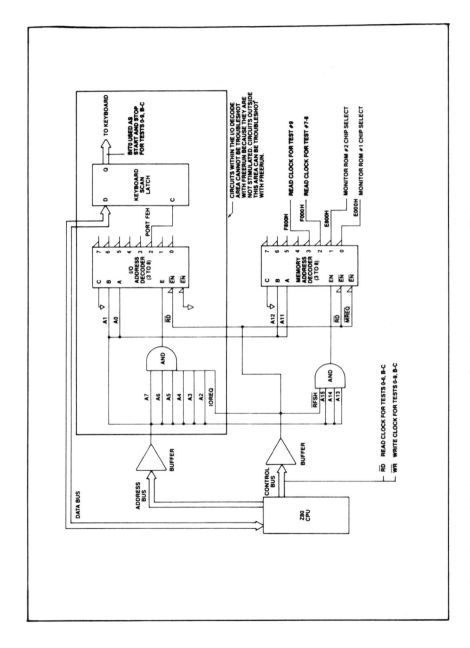

Fig. 15-13. Troubleshooting tests employ this program-controlled gating. (Courtesy, Hewlett-Packard.)

FEH. The programs set and reset the bit to create edges that can be detected by the signature multimeter's Start and Stop inputs. Start is selected to trigger on a rising edge and Stop triggers on a falling edge. *Setting the bit at the beginning of the troubleshooting test opens the Gate while resetting the bit immediately after the last test step closes the Gate.*

Figs. 15-14 and 15-16 show the Z80 code that creates the Start and Stop edges. The Clock connection depends on which test is run, as explained in Figs. 15-14, 15-15, and 15-16. Start, Stop, and Clock connections for test A are shown in the separate description of that test.

With reference to Fig. 15-14, for tests 0–6 and B–C, two Clocks ($\overline{\text{RD}}$ and $\overline{\text{WR}}$) are used to detect the Start and Stop edges. A $\overline{\text{RD}}$ Clock occurs with each op-code fetch of the Z80 which is more than adequate to detect the Start and Stop edges. (A clock edge must occur both before and after both the Start and Stop edges to ensure detection.) A $\overline{\text{WR}}$ Clock occurs when the I/O port FEH and the device being tested are written. A $\overline{\text{WR}}$ Clock does not occur for these tests. Similar code also applies to tests 0–6 and B–C.

Consider next the troubleshooting block diagrams shown in Fig. 15-15. In (a), the Z80 gains access to the Screen RAM to modify or examine the ASCII characters that appear on the CRT.

In (b), the Z80 accesses Graphics RAM to modify or examine the user-defined font stored there.

In (c), the Video Generator accesses the Screen RAM and Font RAM simultaneously to convert the ASCII characters in Screen RAM into standard text font for display on the CRT.

In (d), Graphics RAM is accessed only if non-ASCII characters are stored in Screen RAM.

In (e), these nodes are shared between the Z80 and the Video Generator. The signature multimeter requires a Clock that will sample data on the node only when the Z80 has access to RAM. Gating the Z80's $\overline{\text{RD}}$ control signal with the corresponding address decode for the RAM creates the required Clock. If $\overline{\text{RD}}$ alone were used to sample the asynchronous data on these nodes, then Video Generator data would also be sampled, resulting in unstable signatures.

With reference to Fig. 15-16, *generation of the Start and Stop edges for troubleshooting tests 7–9 is similar to tests 0–6 and B–C of Fig. 15-14.* In this case, extra code has been added between the generation of Start and Stop because of the gated Clock. The gated $\overline{\text{RD}}$ Clock used in these troubleshooting tests occurs only when the device being tested is read. The extra code adds both a read and a write access to the device under test between the Start and Stop edges to ensure detection.

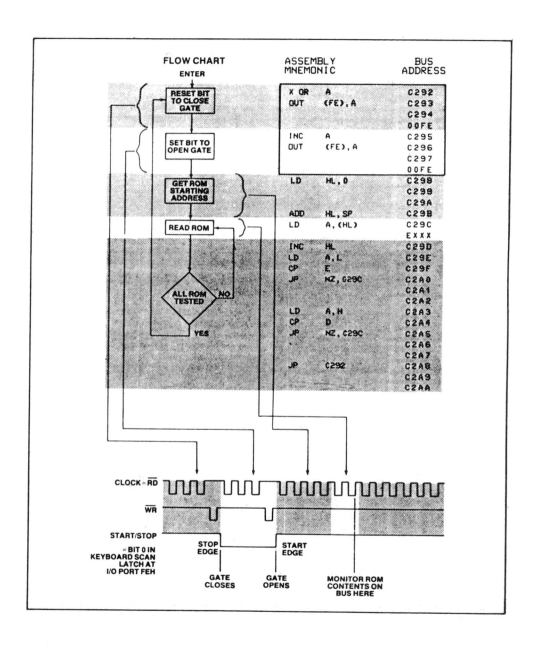

Fig. 15-14. Z80 troubleshooting code that creates the Start and Stop edges. (Courtesy, Hewlett-Packard.)

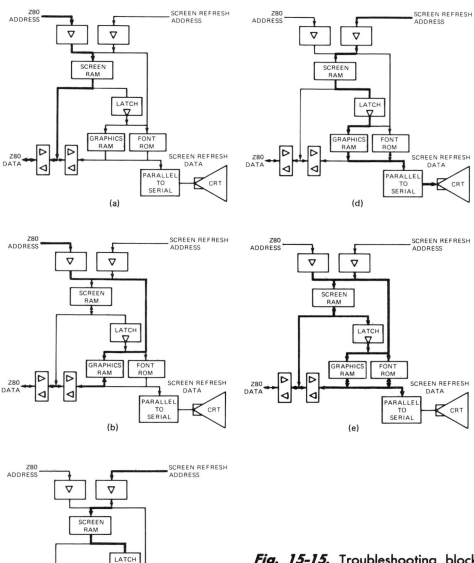

Fig. 15-15. Troubleshooting block diagrams showing signal flow when the Z80 or the Video Generator accesses the Screen RAM, Graphics RAM, or Font RAM; see text for details. (Courtesy, Hewlett-Packard.)

DETECTING START, STOP, AND DATA WITH THE CLOCK

Troubleshooting guidelines for choosing a Clock are:

1. A clock edge must occur both before and after the Start and Stop edges to assure detection and correct Gate action. The troubleshooter should make certain that this requirement is met when gated Clocks (defined below) are used.

2. The Clock must be synchronous to the Start, Stop, and Data inputs that it samples. This guideline is generally met if $\overline{RD}$ or $\overline{WR}$ from the Z80 is used as the Clock when troubleshooting any circuits that are accessed by the Z80.

3. Choose a Clock that will avoid sampling a three-state node when in its third state. This is generally accomplished by creating or using a gated Clock.

Gated Clock Action

A gated Clock is defined as a combination or gating of a constantly occurring clock, such as the Z80's $\overline{RD}$ or $\overline{WR}$ lines, with other signals, such as address decodes, *so that the signature multimeter is synchronized to the data of interest during the troubleshooting test.* Tests 0–6 and B–C do not require a gated Clock. They use $\overline{RD}$ and $\overline{WR}$ directly from the Z80 as their Clock as shown in Figs. 15-13 and 15-14. When $\overline{RD}$ was tried as a Clock for tests 7–9, the Gate light was flashing, indicating that the Start and Stop edges were being detected properly, but unstable signatures were also occurring because:

1. The Screen and Graphics RAM are both dual-ported and are accessed by two processes that are asynchronous to each other. The Z80 occasionally accesses the RAMs to store characters and graphics font for eventual display on the screen. The Video Generator Timing circuits also gain access to the RAM so that the characters and font stored there are displayed on the CRT on a continuing basis.

2. $\overline{RD}$ is active during the Z80's op-code fetches from ROM Pac as well as during a read of the RAM while the SA troubleshooting test is made. When $\overline{RD}$ is used as a Clock while probing the RAM circuits, data bits will be entered into the signature multimeter that are associated with the CRT refresh process (because of the Clock during op-code fetch) when what is sought is the data bits associated with the troubleshooting test.

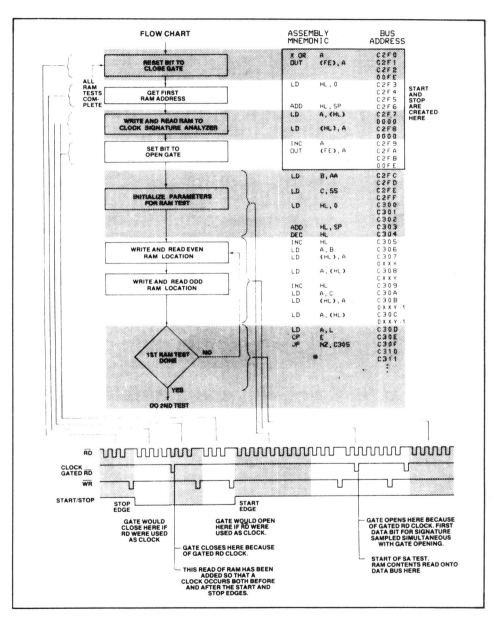

Fig. 15-16. Generation of Start and Stop edges for troubleshooting tests 7-9. (Courtesy, Hewlett-Packard.)

Stabilized Signatures

To obtain stable signatures, a gated Clock is required to sample RAM data only when the Z80 has access to the RAMs and not when the screen refresh process takes place nor when op-code is fetched.

To "window out" this unwanted data during the signature measurement cycle, $\overline{RD}$ is gated with the address decode of the RAM that the troubleshooter is testing. As is often the case, the gated clock in this example was already available in the address decode circuits for the RAM. In turn, no modifications to the circuit were required.

The resulting gated Clock occurs only when the RAM is accessed by the Z80. In this example, this should have resulted in stable signatures, but when tested, there wasn't even a Gate. Changing to a gated Clock also eliminated the Clock edges around both the Start and Stop edges. To solve this troubleshooting problem, a Clock cycle (an access to the RAM being tested) was added between the generation of the Start and Stop edges in tests 7–9 to ensure their detection as shown in Fig. 15-16.

Because the Screen RAM and Graphics RAM have different address decodes, two separate clocks are used, depending upon which RAM is being tested. *It would be convenient for the troubleshooter not to be required to move the clock, if at all possible. However, because of the retrofit situation, this was not possible.*

FAULT ISOLATION OF BUSED DEVICES

The way in which signature-multimeter tests are organized can make a difference in the ease of isolating a fault in a device that communicates over a data bus. *Signature-analysis troubleshooting tests are generally written in one of two different ways, depending upon the troubleshooting environment:*

1. Go/no-go indication of all bused devices. All bused devices are tested at the same time within one SA loop so that:
    a. If there is no fault, further testing is not required.
    b. If there is a fault, the failure is indicated to be within a limited area of the PC board.
2. Fault isolation of a specific bused device. *The troubleshooter knows within which area of the board the fault lies, and he is proceeding to locate the device or process fault causing the problem.*

For example, consider the Monitor ROM tests 0–1. They are written to test each Monitor RAM separately. However, consider that both RAMs may be tested within the same SA Loop. In other words, the contents of both RAMs are read back onto the data bus between the same Start and Stop. When the troubleshooting test is run, a go/no-go indication can be obtained from eight signatures taken on the data bus.

Correct signatures indicate that everything is correct for both ROMs. Incorrect signatures would indicate a failure in one of the ROMs or in the supporting circuitry. *But the troubleshooter does not know which ROM has failed until the contents of each ROM is individually examined with signatures.* There are several ways to do this:

1. Remove all ROMs from their sockets or disable all chip selects. Then add one ROM at a time to the circuit until incorrect signatures reoccur on the data bus.
2. Freerun the Z80 and "window" around each ROM's data by moving Start and Stop to each chip select until incorrect signatures occur.
3. Create a separate test for each ROM so that only that ROM's data is placed on the bus. Start, Stop, and Clock can remain connected to the same signals if under program control.

Separate Tests (Figure 15-17)

Separate troubleshooting tests were written for several reasons, in this example:

1. The condition of each ROM and supporting circuitry is determined quickly by running each test and taking only eight data bus signatures.
2. Diagnostics other than SA stimulus routines had already limited the failure to ROM. *The troubleshooter was now looking for the device or process fault causing the failure.*
3. It was simpler to select a new troubleshooting test to run than to remove parts from the board or move Start, Stop, and Clock around from chip select to chip select.
4. No modifications to the board or hardware could be added to allow the ROM chip selects to be disabled because of the retrofit situation.

Separate troubleshooting tests were also written for the Processor RAM of tests 2–6. They are also implemented to find the one bused RAM out of several that could be causing the fault. Separating the tests also made easy troubleshooting tests of optional sizes of Processor RAM.

Each socket for a RAM can accept a 4K or 16K dynamic RAM part, or no part at all, allowing Processor RAM to vary from 4K to 48K bytes total. Each

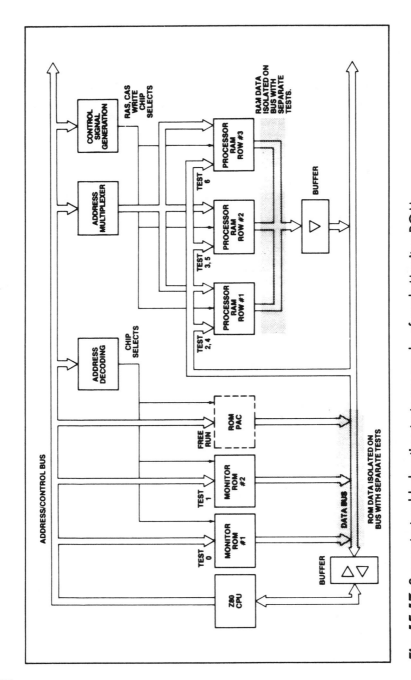

Fig. 15-17. Separate troubleshooting tests are made of each Monitor ROM and each row of Processor RAM.

variation of Processor RAM requires a new signature set. Since the Processor RAM troubleshooting tests are independent of the configuration, so is the signature documentation.

READ AND WRITE AS CLOCK ASSISTS FAULT LOCATION

The signature-analysis troubleshooting test both reads and writes devices such as RAM, so that the Z80's $\overline{RD}$ and $\overline{WR}$ outputs can be used as the Clock to determine if the fault is caused by the RAM being incorrectly read or written. When $\overline{RD}$ is used as the Clock, and signatures on the data bus are correct, the RAM is both being read and written correctly.

When signatures are incorrect, the Clock is moved to $\overline{WR}$ to check the signatures on all inputs to the RAM, including control lines. If all signatures are correct, the problem exists with reading RAM. The Clock is moved back to $\overline{RD}$ to isolate the problem caused by reading of the RAM. *It may be the RAM itself, the control line inputs to the RAM and the support circuits that generate them, or a process fault.*

With reference to Fig. 15-17, each Monitor ROM and each row of Processor RAM is tested separately by the troubleshooter to allow easier fault location in these bused devices. This ensures that the only data on any node comes from the device being tested, and nothing else. (Except for the program that is executing from ROM Pac, which has to be good for the program to run. It is tested with Freerun when it is bad.)

A faulty device being tested is isolated by following incorrect signatures back to the source of the fault. Similarly, when data comes from a device that shouldn't be on the bus, it is detected as an incorrect signature and is also traced to the fault. $\overline{RD}$ and $\overline{WR}$ as Clocks also sort out faults. When incorrect signatures appear on the outputs of the RAM during a test using $\overline{RD}$ as a Clock, sometimes one or more of the RAM cells is bad, or control signals into the RAM are faulty (such as RAS, CAS, and Chip Select), or the data was incorrectly written into the RAM.

To isolate the fault, $\overline{WR}$ is used as a Clock to check signatures on the inputs that could affect writing of the RAM. (For example, the data bus inputs and control lines such as RAS, CAS, WRITE, and Chip select.) If they have the correct signatures, the problem has something to do with reading RAM.

Next, with reference to Fig. 15-18, observe the program for the static video pattern to write it into RAM. All possible characters and all possible patterns of a user-defined font are written into Screen RAM and Graphics RAM, respectively. The program then enters a small loop that keeps the Z80 from further interaction with either RAM. This maintains the node activity limited to the CRT refresh process so that signatures are stable.

Nodes stimulated by the CRT refresh process while the static video pattern is displayed on the CRT are shown in Fig. 15-19. These Start, Stop, and Clock connections form a Gate that is open for one complete refresh cycle of the CRT, allowing the signature multimeter to detect errors in any of the circuits, including all the font patterns in ASCII Font ROM. When the Timing Generators fail, Start and Stop are no longer generated. *In that case, Start and Stop are moved by the troubleshooter to the connections shown in the following diagrams, closer to the kernel circuits of the Video Generator.*

Observe the Freerun troubleshooting test depicted in Fig. 15-20. Grounding one point causes these Vertical Timing Generator counters to "Freerun" through all possible states, instead of counting CRT vertical lines. It does this by eliminating feedback loops. Although grounding the output of a TTL device is not a recommended troubleshooting procedure, it was not possible in this example to design-in a jumper that would disconnect the output from the circuit and ground the remaining inputs. *To troubleshoot the freerunning counters, Clock is connected to the counter's Clock input (the MSB of the Horizontal Timing Generator in the next diagram).*

The Data input is placed on a source of logic-high, such as +5 vdc. Start and Stop are both moved to the circuit node under test to take a signature. The signature for any node then represents the number of Clock edges between Start and Stop. If incorrect signatures occur for all nodes of these counters, then Start, Stop, and Clock are moved as shown in the following diagram.

Next, observe the Freerunning Horizontal Timing Generator counter troubleshooting test depicted in Fig. 15-21. Freerunning the Horizontal Timing Generator counters is similar to that of the Vertical Timing Generator counters of the preceding figure. Grounding one point Freeruns the counters. Clock is connected to the counter's clock input, the source of the Video Clock. The Data input is placed on +5 vdc, and *the troubleshooter moves Start and Stop from node to node to take signatures.* These counters only require that the crystal oscillator of the Video Clock Generator be operating for Freerun to occur.

PARALLEL PORT, TROUBLESHOOTING TEST B

In this example, external hardware was required to stimulate the Input Port. Wires on an external connector loop the patterns that are written to the Output Port back to the Input Port. Timing requirements of the Handshake control lines made it impossible to simply loop their outputs back to the inputs with similar wires on the connectors.

Fig. 15-18. Program for writing the static video pattern into RAM for troubleshooting tests. (Courtesy, Hewlett-Packard.)

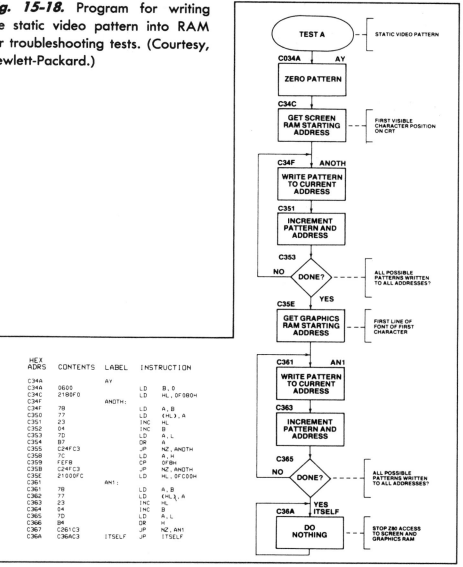

HEX ADRS	CONTENTS	LABEL	INSTRUCTION	
C34A		AY		
C34A	0600		LD	B, 0
C34C	2180F0		LD	HL, 0F080H
C34F		ANOTH:		
C34F	78		LD	A, B
C350	77		LD	(HL), A
C351	23		INC	HL
C352	04		INC	B
C353	7D		LD	A, L
C354	B7		OR	A
C355	C24FC3		JP	NZ, ANOTH
C358	7C		LD	A, H
C359	FEF8		CP	0F8H
C35B	C24FC3		JP	NZ, ANOTH
C35E	21000FC		LD	HL, 0FC00H
C361		AN1:		
C361	78		LD	A, B
C362	77		LD	(HL), A
C363	23		INC	HL
C364	04		INC	B
C365	7D		LD	A, L
C366	B4		OR	H
C367	C261C3		JP	NZ, AN1
C36A	C36AC3	ITSELF	JP	ITSELF

The troubleshooter decided not to add the ICs that would be required to fully stimulate the handshake circuits. Two things determined this—first, the extra hardware was not available, and, second, the handshake circuits consist of one IC that can be checked out by a logic probe, or equivalent tester.

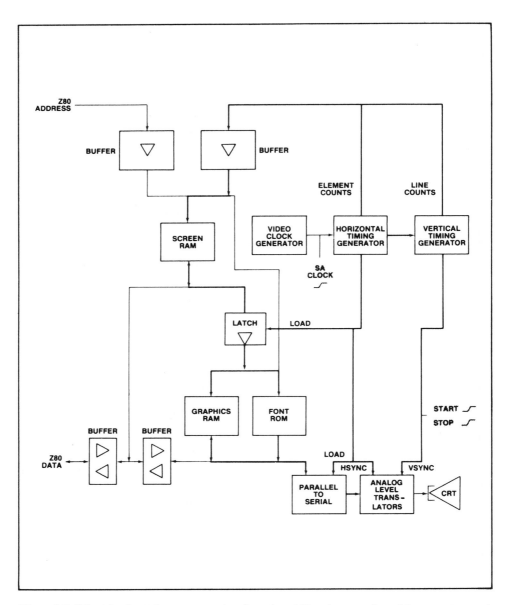

Fig. 15-19. Nodes that are stimulated while the static video pattern is displayed. (Courtesy, Hewlett-Packard.)

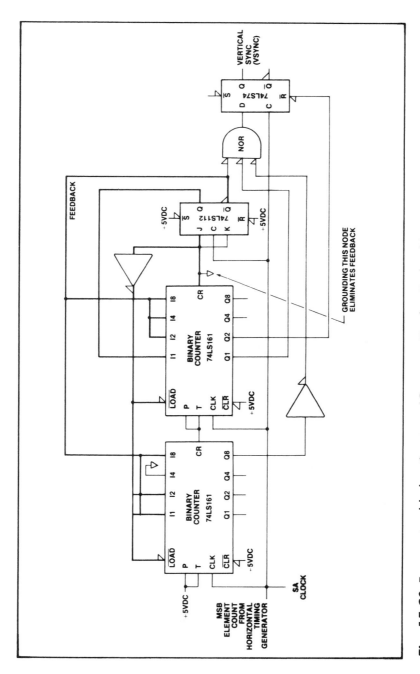

Fig. 15-20. Freerun troubleshooting test. (Courtesy, Hewlett-Packard.)

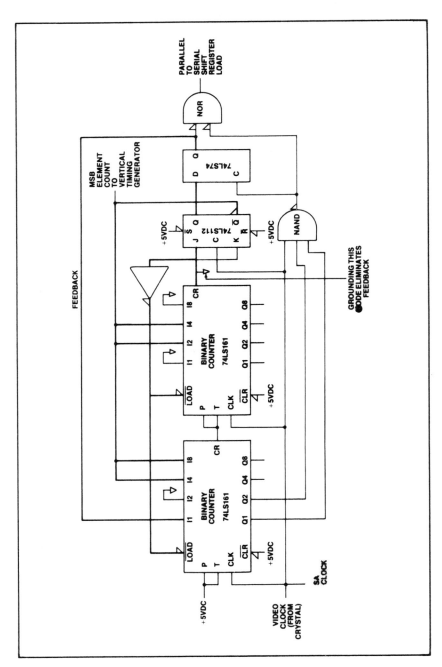

Fig. 15-21. Freerunning the Horizontal Timing Generator counters. (Courtesy, Hewlett-Packard.)

Next, observe the troubleshooting program shown in Fig. 15-22. This program stimulates both the Output and Input Parallel Ports by continuously writing all possible patterns to the Output Port. The program also reads the Input Port, whether it is stimulated or not. The Input Port is stimulated by looping the Output Port back to the Input Port using the connector shown in the following diagram.

With reference to Fig. 15-23, note the circuits that are stimulated by the Parallel Port troubleshooting test. Start and Stop are connected to a bit in the Keyboard Scan Latch and are controlled by the program as shown in the section headed The Hardware and Software Behind Start, Stop, and Clock.

When the troubleshooter puts the loop-back connector on, signatures are taken on the data bus using $\overline{RD}$ as a Clock. If signatures are correct, then both the Output and Input port are operating correctly. If signatures are incorrect, the connector is removed by the troubleshooter, and signatures are taken on the Output Port using $\overline{WR}$ as the clock.

Repairs are made as required, based on the troubleshooting data that is obtained. The loopback connector is then replaced to check the Input Port for problems associated with reading it. Note that the Handshake circuitry is not stimulated by this test.

SERIAL RS-232C PORT, TROUBLESHOOTING TEST C

This test stimulates the Universal Asynchronous Receiver Transmitter (UART) for SA troubleshooting. UARTs are generally considered to be troubleshooting problems because of the lack of synchronization between the parallel side and the serial side of the port. However, the UART in this example (and in most applications) can be checked with SA as follows:

1. The serial output is connected to the serial input to take advantage of the loop-back technique for port testing, described previously. The program is seen in Fig. 15-24, and the UART loop-back configuration is shown in Fig. 15-25.

2. The stimulus program for troubleshooting test C writes checkerboard patterns to the UART, and then reads them back onto the data bus, allowing a fixed time for loop-back transmission of the serial words.

3. The first troubleshooting test setup allows a go/no-go check on the UART and support circuits. Connect Start and Stop to the keyboard scan latch as previously shown. Connect Clock to $\overline{RD}$. Take signatures on data bus lines. If bus signatures are correct, then the UART and de-

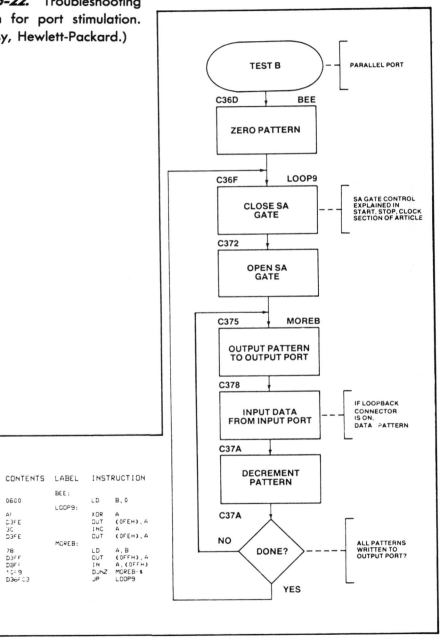

Fig. 15-22. Troubleshooting program for port stimulation. (Courtesy, Hewlett-Packard.)

TEST B — PARALLEL PORT

C36D   BEE

ZERO PATTERN

C36F   LOOP9

CLOSE SA GATE — SA GATE CONTROL EXPLAINED IN START, STOP, CLOCK SECTION OF ARTICLE

C372

OPEN SA GATE

C375   MOREB

OUTPUT PATTERN TO OUTPUT PORT

C378

INPUT DATA FROM INPUT PORT — IF LOOPBACK CONNECTOR IS ON, DATA = PATTERN

C37A

DECREMENT PATTERN

C37A

NO   DONE?   — ALL PATTERNS WRITTEN TO OUTPUT PORT?

YES

HEX ADRS	CONTENTS	LABEL	INSTRUCTION	
C36D		BEE:		
C36D	0600		LD	B, 0
C36F		LOOP9:		
C36F	AF		XOR	A
C370	D3FE		OUT	(OFEH), A
C372	3C		INC	A
C373	D3FE		OUT	(OFEH), A
C375		MOREB:		
C375	78		LD	A, B
C376	D3FF		OUT	(OFFH), A
C378	DBFF		IN	A, (OFFH)
C37A	10F9		DJNZ	MOREB-$
C37C	D36FC3		JP	LOOP9

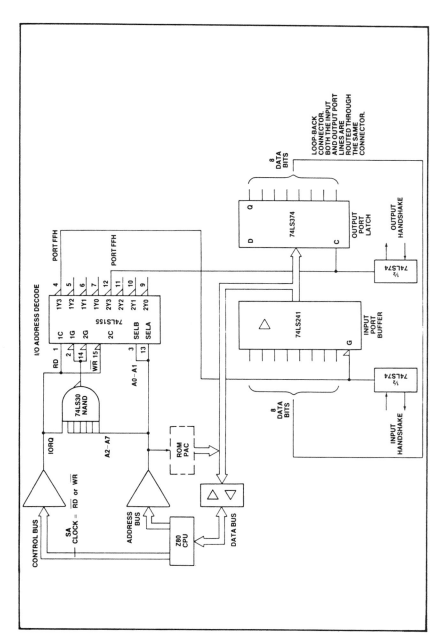

Fig. 15-23. Circuits stimulated by the port troubleshooting test. (Courtesy, Hewlett-Packard.)

coder are okay. If incorrect, then take signatures on the decoder outputs. If decoder signatures are incorrect, suspect the decoder. *If correct, then set up the second troubleshooting test.*

4. The second troubleshooting test setup allows verification of a UART chip failure. Connect Start to the serial output line, TSO, which will open the Gate on the first serial output bit (the start bit). Connect Stop to the TBE output, which indicates the end of a serial output word. Connect Clock to the UART Clock, pin TCP. *Take signatures on the serial side of the UART for node-level troubleshooting and fault isolation.*

With reference to Fig. 15-24, observe how the inputs and outputs of a UART are stimulated by the troubleshooting program, along with the control and status registers. The UART is first set to send and receive serial words with eight data bits, even parity, and two stop bits at 1200 baud. Next, the program writes the word AAH into the UART and waits for its transmission to complete. Then the status word is read onto the data bus along with the serial word receiver, and then the status word again. Finally, 55H is loaded for transmission similar to the word AAH. The troubleshooting program then jumps back to the beginning of the loop upon completion.

With reference to Fig. 15-25, note that in Test C, the UART serial output is looped back into the serial input, as shown. The stimulus exercises the entire loop. Start, Stop, and Clock connections for troubleshooting both the parallel and serial sides of the UART were noted in the foregoing text.

Note that although a home computer operating with a Z80 microprocessor has been featured in the foregoing troubleshooting discussion, the signature multimeter can be applied in a similar manner to almost all microprocessor-based systems. The particular computer considered in this chapter is called the Sorcerer II, and is manufactured by Exidy Corporation in Sunnyvale, California.

The signature multimeter can be applied in the general manner that has been described for troubleshooting video games, digital voltmeters, or other microprocessor-based equipment.

OPENING UP A CAN OF WORMS

Personal-computer owners should be cautioned not to attempt to work on their computers until they have become professional digital troubleshooters. A personal computer can be compared to a can of worms in this regard. Opening up a personal computer could lead to voiding the warranty and/or expensive repairs.

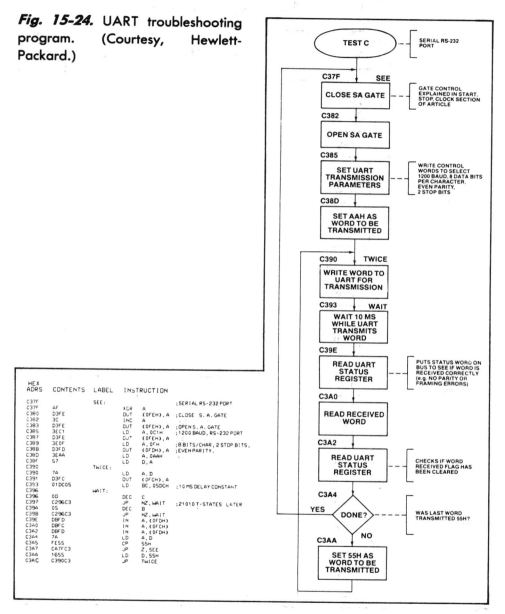

Fig. 15-24. UART troubleshooting program. (Courtesy, Hewlett-Packard.)

Note on Logic State Analyzers

An important advantage of the digital signature multimeter is that the trouble-

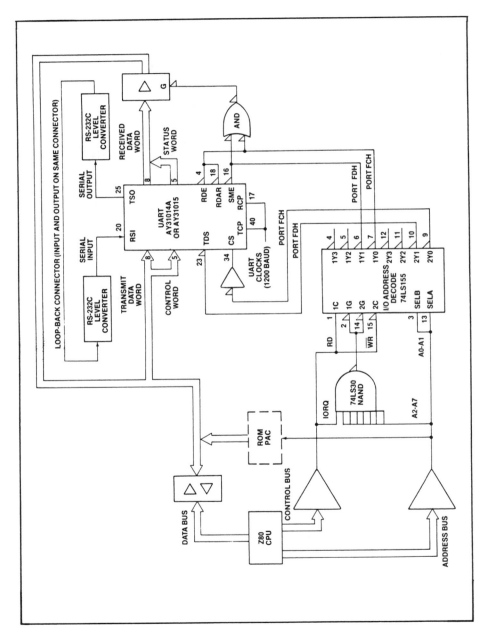

Fig. 15-25. UART troubleshooting arrangement in Test C. (Courtesy, Hewlett-Packard.)

*shooter does not need to have an in-depth understanding of microcomputer oper-
ation in order to check out the system and localize defective nodes.*

*On the other hand, as explained above, not all microprocessor systems can be
checked at the outset with a digital signature multimeter—it is often necessary
to retrofit the system before it can be tested by signature analysis.*

*If it is desired to check out a microprocessor system that is not adapted to sig-
nature analysis, a logic state analyzer can be used. The chief drawback to logic
state analysis is that the troubleshooter must have an in-depth understanding of
microcomputer operation.*

A logic state analyzer is a form of "intelligent oscilloscope" that displays
streams of data flow, as exemplified in Fig. 15-26. Four fundamental functions
are provided by a logic state analyzer:

1. A display of data is provided from the data bus, or other bus in the
   microcomputer (Fig. 15-26).

2. A reference point is provided. This is a trigger point that is sensibly related to the data that is to be displayed on the screen, or, it is a method of
   defining a unique trigger point within a data sequence.

```
11  101  010          11  101  010
01  100  011          01  100  011
01  100  100          01  100  100
00  100  111          00  100  111

10  101  011          10  101  011
10  101  100          10  101  100
10  101  111          10  101  111
10  110  001          10  110  001

01  110  011          01  110  011
01  110  101          01  110  101
01  110  100          01  110  100
01  110  111          01  110  111

01  111  001          01  111  001
00  111  000          00  111  000
10  111  011          10  111  011
10  111  110          10  111  110
```

Fig. 15-26. A data table processed in a microcomputer.

3. An indexing method is provided. This indexing action permits the troubleshooter to move the display window forward or backward along the data stream with respect to the reference point.

4. Data storage is provided. In other words, the logic state analyzer contains a memory whereby a sizeable portion of a data stream can be stored. In turn, the troubleshooter can check the data processing action, and can "call back" single-shot events for detailed analysis.

INDEX

A

Absolute maximum rating, 194
Accessing, 240
Accumulator, 136, 149
Action
    clamp, 163
    counter, 47
    flip-flop, 20
    gate, 64
Active
    high, 38, 51
        flip-flop, 104
    load, 106
    low, 38, 51, 220
Activity
    bus, 180
    counter, 47, 56
    current, 188
    digital, 61, 64
    pulse, 170, 196
A-D conversion, 80, 229
Adder
    binary, 149, 177
    full, 151
    half, 149
    parallel, 149, 156

    serial, 154
Addend, 156
Addressable latch, 105, 115
Address
    bus, 177
    input, 217
Algorithmic state machine, 229
ALU, 177
Analog-to-Gray converter, 82
AND
    dot, 94
    expandable, 34
    gate, 31
    implied, 94
    phantom, 94
AND-OR, 32, 58, 124
    INVERT, 32, 124
Apparent open, 200
Architecture, 177
Arithmetic
    logic unit, 177
    section, 190
Armed probe, 42
ASCII, 80
    font RAM, 231
Assembly language, 243

271